WYCLIF

SELECT ENGLISH WRITINGS

AMS PRESS
NEW YORK

JOHN WYCLIF

From the mezzotint by R. Houston
in Rolt, *Lives of the Reformers*, 1759

W Y C L I F

SELECT ENGLISH WRITINGS

Edited by

HERBERT E. WINN, M.A.

With a Preface by

H. B. WORKMAN, D.D., D.Lit.

OXFORD UNIVERSITY PRESS
LONDON : HUMPHREY MILFORD
1929

Library of Congress Cataloging in Publication Data

Wycliffe, John, d. 1384.
    Wyclif: select English writings.

    Reprint of the 1929 ed. published by Oxford
University Press, London.
    1. Theology—Collected works—Middle Ages, 600-1500.
I. Title.
BR75.W84   1976   230   75-41303
ISBN 0-404-14635-X

Reprinted from the edition of 1929, London
First AMS edition published in 1976

Manufactured in the United States of America

AMS PRESS INC.
NEW YORK, N.Y.

PREFACE

THE importance of Wyclif as one of the forerunners in the revolt against Rome, as well as in the effect of his life upon contemporary politics both in England and Bohemia, has been abundantly illustrated in the number of works and learned articles which have been written about him during the last hundred years, both in this country, Germany, and Bohemia. The labours of the Wyclif Society have also enabled a limited number of experts to become acquainted with his scholastic philosophy and theology, and to give him his right place in that remarkable system. There is, however, another side to Wyclif's labours which give him claim to national regard. In the present volume Mr. Winn seeks once more to emphasize this. His Latin works for the most part are only to be found in continental libraries, especially Prague and Vienna ; his English works, all of them written after his revolt, as might be expected, are to be found only in his native country.

The widely diffused legend that Wyclif himself was the translator of the first English Bible may be put on one side, though he certainly was the leading spirit in the movement which led to its production, while his translation of sections of the New Testament show what he could have done if, instead of leaving the work to his associates, he had done it all himself. Wyclif is certainly one of the founders of English prose. But apart from the Bible, Wyclif has left us many English works of the

highest excellence, not only from the standpoint of their
vigorous idiomatic English, but of great interest from the
light that they shed upon his later opinions, and in some
instances upon contemporary life. Unfortunately the
English works of Wyclif are now almost impossible to
procure. The so-called Wyclif versions of the Bible can
only be found in the greater libraries in the magnificent
but expensive editions by J. Forshall and J. Madden,
published by the Oxford Press in four quarto volumes in
1850. A selection from his reputed English works was
published by T. Arnold, also by the Oxford Press in
three volumes in 1869. This is now completely out of
print, and is also only to be obtained in better libraries.
Many of the works which it contains are certainly not by
Wyclif. A further contribution to Wyclif's English works
was that made by F. D. Matthew, *The English Works
of Wyclif*, published by the Early English Text Society
in 1880. Matthew's work, however, also contained a great
many pamphlets, the larger part in fact, that could not
be attributed to Wyclif himself. This also is out of print.
It is thus impossible for all except scholars advantage-
ously situated either to study Wyclif in his native
tongue, whether from the standpoint of its linguistic and
dialectic development or as embodying his opinions, or
even to get hold of any of his works. The Oxford Press
have sought to remedy this in Mr. Winn's admirably
edited selection of Wyclif's English writings. The care-
fulness and accuracy with which the work has been done,
the greater knowledge that is now possessed of medieval
English than when Arnold wrote, is evident on every

page. It should now be possible for Wyclif's contribution to English prose literature to attain its right place
in schools and colleges. Students of his life will be glad
to welcome this excellent attempt to make Wyclif a
living reality. Only from his English writings is it
possible to form some idea of an otherwise rather illusive
personality who was nevertheless a great Englishman,
both in his courage, independence, and influence.

H. B. WORKMAN.

WESTMINSTER COLLEGE.
October 1929.

Suppono autem quod Evangelium Christi sit cor corporis legis Dei.

Epistola missa Pape Urbano.

I suppose over þis, þat þo Gospel of Crist be hert of þo corps of Gods lawe.

MS. Bodl. 647.

CONTENTS

Contents

INTRODUCTION

LIFE OF WYCLIF

' Had it not been the obstinate perverseness of our prelates against the divine and admirable spirit of Wyclif, to suppress him as a schismatic and innovator, perhaps neither the Bohemian Hus and Jerome—no, nor the names of Luther or of Calvin—had ever been known : the glory of reforming all our neighbours had been completely ours.'

So Milton conjectured, and the sober historian, who limits himself to the realm of fact, must grant to Wyclif the following titles to fame:—He was the last great Oxford Schoolman. He *instigated* the first *complete* translation of the Bible into English. He was one of the first writers of nervous and balanced English prose. Through his Latin writings he exerted a very great influence on Hus,[1] and through Hus, a considerable influence on Luther and the Moravians. Lastly, to use the words of his authoritative biographer, he ' should be regarded as the stern, unbending forerunner and father of the Puritans, Covenanters and Nonconformists of England and America '.[2]

Birthplace.

John Wyclif, son of Roger and Katherine Wyclif, was born *c.* 1328[3] at the village of Wiclif-on-Tees.[4] His

[1] The great Bohemian reformer, burnt at the stake 1415 ; now accepted as the national hero of the new Czecho-Slovakia.

[2] H. B. Workman, ii. 321.

[3] Lewis suggested 1324. H. B. W. i. 21 suggests 1328 chiefly because an earlier date would make Wyclif unusually old when he took his doctorate in 1372.

[4] There is some doubt as to birthplace. Leland, in his *Collectanea*, points to ' Wiclif ' as the place *unde originem duxit*. In his *Itinerary* is the following :

> Wyclif a meane gentilman dwellith at a little village caullid Wiclif
> [They] say that [Joh]n Wiclif Haereticus [was borne at Ipreswel a poore village a good myle from Richemont]

family held the manor and living of Wiclif in the ' honour ' of Richmond. The future reformer was nurtured in bleak and wild country whose inhabitants suffered terribly from the raids of Scottish marauders. In the year of the marriage of his parents (1319), 3,000 Yorkshiremen were slain at Boroughbridge and, in the previous year, North-allerton was burned and Richmondshire devastated. The fighting qualities developed in Yorkshiremen by such a stern environment were illustriously exhibited in Wyclif's mind.

At Oxford.

Wyclif probably went up to Oxford somewhere about the year 1345. Three colleges, Queen's, Merton, and Balliol, claim him as an alumnus. To investigate these rival claims would occupy too much space ; but one in-disputable fact fortunately emerges : that by 1360 Wyclif had become Master of Balliol College.

When Wyclif arrived in Oxford, the University pos-sessed six foundations—University, Balliol, Merton, Exeter, Oriel, Queen's—and a multiplicity of halls and inns.[1] It could claim, with a large degree of justice, to be the rival of Paris. It already numbered among its distinguished sons Grosseteste, Duns Scotus, Ockham, Fitz-ralph, Bradwardine, and Roger Bacon.

Oxford, in Wyclif's day, consisted of a huddled mass of mean houses, honeycombed by dark and narrow streets, down the middle of which ran a noisome, open sewer, such as is still to be met with in insanitary Eastern cities. The now spacious ' Broad ' was the town ditch. On its far side lay Balliol, which Wyclif presided over for a few years.

The additions are by Stow the antiquary. Leland's MS. was rotted by damp in Stow's time. I suggest that Stow should have read ' was borne her ', i. e. at Wiclif. The jotting on Ipreswel would then be separate. Vide *Itinerary*, ed. Toulmin-Smith, iv. 28.

[1] See the interesting map of Academical Oxford given as frontispiece in Mallet's *A History of the University of Oxford*. By 1440 there were ninety-one halls.

During his long residence at Oxford he underwent the rigid intellectual discipline of fourteenth-century Scholasticism. First, as a student in Arts, he 'ground at grammar' and logic ; then, as a Bachelor, he lectured on certain prescribed portions of Aristotle, and was finally awarded the degree of Regent Master of Arts in 1361. There followed a course of equally long duration in Theology. From 1363 to 1366 Wyclif applied himself to the text of the Vulgate ; then for two years to the *Sentences* of Peter Lombard, the great medieval textbook on the Scriptures. After this he lectured for several years on the Bible and the *Sentences*, and after various public 'disputations' was granted the full Doctorate in Theology in 1372. Such a long course of academic discipline could not fail to leave its mark on his mind. In this period he acquired that bent for subtle disquisition and logical rigidity of mental process which characterized even his English writings, though his Latin writings exhibit these qualities in a much more marked degree. Certain interruptions occurred in Wyclif's course of study. These were due partly to external circumstances such as the terrible Black Death of 1349 and the Great Slaughter[1] of 1355, and partly to the fact that in 1361 Wyclif left Balliol to take the college living of Fillingham, then of Ludgershall in 1368. As rector of these parishes Wyclif was obliged to obtain leave of absence from his bishop in order to prosecute his theological studies at Oxford.

In the King's service.

The Oxford doctor and parish rector now took a momentous step. In 1372 he entered the King's service and commenced that series of public actions and writings which were to influence, so markedly, the development of English, and, indeed, European life and thought. In 1374 the Crown rewarded him for his services with the

---

[1] A most violent affray between 'town' and 'gown' in which eighty-six 'gownsmen' were killed.

Rectory of Lutterworth, which Wyclif held until his death. He seems to have attached himself to the anti-clerical party of the day. At any rate we first see him in his public capacity as the mouthpiece of the nation against Papal exactions. The occasion was as follows:—
In 1374 Gregory XI boldly demanded the payment of the tribute, which had been wrung by Innocent III in 1213, from the defeated and excommunicated King John. Wyclif strongly opposed the Papal claims,[1] maintaining (1) that the Pope ought to be chief follower of the Christ who abjured all earthly possessions;[2] (2) that chosen laymen should administer the temporalities of the Church; (3) that every one should hold his possessions directly from Christ 'since he is the chief Lord, who grants to every living creature that which he holds'; (4) that the superfluity of ecclesiastical wealth should be divided among the poor.

Thus early appeared some of his most characteristic doctrines.

An incident in the negotiations between the English Crown and the Papacy was the mission to Bruges, in the summer of 1374. The name of Wyclif was placed second in the list of those who were to form the commission. But in the actual negotiations he appears to have proved too unaccommodating, for he was not included in a second mission which was dispatched in the following year.

Wyclif spent the next two years, 1375 and 1376, at Oxford, in developing his ideas on the relationship of Church and State, and of both to God. These he embodied in two lengthy treatises *de Dominio Divino* and *de Civili Dominio.*

Late in 1376 he appeared in London and preached in the interests of John of Gaunt, though the latter was engaged at the time in undoing the work of the Good Parliament. To us the Reformer and the selfish duke

---

[1] See *Op. Min.*, ed. Loserth, pp. 405–30: *Determinatio ad argumenta magistri Outredi,* and *Determinatio ad argumenta Wilelmi Vyrinham.*

[2] 'Debet enim Papa esse praecipuus sequax Christi. Ipse (Christus) noluit esse proprietarius civilis dominii.'

appear a strangely assorted couple ; yet their association lasted for many years. It is probable that he cherished the hope that John of Gaunt would carry out a wholesale scheme of ecclesiastical disendowment and reform.

Attacked by the Church.

During the next five years (1377–82), many attacks were made on Wyclif by the Church. The protagonists were Courtenay, Bishop of London, and various learned monks, backed by the authority of the Pope. Wyclif, for his part, was loyally supported by John of Gaunt and the 'seculars' at Oxford like Nicholas of Hereford, Repingdon, Aston, and John Purvey. The king and the citizens of London also took his side for about two years. In February 1377 he was arraigned by Courtenay at St. Paul's. John of Gaunt, however, appeared in person as his champion. The proceedings ended in a *mêlée* from which Wyclif was carried off by John of Gaunt's retainers. On May 22, Gregory XI issued bulls[1] against Wyclif, denouncing him as a heretic and citing him to Rome. No action was taken, however, till December, when a reluctant University confined Wyclif to his rooms in Blackhall. But in March 1378, a council of bishops was only prevented from adopting stronger punitive measures by a message from Joan of Kent, the widow of the Black Prince.

It is interesting to note that about the same time King Richard addressed an inquiry to Wyclif asking him 'utrum regnum Angliae possit legitime, imminente necessitate suae defensionis, thesaurum regni detinere ne deferatur ad exteros'.[2] Wyclif, of course, replied vigorously in the affirmative.

---

[1] Gregory XI required the said John Wyclif to be laid in gaol and kept in faithful custody in chains. A schedule of eighteen erroneous ' propositions and conclusions ' accompanied the bulls. These were abstracted 'for the most part, some of them word for word, from Wyclif's *de Civili Dominio*. They are concerned with the politics not the theology of the Church.' H. B. W. i. 297-8.

[2] *Fasc. Ziz.*, p. 258.

He was never so strong in his life as he was in this year, when he stood as the national champion against the Papacy, and spoke the national feeling against the abuses of the Church at home. Men had not had time to see how far he was leading them, and were content with the general direction. In later years, when he expounded one by one the doctrines peculiar to later Protestantism, he formed a powerful sect, but he ceased to lead the nation or to enjoy the patronage of the government.[1]

In 1379 Wyclif began to deny the orthodox belief as to Transubstantiation—the central doctrine of the Medieval Church. This alienated some of his most powerful friends, notably John of Gaunt, who was afraid to countenance an arch-heretic. It also put a formidable weapon in the hands of his opponents. Consequently, in 1380, a committee of twelve Oxford doctors, six of whom were friars, *publice in scholis Augustinensium*,[2] condemned Wyclif as a heretic. Nothing daunted, he set forth his views in a Latin *Confessio*;[3] but the opposition growing more violent, he left Oxford for ever.

In his retirement at Lutterworth, however, his polemics against the Church became still stronger and more copious. Repingdon and Hereford continued to champion his views at Oxford. The Church, therefore, in May 1382, condemned all three in the famous Synod of Blackfriars—the 'earthquake council'. Repingdon was forced to recant; Hereford fled to Rome; but Wyclif was left unmolested at Lutterworth.

Last Years.

During his last years at Lutterworth, Wyclif ministered as a parish priest, thus fulfilling the pastoral ideal he had himself so often prescribed. But the cure of souls only occupied a small part of his time and energy. He instructed and dispatched far and wide his Poor Priests, whose ministrations among the common people laid the

---

[1] Trevelyan, *England in the Age of Wycliffe*, p. 81.
[2] *Fasc. Ziz.*, p. 113. [3] Ibid., p. 115 f.

foundations of that Lollard mode of thought and practice which lasted down to the period of the Reformation. His brain was as active as ever. With the assistance of his secretary, Purvey, he poured out polemic after polemic, reiterating with ever-growing severity his strictures on an unevangelical, propertied, and corrupt Church. He completed in thirteen volumes the *Summa* of his Latin writings. This is the period, also, to which we owe his English Sermons, and, incorporated in them, his own personal experiments in Bible translation. An event in the political history of 1382–3 affected him strongly, namely Bishop Spenser's Crusade.[1] This miserable venture, blessed by Pope Urban VI and preached by the friars, intensified Wyclif's scorn both for the Roman Pontiff and for the Mendicant Orders. The end, however, was near :

> The same Wyclif was paralysed for two years before his death, and he died in the year of our Lord, 1384, . . . on the day of the Holy Innocents, as he was hearing mass in his church at Lyttyrwort, at the time of the elevation of the host, he fell down, smitten by a severe paralysis, especially in the tongue, so that neither then nor afterwards could he speak, to the moment of his death.[2]

He was buried at Lutterworth, but was not allowed to rest undisturbed. In 1410 his works were burnt at Prague and at Carfax, Oxford ; while in 1415 the Council of Constance ordered his bones to be dug up and scattered to the four winds. This was not performed until 1428, when Fleming, bishop of Lincoln, carried out the loathsome operation. Let Fuller conclude :

> Hitherto the corpse of John Wickliffe had quietly slept in

[1] See pp. 171, 172.

[2] Attested on oath by John Horn, Wyclif's curate, before Dr. Thomas Gascoigne 1441. Cf. the monk Walsingham's account, *Historia Anglicana*, ii. 119 : Die Sancti Thomae . . . organum diabolicum, hostis Ecclesiae, confusio vulgi, haereticorum idolum, hypocritarum speculum, schismatis incentor, odii seminator, mendacii fabricator, Johannes de Wiclif, dum in Sanctum Thomam, ut dicitur, . . . orationes et blasphemias vellet evomere, repente iudicio Dei percussus, sensit paralysim omnia membra sua generaliter invasisse.

his grave about one and fourty years after his death, till his body was reduced to bones and his bones almost to dust. . . . But now such the Spleen of the Council of Constance . . . as they ordered his bones (with this charitable caution, if it may be discerned from the bodies of other faithful people) to be taken out of the ground and thrown farre off from any Christian buriall. In obedience hereunto, Richard Fleming Bishop of Lincolne, Diocesan of Lutterworth sent his Officers . . . to ungrave him accordingly.   To Lutterworth they come, Sumner, Commissarie Official, Chancellour, Proctors, Doctors, and the Servants (so that the Remnant of the body would not hold out a bone amongst so many hands) take what was left out of the grave, and burnt them to ashes, and cast them into Swift a Neighbouring Brook running hard by. Thus this Brook hath convey'd his Ashes into Avon ; Avon into Severn ; Severn into the narrow Seas ; they, into the main Ocean.   And thus the Ashes of Wickliff are the Emblem of his Doctrine, which now is dispersed all the World over.[1]

WYCLIF AND HIS WORLD
The People.

The substratum of society in Wyclif's day was the mass of the peasantry—three-quarters of the whole population.   Their daily business was :

> To kepe kyne in þe felde · þe corne fro þe bestes,
>
> Diken and delven · or dyngen uppon sheves,
>
> Or helpe make morter · or bere mukke afelde.[2]

Some were honest toilers :

> Some putten hem to þe plow · pleyed ful selde,
>
> In settyng and in sowyng · swonken ful harde.[3]

But many shirked work ; they

> feyned hem blynde

---

[1] Fuller, *Church History of Britain*, ii. 424.

[2] *Piers Plowman*, vi. 142.

[3] Ibid., Prologue, l. 20. The reader who wishes to reconstruct in imagination the world of Wyclif has two invaluable aids—Chaucer and Langland. His best and quickest way, therefore, of getting into living contact with the men and women of the Reformer's day is to read the two famous *Prologues*. In Langland's *Prologue* he will find all the classes of fourteenth-century society touched off by some vivid phrase, while in Chaucer he will meet with individuals as they moved, worked, and talked.

Somme leyde here legges aliri · as suche loseles
    conneth,
And made her mone to Pieres · and preyde him of
    grace:
'For we have no lymes to laboure with.'[1]
Some, 'that loth were to swynke',

Clotheden hem in copis · to ben knowen from othere,
And shopen hem heremites · here ese to have.[2]

Let us look for a moment at the lot of the honest
toilers. They would belong to some manor, owned
either by a 'possessioner' abbot or secular lord. Of
this manor they might be the chattels, for half the
peasantry were unfree. They would live. in an un-
comfortable hovel without chimney or glazed window,
and eke out a bare subsistence by tilling their little
strips of ground; by keeping a few swine which would
feed cheaply on mast in the neighbouring wood; and
by grazing a few beasts on the common. But their
small wealth would be considerably depleted by the
dues and exactions demanded by lords secular and
spiritual. To the village priest they would be expected
to pay tithes and special fees at births, marriages, and
deaths. To their feudal lord they would be constrained
to render a *merchet*, i.e. a fine, whenever a daughter
married. Even if a peasant wished to send a son to
school he would be obliged to pay a fine. For in
fourteenth-century England the children of a serf were
considered to be the chattels of the overlord. An extract
from the records of the Abbey of Glastonbury will
illustrate the hardships which fell to the lot of the
peasants. The lord, in this case, is an abbot:

Be it noted that each customary tenant [of Wrington,
Glastonbury], as often as he shall have brewed one full
brew, shall give to my lord abbot 4*d*. under the name of
tolcestre. *Item*, each customary tenant shall give mast-

---

[1] *Passus*, vi. 122 f.   [2] Prologue, 56.

money for his pigs, as appeareth more fully in the Ancient Customal. *Item*, be it noted that the customary tenants are bound to grind their corn at my lord's mill, or to pay a yearly tribute in money, viz. each holder of a yardland 2*s.* 8*d.* [&c., down to the lowest cotter at 4*d.*]. Be it noted also that, when any shall die, my lord shall take his heriot, to wit his best beast. And, if there be no beast, from the owner of a yardland or half a yardland, he shall have one acre of corn ; and from any lesser tenant, if he have so much land in cultivation, the lord shall have half an acre of his best corn.[1] . . .

The peasantry of Wyclif's day suffered severely at the hands of their overlords immediate and remote. Their wrongs must indeed have been great and widespread to cause the rising of 1381—the famous Peasants' Revolt. The dishonest measures by which the rebels were dispersed, and the cruelty with which they were subsequently punished, point unmistakably to the spirit of the governing classes of the time.

Yet, under a generous and sympathetic lord, in times of plenty, the manorial system worked well. The peasants had their rights as well as their duties ; and they had ample opportunity for relaxation in the form of sports and feasts. Wyclif was a supporter of the manorial system in its best form—he was no communist like John Ball. Thus in *de Papa* he says : 'Þe ordre of kyngis and dukis and knyȝtis, and of servauntes to hem, ben groundid in Goddis lawe.'

On the other hand he was opposed to serfdom. He was, indeed, the only medieval philosopher who objected to it on principle.[2] And, further, he demanded that lords should be just, sympathetic, and lenient. 'If þou be a lord, loke þou lyve a riȝtful lif in þin owne persone, boþe anentis God and man—doyng reson and equité and good conscience to alle men.'[3] But equally he required

---

[1] Quoted by Coulton, *Medieval Village*, pp. 36, 37.
[2] Ibid., p. 155.
[3] *A Schort Reule of Lif.* S. E. W. iii. 204.

from the 'laborer' hard work and loyal service. He would have approved of Chaucer's Plowman:

> With him ther was a Plowman, was his brother,
> That hadde y-lad of dong ful many a fother,
> A trewe swynkere and a good was he,
> Lyvynge in pees and parfit charitee.[1]

War and 'Chivalry'.

> þanne come þere a Kyng · Knyȝthod hym ladde.
> *Piers Plowman*, Prologue.

Feudalism was a simple and effective means of government. It was also a quick and ready means of war. To the barons and knights of Wyclif's day war provided an exciting diversion in which large prizes were to be won by the fortunate and skilful. France, 'our dear enemy', furnished a field for exhibitions *à outrance* of that military prowess which had been acquired by hard daily practice in the castle grounds, and in the realistic combats of the tournament, where, before the eyes of a brilliant assembly of knights and ladies, the aspirant to honour could display his skill in unhorsing his opponent. English knights of Wyclif's day fought not only in such pitched battles with the French as Crecy and Poitiers: they travelled over Europe in their eagerness for the dangerous war-game. Chaucer's knight is typical:

> In Lettow hadde he reysed and in Ruce,
> No Cristen man so ofte of his degree.
> In Gernade at the siege eek hadde he be
> Of Algezir, and riden in Belmarye.

Chivalry was associated with a large body of rules of etiquette and possessed a high ethical code. The knight in Chaucer's Prologue

> loved chivalrye
> Trouthe and honour, fredom and curteisye.

[1] *Prologue*, 529 f.

But in actual warfare these ideals were not always, or even often, carried out. That pattern of knighthood, the Black Prince, put to the sword men, women, and children at Limoges. Henry of Lancaster, the beau idéal of chivalry, butchered men, women, and children at Poitiers. Chivalry, in fact, was largely a sham.

Wyclif was strongly opposed to war. Above the ethics of chivalry he placed the ethics of the Gospels. It is true that in *de Officio Regis* he endeavoured subtly to determine when a king might be justified in waging war, but he came to the final conclusion that 'it is more conformable to the law of Christ not to war'. The many military expeditions to France provoked his horror. Shortly after his return from Bruges, he broke through his usual reserve to protest that 'the Great Company devastating France is hateful to God'. The extract at p. 114 shows him applying to the problem of war his usual test—the words of the Gospel. He decides that a soldier on active service cannot rightly use the Lord's Prayer.

Towns and Guilds.

> And somme chosen chaffare · they cheven the bettere
> As it semeth to owne sy3t · that suche men thryveth.
> *Piers Plowman*, Prologue.

Wyclif's life witnessed the expansion in size and dignity of the towns. This was due largely to the increase of trade, especially the export of wool to the Low Countries. The free cities of Ghent and Bruges served at once as our chief foreign marts and as the model for ambitious corporations. In the fourteenth century existing corporations, like that of London, received a large extension of privileges, and many rising towns were granted charters. Some like York and Southampton became counties with Sheriffs of their own. The king found it politic to grant these privileges. Towns which had grown up under the shadow of an abbey were not so fortunate, for the abbots resented the loss of power that came from the creation of a mayoralty.

In the towns flourished the numerous guilds—each possessing its special ' mistery '. The guilds of medieval England were close corporations of immense power. These organizations not only determined conditions of apprenticeship and quality and price of goods but looked after the social and religious well-being of their members. Wyclif notices this in a sermon [1] :

>   ȝit þes ȝoldes, founden of men, helpen al þer breþeren in nede boþe of temporal goodis and laten hem dwelle in Cristis ordre.

The attitude of Wyclif to merchants and tradesmen, busily engaged in piling up wealth, was naturally critical. The extracts at p. 104 point to the way in which guilds imposed on the public. Wyclif, as the zealous follower of the Christ who threw the money-changers out of the Temple, would sympathize with his own disciple who wrote :

>   Marchauntis and riche men of þis wikked world fallen in moche ypocrisé ; for þei traveilen nyȝt and day, bi watir and lond, in cold and in hete, bi false sotiltis and cautelis, and grete sweringes, nedles and false, for to gete muche drit or muk of þis world ; to gete riche wyves and purchase londis and rentis, and dwelle in pore mennus dette after þat þei hav desceyved hem in byynge of here catel.[2]

The Church.

Such were the chief secular portions of Wyclif's world. It remains to indicate the structure and condition of the vast and imposing Church, for this was the chief object of the Reformer's denunciations.

The Roman Church was now an ancient institution. About two hundred Popes had presided over the religious discipline of Western Europe. They had established contact with the society of the time at a thousand points.

[1] Þe Firste Sundai Gospel in Advent.
[2] *On the Leaven of the Pharisees,* c. 1383. Matt., pp. 24, 25.

It is difficult for people of to-day, who have grown up under a secular régime, to realize to what an extent the Medieval Church dominated the life of the time. Kings stood in awe of the Popes. John was beaten to his knees by Innocent III in 1213, but even Edward III and Richard II, a century and a half later, were careful to refuse the Papal demand for the John-tribute as diplomatically as possible. Through his cardinals who held wealthy ecclesiastical benefices in England, through the friars and monks who were under his authority, and through pardoners with their indulgences ' al hoote ', the Pope wielded an immense authority in England. The archbishops and the bishops upheld the power of the Pope because he served as their chief buttress in their struggle with the lay officers of State. When Courtenay, Bishop of London, defied John of Gaunt, on the occasion of Wyclif's trial at St. Paul's,[1] he did so in the secure knowledge that behind him was the might of the Papacy. This was the institution that Wyclif, with courage equal to that of Luther, dared openly to defy.

During the first fifty years of Wyclif's life the Popes were in ' the Babylonish Captivity ' at the ' sinful city of Avignon '.

> The degradation of the Papacy was complete . . . the living Popes and Cardinals soon attained a reputation for debauchery and avarice. At their iniquitous court, benefices in every country of Catholic Europe were put up for sale, and the income spent in licentious splendour. In the year in which Clement the Sixth ascended the throne it was said that a hundred thousand clergy came to Avignon to traffic in simony.[2]

In 1376 Gregory XI left Avignon for Rome and thus ended the Captivity. He hesitated to enter the city of his predecessors, and did not take up his residence in the

---

[1] 19 Feb. 1377.
[2] Trevelyan, *England in the Age of Wycliffe*, p. 76.

Vatican until the 17th January 1377. He died early in the next year (27th March), and Urban VI was elected in his place. The French cardinals, however, chose a rival Pope, Clement VII, who continued to hold his court at Avignon. War broke out almost immediately between the two competing heads of Christendom, and Europe was presented with the shameful spectacle of a Pope and Antipope preaching crusades against each other. This Great Schism, as it was called, did more than anything else to confirm Wyclif in his opposition to the Papacy. In the following year he wrote a Latin treatise, *de Potestate Pape*, by which his breach with Rome became complete.

Wyclif poured some of his strongest and most reiterated denunciations on the monks and the friars. He disapproved of the monks partly because of their vast possessions [1] and partly because they failed in the chief office of a priest—the preaching of God's Word. Shut up as they were behind stone walls, they failed to maintain any vital contact with the spiritual life of the people. The friars, in his opinion, influenced the religious life of the people by bad methods. They reduced confession to a farce, but, worse than anything else, they twisted the words of the Bible, and pleased their auditors with fables.

---

[1] 'The attacks of Wyclif upon the " possessioners ", as he called the monks . . . were unceasing. The Lollards pointed out that monasteries " be grounded upon labour of their hand by their own rule ", but now the work was done by others. For manual work their clothes were altogether unsuitable : " four or five needy men might well be clothed with one cope and hood of a monk, and that large cloth serveth to gird wind and let [prevent] him to go and do his deeds." He pointed to their vast wealth and asked whether the monks were faithful stewards. . . . With characteristic exaggeration he stated that the whole population of England could be maintained out of their income, which, instead, was wasted on gluttony, gay clothes, hounds, hawks, minstrels, and other luxuries. The Lollards protested that though the monasteries " had almost all lordship amortized to them yet they will not pay tax nor tribute to the King for maintenance of the realm." They claimed that charity funds were diverted into monastic coffers. But it should be noted that Wyclif brings no special charge of immorality against the monks. Their crime was the self-satisfied unspirituality which he dubbed as " the religion of fat cows ", with nothing in it that helped to subdue the flesh.' H. B. Workman, ii. 94, 95.

Langland, it is interesting to note, brings the same charge
against them. In the ' faire felde ful of folke ' he found

> freris · alle þe foure ordres,
> Preched þe peple · for profit of hemselven,
> Glosed þe gospel · as hem good lyked,
> For coveitise of copis · construed it as þei wolde.

The English bishops of the fourteenth century also
came under Wyclif's condemnation because of their
assumption of secular offices. They were not as a rule
vicious men, but they laboured less at the cure of souls
than at the King's business. Wykeham is an outstanding
example. He was appointed Chancellor of England and
Bishop of Winchester on almost the same day. His
wealth was immense. His duties, as the king's minister,
kept him away from his diocese. Bishops, like Wykeham,
were dubbed by Wyclif ' Caesarean '. He was of opinion
that their wealth should be taken from them and their
energies confined to spiritual ministrations. The bishops
were so fully employed by their State duties that they had
no spare time in which to preside over their ecclesiastical
courts. Their functions were therefore deputed to archdea-
cons, who were often alien cardinals. To these ecclesiastical
courts ' Sumnours ' haled not only peasants who had failed
to pay their tithes, but also men and women guilty of
various offences—adultery, slander, witchcraft, and so on.
To the same courts also belonged the overseeing of wills
and contracts. From the squabbles which thus ensued,
clerics and religion were brought into disrepute.

Such in broad outline was the world as Wyclif saw it.
He desired its reform from top to bottom. The Church,
he maintained, should be stripped of its endowments and
these divided among the poor. Temporalities should be
entirely in the hands of the king and secular lords. The
preaching of the Gospels should be performed by pastors
who should be kept thoroughly evangelical in spirit by
depending for clothing and sustenance on the voluntary
grants of their flock. The king's courts should assume

all the business of judicial administration, and all secular offices should be filled by laymen. King and nobles should treat their servants justly and sympathetically, and servants should respond by loyal and willing labour.

He found his authority for these reforms in ' Goddis lawe ', which to him was the paramount rule of life. It was from his interpretation of this law that he formulated the great Protestant ideal of freedom from authority and validity of the private judgement. Wyclif's final ideal of society was a reconstruction of the simple communism of the earliest Christians, described in the *Acts of the Apostles*. He desired a Christian commonwealth, whose members would guide their life simply and solely by the precepts of Christ, by the interpretation which their conscience demanded of the words of God. Pursued to its logical consequences this is a revolutionary principle, for it places ' God's law ' not only above ' Pope's law ' but above ' King's law ' too. The individual, basing his decisions on a conscientious reading of the Scriptures, becomes for himself the final authority in all private and public affairs. This is the traditional Protestant ideal —' the Protestantism of the Protestant religion '—and Wyclif in his last year did not scruple to express it plainly. The following passage from *þe Chirche and hir Membris* may be taken as one example :

Herefore we wolen seie opinli þe sentence þat we conseyven ; and ȝif God wole vouchesaaf, it mai after be declarid more. Oure grounde is comune bileve, þat Crist is boþe God and man, and so He is þe beste man, þe wyserst man, and moost vertuous, þat ever was or ever shal be. And He is Heed of þe Chirche ; and He ordeynede a lawe to men, and confermede it wiþ His life, for to reule Holi Chirche, and teche hou þat men shulde lyve ; *and al þis mut passe al oþir, siþ þe Auctor is þe beste.* And grutche we not þat many men þenken ful hevy wiþ þis sentence, for so þei diden in Cristis tyme, boþe wiþ His lyf and wiþ His lawe. . . . Us þinkiþ þat þe Chirche shulde here holde þe ordenaunce of Crist ; *and ever þe streiter þat it helde þat, evere be betir it were to it.*

THE ENGLISH WRITINGS

A very large number of English writings, including
a complete translation of the Bible into English, has
been attributed in the past to Wyclif. Shirley ascribed
to the Reformer sixty-five English works.[1] Arnold in
his *Select English Works*[2] reduced the number very
considerably, but omitted several tracts which may be
considered authentic.[3] These were, fortunately, printed
by Matthew in a volume published by the Early English
Text Society;[4] but Matthew also printed many tracts
which must be attributed to followers of Wyclif, for
though the broad message is Wycliffite, yet the style is
cruder than his and the emphasis differently placed.

This book of selections, apart from a few specified
pieces by Hereford and Purvey, is restricted to what may
be called with a high degree of probability, Wyclif's
genuine works. These may be divided into two classes : —

1. Writings with a Latin parallel or original.
2. Original writings in English.

In the first class may be placed the (1) *Sermons*, (2) *þe
Chirche and hir Membris*, (3) *de Papa*, (4) *Letter to Pope
Urban*, (5) *Five Questions on Love*, (6) *Wyclif's Confessio*,
(7) *On Confession*, (8) *Of Dominion*, (9) *de Officio Pasto-
rali*, (10) *A Petition to King and Parliament*. To the
second group belong (11) *þe Ten Comaundementis*, (12)
Ave Maria, (13) *Of Weddid Men and Wifis*, (14) *Of
Feigned Contemplative Life*, (15) *Of Servauntis and
Lordis*.

Of prime importance in the consideration of the
writings with a Latin parallel or original is Wyclif's statement at the beginning of his *Speculum Secularium Domi-*

---

[1] *Catalogue of the Original Works of John Wyclif*, Oxford, 1865. An
early and very erroneous list was given by Bishop Bale in his *Illustrium
Britanniae Scriptorum Summarium*, Basle, 1559.

[2] Oxford, 1869.

[3] e. g. *de Papa* and *de Officio Pastorali*.

[4] *English Writings of Wyclif Hitherto Unprinted*, 1880.

norum: 'In order that the truth may be more widely spread abroad, it behoves the faithful to set forth their opinions both in Latin and in the vernacular.' [1] Indeed, he often prepared a triple series of writings—one a lengthy Latin treatise, addressed to a scholastic audience; the second a short Latin summary intended for a lettered but less leisured circle of readers; the third a popular presentation of his ideas in English. Such a series may be found in *de Potestate Pape, de Ordine Christiano, de Papa*; in *de Ecclesia, de Fide Catholica*, and *Þe Chirche and hir Membris*; and in *de Eucharistia, de Eucharistia et Poenitentia*, and *Of Confession*.

The degree of correspondence between Wyclif's Latin and English writings printed in this book varies considerably. Only two, the *Letter to Pope Urban* and *Five Questions on Love* are close translations. *De Officio Pastorali* is, in most of its chapters, a fairly close paraphrase; *On Confession* and *de Papa* bear an undoubted general resemblance to *de Eucharistia et Poenitentia* and *de Ordine Christiano* respectively; while *Þe Chirche and hir Membris* contains many passages which resemble those in the two short Latin treatises *de Fide Catholica* and *Responsiones ad Argumenta Emuli Veritatis*. *Of Dominion* does not seem to correspond to any Latin tract of similar length, but merely gives a few of the basic ideas which are set forth in the long and elaborate Latin work *de Dominio Divino*.

The largest body of writings with Latin parallels is the *English Sermons*, which occupy vols. i and ii of Arnold's *Select English Works of John Wyclif*. A considerable number of these correspond to Latin sermons written by Wyclif. But, again, the English is not a translation of

---

[1] *Op. Min.* 74. Ut veritas sit nota planius atque diffusius, necessitantur fideles sententiam quam premittunt enucleare tam in lingua latina quam etiam in vulgari. Cf. also *de Triplici Vinculo Amoris*: Patet eorum stulticia, qui volunt damnare scripta tamquam heretica propter hoc, quod scribuntur in anglico et acute tangunt peccata que conturbant illam provinciam. The folly is very plain of those who wish to condemn writings as heretical because they are written in English and pierce through the evils which disturb the state.

the Latin. In the *English Sermons* Wyclif has merely
treated much more briefly and, on the whole, in a much
more popular manner some of the ideas which occur in
the Latin sermons. For example, Sermons A and D in
Section IV of this book correspond to Nos. xxx and
xxxii of the *Sermones*. Sermon A and Sermo XXX
both treat of the 'double procession' of the Holy Spirit
and of the matter of persecution. The Latin contains
also a lengthy discussion of the five senses and their
function in the spiritual life. This is omitted from A
but appears in 'Of Oon Confessor and Bishop', one of
the last sermons in *Commune Sanctorum*.[1] Sermon D in
this book and No. xxxii in the Latin both treat of the
doctrine of the Trinity and carnal and spiritual birth.
All the Latin Sermons are much longer than their
English counterparts and are much more scholastic in
form and content.

The existence of corresponding Latin works lends an
authority to Nos. i–x on our list as regards their substance. The question remains whether they were actually
written down in English by Wyclif himself, or whether
some close disciple, as for instance Purvey,[2] did the
work of adaptation to a popular audience. This difficult
question must be answered partly on general considera-
tions of purpose, thought, and style, and partly on special
evidence for particular works. This is set out briefly
below, and we may anticipate the result by saying that,
except in the *Letter to Pope Urban* (which being a *translation* is genuine as regards matter), and *Wyclif's Confessio*, not only are the writings authoritative in substance
but they may also be accepted, with reasonable confidence, as authentic specimens of Wyclif's mode of expression in English.

The most obviously genuine works, from their tone,
content, and style, are the *English Sermons* and the very

[1] S. E. W. i. 261 f. Cf. also Sermon B, p. 46 f.
[2] Netter of Walden affirms that Purvey 'was called the glossator and
translator of Wyclif, for he was the continual Achates of Wyclif right
down till his death and drank in his most secret teaching'.

important tract *Þe Chirche and hir Membris*. No serious student of the Latin and English works could doubt that the Reformer himself wrote the latter. It is stamped with the personality of Wyclif and is thoroughly authoritative in tone. Arnold gives an excellent summary of the reasons for regarding the *English Sermons* as genuine:

> The authenticity of these sermons, taken as a whole, cannot reasonably be questioned . . . they have all come down to us accompanied by the tradition of his authorship and have never been ascribed to any one else . . . the weight of internal evidence tends strongly in the same direction ; the authoritative tone, the proneness to subtle and recondite distinctions, so completely in harmony with what we know of Wyclif's fame in the schools, the special hostility to friars, the allusions to contemporary events, such as the crusade of Bishop Spenser, and the grant of papal indulgences to those engaged in it—events which occurred in 1383—lastly, a distinct reference, at the end of Sermon XXX, to a Latin work by the writer, which, it can hardly be doubted, was the *De Veritate* [*Sacrae*] *Scripturae* [1]—all these converging proofs . . . appear to establish Wyclif in the authorship of the Sermons beyond all reasonable doubt.[2]

Wyclif attached great importance to his ' plain sermons for the people '. This appears from a sentence in the preface to his Latin Sermons : ' That the law of God may be spread abroad, it seems fitting in the end of our days, in the respite which we now enjoy from scholastic labours, to bend our efforts to collecting our plain sermons for the people.'

One point, which at first sight militates against the genuineness of the Sermons, was pointed out by Arnold, namely, that there are references in three sermons [3] to the killing and burning of heretics. Now it has long been supposed that Sawtre, who was burnt on 2 March 1401, eight days before the passing of *de Haeretico Combu-*

---

[1] In þis mater [i. e. the authority of Scripture] we have ynow stryſen in Latyn wiþ adversaries of Goddis lawe.

[2] S. E. W. i, pp. xiii–xv. [3] S. E. W. i. 200, 205, 211.

rendo, was the first Lollard victim in England to suffer such extreme punishment. Wyclif died in 1384. Can he therefore have written the sermons containing these passages? Arnold boldly argued that there must have been cases of killing and burning for heresy in England before Wyclif's death. The truth probably is that Wyclif is speaking from a European standpoint. Burnings for heresy had been frequent on the Continent for many years previous. ' John XXII laid it down that it was a heresy to be punished by burning to deny his rights of binding and loosing at will. This papal claim was at once challenged by two of the leaders of the Spiritual Franciscans, Michael of Cesena (†1342) and Ockham. Hundreds went to the stake at Carcassonne, Narbonne, Marseilles, and Venice rather than acknowledge John's decrees. Rumours of these burnings reached England.'[1] When Wyclif was at Oxford he would also hear of the burning of two Spiritual Franciscans at Avignon, May 1355, and at Viterbo, 2 September 1368.[2]

In any case it seems impossible to rule out the English Sermons from the canon of Wyclif's works because of these references to burnings of Poor Priests, for similar references occur in his undoubted Latin works, e. g. in *de Blasphemia*: ' A new type of martyrdom has been engineered by the false friars, namely, that whoever is arraigned on a charge of heresy must answer simply " Yes " or " No ". If he maintains his heresy he must be given immediately to the flames without any further reply.'[3]

[1] H. B. W. ii. 100.

[2] Mollat-Baluze, i. 117–18:
The authority for the burning of heretics was given by a ' Constitutio ' of Frederick II, dated Nov. 22, 1220, supplemented by a ' Constitutio ' of March 1224 which contains the words ' ignis judicio concremandus '. Cf. Lyndwood, *Provinciale* 293: ' Debent comburi vel igne cremari, ut patet in quadam constitutione Frederici, quae incipit " ut commissi ".' A series of Papal bulls made these constitutions of Frederick the common law of Europe. Wyclif, who shows considerable knowledge of canon law, would have in mind these edicts against heretics, when speaking of burnings for heresy.

[3] *de Blasph.*, p. 73. ' Iam enim machinatum est per falsos fratres novum

Thus we have in the *Sermons* a valuable criterion by which other writings may be tested. E. Jones (*Anglia*, vol. xxx) has attempted to utilize the style of the *Sermons* as a touchstone of genuine writings and, as a result of his inquiry, he has decided that the following tracts printed in this book are genuine : *de Papa, Þe Ten Comaundementis, Five Questions on Love, Ave Maria,*[1] and *Þe Chirche and hir Membris.* Workman agrees as to the authenticity of all these works.[2]

In the following paragraphs some details are given bearing on the date, dialect, literary characteristics, &c., of each of the writings from which extracts have been taken :

Þe Chirche and hir Membris. The reference to 'þis laste journé þat Englishmen maden into Flandres', i. e. Spenser's Crusade, seems to fix the date as early in 1384. This is confirmed by the strong resemblances to *de Fide Catholica*, written, according to Loserth,[3] in the summer of 1383, and to *Responsiones ad Argumenta Emuli Veritatis*, written, according to the same authority,[4] in 1384.

de Papa. Matthew remarks:[5] ' I have no doubt that this tract is genuine. . . . . Not only are the views Wyclif's; the arguments and illustrations are such as he frequently uses in his authentic writings. . . . The date of the tract is probably about 1380. The reference to the doctrine of Transubstantiation shows that Wyclif had already made up his mind on this point, but the Schism is spoken òf in a tone which implies that it was still recent.' The reference to the Schism, ' dyvysioun of þes popis þat is nou *late* fallun ', seems to indicate 1379 rather than 1380. This is the date of the elaborate Latin treatise, *de Potestate Papa*, of which *de Papa* is the popular English form.

genns martyrii, quod quicunque fuerit impetitus super heretica pravitate debet ille simpliciter concedere vel negare ; quo concesso, debet indilate exponi ad ignem sine responso ulteriori.' Cf. also *Supp. Trialogi*, p. 455.

[1] Not the one printed in this book. The differences, however, are dialectal, not stylistic.

[2] H. B. W., Appendix C.   [3] *Op. Min.*, p. xxi.

[4] Ibid., p. xxxvii.   [5] Matt., p. 458.

De Officio Pastorali (English) corresponds to the Latin tract [1] of the same name, but it differs from its counterpart in the ordering of its chapters, and the presentation is throughout adapted to an unacademic audience. Ch. xv, printed pp. 19, 20. is entirely new. It deals with the question of translation of the Scriptures into English. This chapter has been attributed by Deanesly to Purvey. 'Chapter 15 in the English form is an interpolation, with no counterpart in the Latin. It is introduced with some irrelevance to defend the English translation of the Bible—not one of the normal subjects of Lollard apologetic.'[2] The chapter seems, however, to come naturally enough after the discussion at the end of ch. xiv. There the writer enters a protest against academic learning. The apostles, he says, took no degree. 'Mannus lawe tauȝt in scolis lettiþ Goddis lawe to growe ... men of scole travelen veynly for to gete newe sutiltees ... and the profit of hooly chirche is put abac.' Further, in deciding the authorship the date of the tract should be taken into consideration. Wyclif seems to have written the Latin and English forms practically simultaneously in accordance with his precept quoted above.[3] Lechler dates the Latin tract not later than 1378, and the sentence in the last chapter of the English form, 'Þe Pope dwelliþ in Auynoun [Avignon]', places the upward limit of its writing late in 1376, for Gregory XI, the last of the Avignonese Pontiffs to be recognized in England, quitted Avignon late in 1376 and took up his residence in Rome early in 1377. Now we know from the opening of the *Speculum* (written *c.* 1378), and numerous references in the *de Veritate Sacrae Scripturae* (written 1378), that Wyclif's mind had been turning, for some time past, to the question of Biblical translation. It would be natural, therefore, for him to write ch. xv about the year 1377. Many phrases of this chapter resemble those in the *Speculum*. It is true that certain of the arguments in Purvey's *General Prologue* resemble those in ch. xv.

[1] Edited by Lechler, Leipsic, 1863.   [2] Deanesly, p. 378.
[3] p. xxx, ut veritas, &c., written 1378.

But this similarity is no doubt due to the fact that Wyclif discussed the arguments for a vernacular rendering of the Bible with his disciple, while the latter acted as his secretary at Lutterworth. Ch. xv may therefore be assigned to Wyclif with the utmost confidence, and it is likely, from the date, style, and details of treatment, that the remainder of the English form of *de Officio Pastorali* is due also to his hand.

The Ave Maria is another early writing. The form in which it appears in this book is that in which it occurs in the *Lay Folks' Catechism*.[1] Arnold printed a South Midland form[2] based upon MS. Bodl. 789. The tract also occurs in MS. Harleian 2385 with the name Wyclif inscribed at the end.

Þe **Ten Comaundementis** is also an early composition. It is interesting to note how, in the hands of Wyclif, what might have been a mere commentary has become a Lollard document. Many characteristic doctrines of Wyclif are introduced, e. g. 'He þat stondiþ in grace is verrey lord of þingis'. Jones thinks the style of the piece to be without doubt Wyclif's.

Of Feigned Contemplative Life. From the tone and the ideas introduced this appears to be an early work.[3] The opinions expressed are typical of Wyclif, e. g. the objection to 'Salisbury uss'; the injunction to priests: 'prestis . . . han expresse þe comaundement of God and men to preche þe Gospel'; the scorn for monks: 'Lord! what cursed spirit of lesyngis stiriþ prestis to close hem in stonys or wallis for al here lif, siþ Crist comaundiþ to alle His apostlis and prestis to go into alle þe world and preche þe Gospel.' The style is such as we should expect in an early composition.

Of Weddid Men and Wifiis. This piece is found in MS. 296. C.C.C. Cambridge, along with several other genuine writings. The volume in which it is contained was presented to Corpus Christi College by Archbishop

[1] See p. 165.
[2] S. E. W. iii. 111.
[3] Cf. Matt., p. 187.

Parker in the sixteenth century. Arnold, in discussing
its authenticity, points out as 'a suspicious circumstance'
the fact that St. Augustine is called 'Seynt Austyn'
instead of simply 'Austyn'. But Augustine appears as
'Seynt Austyn' in S. E. W. iii. 105, 223, and ii. 263, 174.
Workman includes this piece among the genuine writings.

A Petition to King and Parliament. Workman remarks: When Parliament assembled (7 May 1382), 'the
heresiarch of execrable memory' laid a memorial [1] before
its members in which he reaffirmed doctrines 'which
would make the ears of a faithful hearer tingle'. . . .
Along with this more formal petition or broadsheet,
Wyclif published an English *Complaint*. This document,
which was either never completed or has come down to
us in an imperfect condition, is in the form of a petition.
[H. B. W. ii. 250, 251].

Of Dominion. This short tract presents in a popular
English dress some of the main ideas which occur in
several elaborate Latin treatises [2] dealing with Wyclif's
theory of 'dominion'. From its style and thought the
piece may be assigned with confidence to the Reformer.

On Confession corresponds to the short Latin treatise
de Eucharistia et Penitentia sive de Confessione.[3] The
English tract is not a translation of the Latin or even a
close paraphrase, but the connexion of the two is not to
be doubted. The general argument is the same, and the
chief ideas of the Latin appear in the English. The
special treatment, in the two versions, of Lazarus and
the Ten Lepers would of itself establish the parallelism.
Matthew says: 'The evidence of style seems to me to
mark it as decidedly Wyclif's.'[4] The phraseology of the
attack on priests who claim powers of effecting transubstantiation of the Host, indicates a fairly late date, e. g.
Power þat prestis han standeþ not in transubstansinge of
þe oste, ne in makyng of accidentis for to stonde bi hem-

---

[1] Included by Wyclif in *de Blasphemia*, 270–1, and called *Imprecaciones*.
[2] For a list see p. 60.
[3] Printed with the longer *de Eucharistia*, W. S. P.
[4] Matt., p. 325.

silf; for þis power graunted not God to Crist ne to any apostle.[1]

Of Servantis and Lordis. This tract was probably written by Wyclif soon after the Peasant's Revolt of the summer of 1381. The attitude towards governors and governed is similar to that adopted in the Latin works, notably *de Blasphemia*, ch. xiii.[2] The advice given to lords and servants closely resembles that contained in another genuine Wyclif tract, *A Schort Reule of Lif.*[3] Compare, for example: If þou be a lord, loke þou lyve a riȝtful lif in þin owne persone, boþe anentis God and man, keping þe hestis of God, doyng þe werkis of mercy . . . governe wel þi tenantis, and maynteyne hem in riȝt and reson, and be merciful to hem in þer rentys and worldly mercimentis, and suffere not þi officeris to do hem wrong ne extorcions . . . If þou be a laborer, lyve in mekenesse and trewly and wylfully do þi labour; þat if þi lord or þi mayster be an heþen man, þat by þi mekenesse and wilful and trewe servise, he have not to gruche aȝens þe, ne sclandere þi God ne Cristendom.[4]

The Letter to Pope Urban. Of this a Latin original exists written, according to Loserth, in 1378.[5] The English translation was probably made after 1382.[6] The style is crude and the dialect West Midland. The scribe may have been Nicholas Hereford or some other disciple from the West Country.

Five Questions on Love is also a translation. Lechler is of opinion that the English form is the original. This seems unlikely in view of the writer's complaint: 'Alle þes questions ben hard to telle hem trewly in Englische.' Jones rightly considers the style to be that of Wyclif, but it becomes somewhat more cramped than usual owing to the exigencies of close translation.

Wyclif's Confessio corresponds to a long Latin *Confessio* preserved by Netter in *Fasciculi Zizaniorum.*[7] The

---

[1] Matt., p. 345.   [2] See p. 99.   [3] S. E. W. iii. 204-7.
[4] S. E. W. iii. 206-7.
[5] This is discussed more fully on p. 67, footnote.
[6] H. B. W. ii. 315.,   [7] *Fasc. Ziz.*, p. 115 f.

English is not a translation or paraphrase of the Latin, but merely a brief and vigorous statement of some of the main points. The dialect in which the piece is written is North-West Midland. The form we possess is probably a rough copy of Wyclif's original, made by some Western disciple, for use in missionary work in his native region, where, as we know, the Lollards were active.

Nearly all these tracts and treatises were written between 1378–84. These last six years may be designated, therefore, Wyclif's 'English' period. He had now passed through his two preliminary phases as Schoolman and Politician, and had found his true *métier* as English Reformer, appealing to the people at large. It was for this reason that, though he continued to write freely in Latin, he tended more and more, as the years advanced, to employ English as his medium of expression. Development may be perceived in the tone and style of his utterance within even this short period of time. To the beginning belong the milder and more academic exercises, such as the *Ave Maria* and the *Five Questions on Love*. These are followed by the larger and more open criticism of *de Papa*, which, in turn, gives way to the strong style and free denunciation of the *English Sermons*. A final stage is reached in the equally pungent but graver and more imaginative manner of *Þe Chirche and hir Membris*, in which Wyclif appeals, in a touchingly strong and simple manner, to the 'coming-on' of time for the realization of his ideals.

MANUSCRIPTS

Title of MS.	Distin-guishing Letter.[1]	Texts.
Bodl. 788 . . .	A	*English Sermons, Þe Chirche and hir Membris.*
Douce 321 . . .	E	Variant Readings for *Sermons.*
New College, Oxford, 95	Q	Variant Readings for *Letter to Pope Urban.*
Bodl. 647 . . .	W	*On the Seven Deadly Sins, Lincolniensis, Wyclif's Confessio, Letter to Pope Urban.*
Corpus Christi College, Cambridge, 296 . .	X	*Of Weddid Men and Wifis, Þe Grete Sentence of Curs, Of Feigned Contemplative Life, Of Servauntis and Lordis, Petition to King and Parliament.*
Trin. Coll. Dublin C. iii. 12	A A	*Of Dominion.*
Trin. Coll. Dublin C. v. 6	CC	*Of Confession.*
Brit. Mus. Tiberius C. vii	HH	Variant Readings for *Wyclif s Confessio.*
Ashburnham XXVII .	MM	*de Officio Pastorali, de Papa.*

[1] The lettering of Arnold and Matthew has been preserved.

LIST OF ABBREVIATIONS

Deanesly = The Lollard Bible. Deanesly. Camb. Univ. Press, 1920.
Fasc. Ziz. = Fasciculi Zizaniorum, Netter of Walden. Ed. Shirley, Rolls Series, 1858.
H. B. W. = Life of Wyclif, Rev. Ḥ. B. Workman. Oxford, 1926.
K. S. = Fourteenth Century Verse and Prose. Kenneth Sisam. Oxford, 1923.
Matt. = The English Works of Wyclif hitherto unprinted. F. D. Matthew, E. E. T. S., 1880.
Op. Min. = Opera Minora. W. S. P. ed., Loserth, 1913.
S. E. W. = Select English Works of Wyclif. Arnold, 1869.
W. S. P. = Wyclif Society Publications.

SAYINGS OF WYCLIF

These sayings are intended to provide the reader with a key to Wyclif's 'criticism of life'. They illustrate, in a short compass, Wyclif's power of concise and picturesque statement, his moments of real elevation of thought, and his occasional lapses into intolerance and medieval superstition.

A. *Jesus Christ.*

Oure ground is comune bileve, þat Crist is boþe God and man, and so He is þe beste man, þe wyserst man, and moost vertuous, þat ever was or ever shal be. And He is heed of þe Chirche. And He ordeynede a lawe to
5 men, and confermede it wiþ His lyf, for to reule Holi Chirche and teche how þat men shulde lyve. And al þis mut passe al oþir siþ þe Auctor is þe beste.

Þe Chirche and hir Membris.

As bileve [in Christ] is first vertue and ground of al oþer, so unbileve is þe first synne of alle oþer.

Sermons. Þe Fourþe Sondai Gospel aftir Estir.

10 Crist, nobulest man þat may be in erþe, was porest man of alle whan He chese to be bischope.

Þe Seven Werkys of Mercy Bodily.

Take we noon heede to beestis skynnes, ne to enke or oþer ornamentis, but to treuþe þat Crist spake; in which stondiþ oure bileve.

Sermons. Þe Wednesdai in þe Firste Weke in Advent.

15 Algatis, þe birþ of Crist passide oþer dedis þat ever God dide; for it is more to make God man þan to make þis world of nouȝt.

Sermons. Þe Gospels on Cristemasse Morwenyng.

Þus shulde þe Chirche drawe to acord bi Crist, þat lediþ þe daunce of love.

Þe Chirche and hir Membris.

B. *Theological.*

Wel we witun þat God bindiþ not men to bileve ony þing which þei may not undirstonde.

Þe Chirche and hir Membris.

Love and good liif ben needful to riȝt bileeve.

Quicunque Vult.

As long as a man lyveþ just lif, kepynge Goddis hestis and charité, so longe he preieþ wel whatevere he do ; 5 and whoevere lyveþ beste, he preieþ best.

de Precationibus Sacris.

Science of God fediþ men wel, and oþer science is mete for hoggis, and it makiþ men fat here, but not after Domesdai.

Sermons. Þe Saturday Gospel in þe Secunde Weke in Lente.

Crist spekiþ in many tymes how al þat shal be mut 10 nedis be, and how nouȝt may come but þat shal be.

Sermons. On Monedai in þe Fiffe Weke in Lente.

Crist preieþ not for þe world, as for þes men þat shulen be dampned, but for men þat shulen be saved ; for Cristis preier mut nedis be herd.

Sermons. Þe Gospel on Vigile of Witsondai.

Soþeli dampned men in helle done ever good to seintis 15 in hevene, for þer blis is more savery for peynes þat þei seen in hem.

Sermons. Þe Mondai Gospel in þe Firste Weke of Lente.

A parable is a word of stori, þat bi þat hydeþ a spiritual witt.

Sermons. Þe Firste Sonedai Gospel After Trinité Sondai.

Alle þingis ben knowun of God and þat myrrour shewiþ 20 forþ þe moost pryvy þing in þis world.

Sermons. Þe Gospel on Feeste of Oon Martir.

Ever wite we, þat þis oost is verri breed in his kynde, and in figure Goddis bodi, bi vertue of Cristis wordis ;

but þus it is not of Cristis fleish and His blood in His kynde.

Sermons. Þo Saturdai Gospel in Fyfþe Weke in Lente.

Þe dai of dome comeþ ful faste.

Sermons.   Of o Martir and Bishop.

C. *True Priests.*

Þei shulden be moost pore men and moost meke in
5 spirit, and moost profit to Cristis Chirche, for so dide
Peter in Cristis name.

Of Mynystris in þe Chirche.

Croune and cloþ maken no prest, ne the Emperours
bischop wiþ his wordis, but power þat Crist ȝyveþ.

de Papa.

Go we nere to þe witt þat þe Gospel techiþ us and we
10 shall see þat eche preest shulde be viker of Crist, and
take of him oyle of grace, and so in a maner be Crist, and
fede þe puple goostly wiþ þe wordis of God.

Sermons.   Þe Sevenþe Sondai Gospel aftir Trinité.

D. *The Pope.*

Lord, what good doiþ þis gabbyng, þat þe Pope wole
be clepid 'Most Hooly Fadir' here, and bishop 'Most
15 Reverent' man?

Sermons.   Þe þridde Sondai Pistle in Advent

Lord, where þis Pope Urbane hadde Goddis charité
dwelling in him, whan he stirede men to fiȝte and slee
many þousand men, to venge him on þe toþer Pope?

Sermons.   Þe Secunde Sonedai Aftir Trinite.

Dignities and pryvelegies þat ben now grauntid bi þe
20 Pope, but ȝif Crist conferme hem first, ben not worþ a flye
foot.

Sermons.   On Passioun Sondai Pistle.

Men shulden shake awey al þe lawe þat þe Pope haþ
maad, and alle reulis of þes newe ordris, but in as myche
as þei ben groundid in þe Lawe þat God haþ ȝovun.

Sermons.   Þe Pistle on þe Sixte Dai fro Cristemasse.

E. *Friars.*

Crist to purge his Chirche, distriede þes þree sectis, Phariseis, Saduceis, and Essees also, but þe fend bi his cautel haþ brouȝt inne now oþer þree, as monkes, chanouns, and freris, and·many braunchis of hem.

Sermons. In Dai of oon Martir.

It were more suffrable to dwelle amonge Sarazynes or oþir paynym sectis, as doen many Cristen men, þan to dwellen among sectis of þese newe religiouse.

Sermons. Þe Elevenþe Sondi Aftir Trinité.

Þes newe ordris hadden plenté of wisdom þat Crist ȝaf hem for to drynke, but þei grutchiden aȝens þis water, and drunken podel water of þe canel.

Sermons. On Ninþe Sondai Aftir Trinité.

F. *Social.*

Ȝif man have riȝt to þing, þat riȝt comeþ of God to him.

Sermons. Þe þridde Sondai Pistle in Advent.

Just men, þat han Hevene, han alle worldli þingis bi resoun of her Lord ; and so alle unjuste men, þat God ȝyveþ Helle for her service, have not justli, alȝif þei semen to have moche.

Sermons. Þe Gospel of O Confessor and Bishop.

Whoevere faillíþ by defaute of grace, he failiþ riȝt title of þing þat he occupieþ.

Þe Ten Comaundementis.

Þou shalt love þi neiȝbore as þisilf—as many pens ben closid in oo tresoure comonly, so in þis o word of God ben comounly oþir undirstonden.

Sermons. On Fourþe Sondai Aftir Octave on Twelfþe Dai.

It perteyneþ to kyngis first to do worship to God, and siþ to do riȝt to þer servauntis and so to alle men under hem.

Sermons. Þe Nynþe Sondai Gospel After Trinité Sonday.

It were a medeful þing to worldely lordis to forȝyve

dette and discharge þer pore tenauntis of many chargis
þat þei ben inne.

Ibidem.

If þou be a laborer, lyve in mekenesse, and trewly and
wylfully do þi labour.

A Schort Reule of Lif.

G. *Miscellaneous.*

5 O leprous man may foule a flok, and a flok mai foule
a more.

Sermons. Þe Gospel on Feestis of many Confessours.

If a man miȝte bi a privé lesinge save al þis worlde þat
ellis schulde perische, ȝit schulde he not lye for savynge
of þis worlde.

Þe VIII Comaundement.

10 Ydelnesse is þe develis panter, to tempte men to synne.

Of Weddid Men and Wifis.

Fendis men contynuen and maken fals pees to more
werre. Crist proveþ þat oure love shulde be alargid to
oure enemyes.

Sermons. Friday Gospel in Quinquagesme.

Þis Baptist was a witnesse more worþ þan þes philo-
15 sophris, as Plato and Aristotle, boþe in liif and in witt.

Sermons. On Fridai in First Weke of Advent.

Curiousté of science, or unskilful coveitise of cunnynge,
is to dampne.

Sermons. In Dai of Many Martiris.

Seyntis han anoþer knowing þan han dampned men,
þat clerkis clepen intuycioun.

Sermons. Þe Gospel of Ascensioun Evyn.

20 Whanne wymmen ben turnyd fully to goodnesse, ful
hard it is þat ony man passe hem in goodnesse. And as
hard it is þat ony man passe hem in synne, whanne þei
ben turnyd to pride and lecherie and dronkenesse.

Þis is the Ave Maria.

THE TRANSLATION OF THE BIBLE

O Crist! þi lawe is hid ʒit; whan wilt þou 'sende þin aungel to remove þe stone, and shewe þi treuþe to þi folk?
Sermons. Þe Gospel on Palm Sonday.

Et sic prodest multum viatoribus studere evangelium sedule in illa lingua in qua ipsis sententia evangelii magis patet, quia ex fide omnes fideles debent sequi dominum 5 Iesum Christum.
de Amore sive ad Quinque Quaestiones.

Wyclif was driven to the translation of the Bible into English as a logical outcome of two main ideas. In the first place he regarded the Scriptures as the paramount 'rule' of life, all human traditions and teaching being of secondary 10 importance. 'Goddis lawe' outweighed, he thought, both canon law and civil law. 'Christ's law is best and enough, and other laws men should not take, but as branches of God's law.' Secondly, the Reformer maintained that every man is God's tenant-in-chief. Therefore no intermediary—priest, 15 bishop, or Pope—can come between a human being and his Creator. The individual is finally responsible to God alone.

These ideas both find expression in the following passage : 'Those heretics who pretend that the laity need not know God's law but that the knowledge which priests have imparted 20 to them by word of mouth is sufficient, do not deserve to be listened to. For Holy Scripture is the faith of the Church, and the more widely its true meaning becomes known the better it will be. Therefore, since the laity should know the faith, it should be taught in whatever language is most easily 25 comprehended. . . . Christ and His apostles taught the people in the language best known to them. . . . Further, since all Christians, as the apostle teaches in 2 Cor. v. 10, must stand before Christ's tribunal and give an account of all the gifts He bestowed upon them, it is necessary that all the faithful should 30 know those gifts and their use, so that their answer may be plain. No answer by a prelate or attorney will then avail, but each will be required to answer for himself.'

The extract just given occurs in the *Speculum Secularium Dominorum,*[1] written, according to Loserth, about 1378. *De Veritate Sacrae Scripturae,* a lengthy and important treatise written in the same year, contains many passages of similar import.[2] So it is reasonable to suppose that Wyclif had a considerable share in promoting the first complete English version of the Bible which was finished about the year 1382. Further, three important witnesses attest his connexion with this translation.

1. Archbishop Arundel, the great foe of Bible translation, writing in 1411 to the Pope, informed him that Wyclif, the heretic, ' to fill up the measure of. his malice, devised the expedient of a new translation of the Scriptures into the mother tongue '.

2. The continuator of Knyghton, a canon of St. Mary de pré, Leicester, wrote under the year 1382 : ' In those days flourished Master John Wyclyfe, rector of the church of Lutterworth, in the county of Leicester. . . . This master John Wyclyfe translated from Latin into English— the Angle not the angel speech [3]—the Scriptures which Christ gave to the clergy and doctors of the Church that they might sweetly minister to the laity and to weaker persons. . . . Thence by his means it is become vulgar and more open to laymen and women who can read, than it is wont to be to lettered clerks of good intelligence. Thus the pearl of the Gospel is scattered abroad, and trodden underfoot by swine.' [4]

3. Hus, the great Bohemian reformer, who absorbed and died for the doctrine of Wyclif, declared, on the evidence no doubt of Bohemian scholars who had studied at Oxford, that Wyclif ' himself translated the whole Bible from Latin into English '.

What was Wyclif's real share in the translations associated with his name ? Modern research has made it fairly certain that the work of translation was performed by other men. The two chief workers were Nicholas Hereford and John Purvey, both Oxford doctors and intimate friends and disciples of Wyclif. The former must be accorded the honour of commencing the *First Version,* but he was assisted by many friends who

---

[1] *Op. Min.,* p. 74. [2] e. g. ii. 137, 170.
[3] In anglicam linguam non angelicam.
[4] Knyghton, *Chronicon,* ii. 152.

sympathized with the undertaking. According to Forshall and Madden (Preface, p. xlvii) five different scribes, writing in different dialects, contributed to the original MS.—Bodl. 959. A copy of this MS., ending like the original at Baruch iii. 20,[1] bears the words ' Explicit translacionem Nicholay de herford '. 5 This translation we call ' Hereford's ' Version.

Possibly Purvey finished the First Version, though this is a matter of conjecture, but there no longer remains any reasonable ground for doubt that, acting under the direction of Wyclif, during the last years at Lutterworth, he undertook the 10 huge labour of revising the whole of ' Hereford's ' Bible, and finally carried through the design after his master's death,[2] thus producing what is generally known as *The Second Version* but what may also be termed *Purvey's Revision*. For this revision Purvey[3] wrote a *General Prologue* which describes his 15 method of translation and provides introductions to the various books of the Bible. From allusions in this *Prologue* to contemporary events Workman allocates the publication of the *Second Version* to the summer of 1395.[4] A MS. of the New Testament portion—*Caius 343*—bears the date 1397.   20

A few extracts from the versions of ' Hereford ' and Purvey are printed on pp. 14–17. These are preceded by Bible passages in English taken from Wyclif's Sermons. It was Wyclif's custom in these sermons either to preface his whole discourse by a translation of a portion of the Gospel for the day or to 25 adopt the method of ' postillization ', i. e. a sentence by sentence translation and commentary. Altogether he translated in this way a large part of the Gospels, for it must be borne in mind that Wyclif's English Sermons number close upon three hundred. Wyclif, therefore, in addition to instigating the early Lollard 30 versions of the Bible, made a personal contribution to the actual work of translation.

---

[1] Baruch came nearly at the end of the O.T. between Jeremiah and Ezekiel. Hereford probably broke off abruptly when he fled to Rome. See p. 146.

[2] ' Manie gode felawis and kunnynge' assisted in correcting the translation. See p. 26, l. 34.

[3] Purvey's authorship has been established by Deanesly, 260–7, 376 f.

[4] Purvey refers in explicit words to certain scandalous results of celibacy ' as it was made known at the last Parliament '. This no doubt alludes to the third of the *Conclusions* of the Lollards presented to the Parliament of Jan.–Feb. 1395.

The merits of the three versions will appear from an examination of the parallel passages given in the text. That of 'Hereford' obviously takes the lowest rank. The translator, in endeavouring to achieve a word-for-word rendering, has lost all
5 pretence to an idiomatic English style. Purvey, on the other hand, as his *General Prologue* shows,[1] strove to remedy this defect. He rejected such characteristic features of the Latin sentence as the Ablative Absolute. While keeping as closely as possible to the sense of his original he endeavoured to
10 attain 'open', i. e. idiomatic, English. He has been much praised for this improved method of translation, but the real contriver of the new type of translation was again Wyclif, for in the Bible passages inserted in his sermons the process of 'opening' has been already carried to a further point than that
15 reached by Purvey. Hence Workman regrets 'that Wyclif did not abandon his polemics, and devote himself to the supreme task of doing the Bible into the vernacular instead of handing it over to his assistants. He would have left behind him a monument more lasting than brass.'

A. *Bible Passages occurring in Wyclif's Sermons.*

I. [THE UNMERCIFUL SERVANT.]

Simile est regnum caelorum homini.—MATT. xviii. 23.

20 Þe kyngdom of hevene, seiþ Crist, is lyke to an erþeli kyng þat wolde ryken wiþ hise servauntis. And whanne he hadde bigun to rekoun, oon was offrid unto him þat owid him ten thousand besantis, and whan he hadde not to paye of, þe lord bad he shulde be soold, his wyf and
25 his children and al þat he hadde, and þat þat he ouȝt þe lord shulde be algatis paid. Þis servant fell doun and praiede þe lord and seide, Have pacience in me, and Y shal quyte þee al. Þe lord hadde mercy on him, and forȝaf him al his dette. Þis servant went out and found
30 oon of hise dettours, þat ouȝt him an hundred pens; and toke him and stranglide him, and bade him paie his dette. And þis servant felle doun and praiede him of pacience, and he shulde bi tyme ȝelde him al þaţ he ouȝte him.

[1] See p. 27.

But þis man wolde not, but wente out and putte him in
prisoun, til he hadde paied þe dette þat he ouȝte him.
And oþir servauntis of þis man, whan þei seyen þis dede,
mourneden ful myche, and tolden al þis to þe lord. And
þe lord clepid him, and seide unto him, Wickide servant, 5
al þi dette Y forȝaf þe, for þou preiedist me ; ne bihoved
þee not to have mercy on þi servant, as Y hadde mercy
on þee? And þe lord was wroþ, and ȝaf him to turmen-
tours, til he hadde paied al þe dette þat he ouȝte him.
On þis manere, seiþ Crist, shal my Fadir of hevene do to 10
you, but ȝif ye forȝyve, ech on to his broþir, of ȝour free
herte.

Sermons.   Þe Two and Twentiþe Sondai Gospel Aftir Trinité.

II. [THE PRODIGAL SON.]

Homo quidam habuit duos.—LUC. xv. 11.

A man hadde two sones ; and þe ȝonger of hem
seide unto his fadir, Fadir, ȝyve me a porcioun of þe
substance þat falliþ me. And þe fadir departide him his 15
goodis. And soone aftir, þis ȝonge sone gederide al þat fel
to him, and wente forþ in pilgrimage in to a fer contré ;
and þer he wastide his goodis, lyvynge in lecherie. And
after þat he hadde endid alle his goodis, þer fel a gret
hungre in þat lond, and he bigan to be nedy. And he 20
wente oute, and clevede to oon of þe citizeins of þat
contré, and þis citisein sente him into his toun, to kepe
swyn. And þis sone coveitide to fille his beli wiþ pese
holes þat þe hogges eten, and no man ȝaf him. And he,
turninge aȝen, seide, How many hynen in my fadirs hous 25
ben ful of loves, and Y perishe here for hungre. Y shal
rise, and go to my fadir, and seie to him, Fadir, I have
synned in heven, and bifore þee ; now Y am not worþi to
be clepid þi sone, make me as oon of þin hynen. And
he roos, and cam to his fadir. And ȝit whanne he was 30
fer, his fadir sawe him, and was moved bi mercy, and
rennyng aȝens his sone, fel on his nekke, and kiste him.
And þe sone seide to him, Fadir, Y have synned in
hevene, and bifore þee ; now Y am not worþi to be clepid

þi sone. And þe fadir seide to his servauntis anoon,
Bringe ȝe forþ þe firste stoole, and cloþe ȝe him, and ȝyve
ȝe a ryng in his hond, and shoon upon his feet. And
bringe ȝe a fat calf, and sle him, and ete we, and fede us;
5 for þis sone of myn was deed, and is quykened aȝen, and
he was perishid, and is foundun. And þei bigunne to
feede hem. And his eldere sone was in þe feeld; and
whanne he cam, and was nyȝ þe hous, he herde a sym-
phonie and oþer noise of mynystralcye. And þis eldere
10 sone clepide oon of þe servauntis, and axide what weren
þes þingis. And he seide to him, Þi broþir is comen,
and þi fadir haþ slayn a fat calf, for he haþ resceyved him
saaf. But þis eldere sone hadde dedeyn, and wolde not
come in; þerfore his fadir wente out, and bigan to preie
15 him. And he answeride, and seide to his fadir, Lo, so
many ȝeeris Y serve to þee, Y passide nevere þi mandement; and þou ȝavest me nevere a kide, for to fede me
wiþ my frendis. But after þat he, þis þi sone, þat mur-
þeride his goodis wiþ hooris, is come, þou hast killid to
20 him a fat calf. And þe fadir seide to him, Sone, þou art
ever more wiþ me, and alle my goodis ben þine. But it
was nede to ete and to make mery, for he, þis þi broþir
was deed, and lyvede aȝen; he was perishid, and is
founden.

Sermons. Þe Saturday Gospel in þe Secunde Weke in Lente.

III. [THE PARABLE OF THE TALENTS.]

Homo quidam peregre proficiscens.—MATT. xxv. 14.

25 A man, seiþ Crist, goinge a pilgrimage, clepide hise
servantis, and ȝaf hem his goodis. And oon he ȝaf fyve
besauntis, and two to anoþer, and to anoþer oon, ech on
after his owne virtue. And whanne he hadde delid þus,
he wente anoon his pilgrimage. And of þes þree ser-
30 vantis, þe first, þat hadde fyve besauntis, wente and
wrouȝte in hem, and gat oþer fyve; þe secounde, þat
hadde two besauntis, wan oþer two ; but he þat took oon,
wente and dalf[1] in þo erþe, and hidde þe monie of his

[1] dalve it *E.*

lord wiþouten encreese. And after long tyme cam þe
lord of þese servantis and rekenede wiþ hem. And þe
firste, þat hadde fyve besauntis, cam to þe lord and offride
him oþer fyve, and seide; Lord þou ȝavest me fyve
besauntis, lo I have geten over[1] oþer fyve. And his 5
lord seide to him ; Wel be þe, good servaunt and trewe ;
for þou was trewe of litil, upon many þingis Y shal putte
þee ; entre in to þe joie of þi lord. Þe secounde cam
nyȝe þat hadde two besauntis, and seide ; Lord þou
ȝavest me two besauntis, lo, oþer two have Y wonne over. 10
And his lord seide to him ; Wel be þee, good servaunt
and trewe ; for þou was trewe of fewe þingis, Y shall putte
þee upon many þingis ; entre into joie of þi lord.

IV. [THE CRUCIFIXION.]

Tunc ergo apprehendit Pilatus Jesum.—JOHN xix.

And þanne toke Pilat Jesus and scourgide Him. And
knyȝtis, foldinge a crowne of þorn, puttiden upon Cristis 15
heed, and cloþiden Him in a cloiþ of purpur. And þei
camen to Him, and seiden 'Heyl þou kyng of Jewis' ; and
þei ȝavun Him buffatis.

Pilat wente out aȝen and seiþ to hem, ' Lo ! Y bringe
Him forþ to ȝou, þat ȝe wite þat Y fynde no cause 20
in Him.' And so Jesus wente out, and baar a crowne of
þornes, and cloiþ of purpur. And Pilat seiþ to hem,
' Lo! þe man '. But whanne bishopis and mynystris
hadden seen Crist, þei crieden, and seiden, ' Picche[2] Him
on þe crosse, picche Him on þe crosse ! ' Pilat seide to hem, 25
' Tak ȝe Him ȝouself, and do ȝe Him on þe cross ; for Y
fynde no cause in Him [to dampne Him to sich deþ].' Þe
Jewis answeriden to Pilat, ' We han a lawe, and after þat
lawe He is worþi to die, for He made Him Goddis sone.'

And whanne Pilat hadde herd þis word, he dredde 30
more, and wente aȝen into þat halle, and seide to Jesus,
' Of whenns art þou ? ' But Jesus ȝaf him noon answere.
Þerfore Pilat seide to Him, ' Spekist þou not to me ?

---

[1] *om. E.*   [2] Putte *E.*

Woost þou not þat Y have power to picche on þe crosse,
and to leeve þee?' Jesus answeride, 'Þou shuldist have
noo power aȝen me, but ȝif it were ȝovun þee from above.
Þerfore he þat trayede me to þee haþ more synne.'

5 Fro þennes forþ souȝte Pilat to delyvere Jesus, but þe
Jewis crieden, and seiden, 'Ȝif þou leevest Him þus, þou
art not þe Emperours frend, for ech man þat makiþ him
king, aȝenseiþ þe Emperour.' And Pilat, whanne he
hadde herd þes wordis, ledde Jesus forþ, and sat for
10 domesman in place þat is seid Licostratos, and in Ebrew
Golgatha. And it was þe Friday of Pask, as it were þe
sixte hour. And Pilat seiþ to þe Jewis, 'Lo! your
kyng.' And þei crieden, 'Take awey! take awey!
picche Him on þe crosse!' Pilat seide to hem, 'Shall Y
15 pitche ȝour kyng on þe crosse?' Þe bishops answeriden,
'We han no kyng but þe Emperour.' Herfore Pilate
toke þanne Crist to hem, to putte Him on þe cros.

Þe Jewis tooken Jesus and ledden Him out. And Crist,
beerynge to Him a cros, went in to þat place þat is clepid
20 Calvarie, and in Ebrew Golgatha; wher þei putten Him
on þe crosse, and wiþ Him two oþer, þeves, on eiþer side, but
in þe myddis Jesus. And Pilat wroot a title, and put it
on þe cros; and it was writun on þis maner, JESUS OF
NAZARETH, KYNG OF JEWIS. And þis title redden many
25 of þe Jewis, for þe place where Jesus was don on þe
crosse was nyȝ þe citee. And it was writun in Ebrew,
Greek, and Latyn. But þe bishopis of Jewis seiden to
Pilat, 'Nyle þou wryte, "King of Jewis", but þat He seide,
"Y am King of Jewis".'

30 Pilat answeride, 'Þat Y have writun, Y have writun'. ·

And þe knyȝtis, whanne þei hadden pitchid Him on þe
crosse, token His cloþis, and maden foure partis, to ech
knyȝt a part. And þei token Cristis cote, and þis cote
was unsewid, woven above altogidere. And þes knyȝttis
35 seiden togidere, 'Kerve we it not, but make we lottis
þerof, to whom it shal falle'; þat þe Scripture shulde be
fulfillid þat seiþ, 'Þei partiden to hem my cloþis, and on
my cloiþ þei castiden lott.' And certis þe knyȝttis diden
þes þingis.

And þer stooden about þe crosse of Jesus His modir, and
His modir [1] sistir, Marie Cleophe,[2] and Marie Mawdeleyn.
And herfore, whanne Jesus hadde seen His modir, and His
disciple stondinge þat He lovede, he seide to His modir,
'Womman, lo here þi sone.' And after He seiþ to Joon, 5
his disciple, 'Lo here þi modir.' And fro þat hour took
þis disciple Marie into his modir.

Afterward Jesus, witinge þat now weren alle þingis
ended, þat þe Scripture were endid, He seiþ, 'Y þirste.'
And a vessil was putt þere ful of eisil. And þei token 10
a spungeful of eisil, putting it aboute wiþ isope, and profide it to His mouþ. And whanne Jesus hadde tastid þis
eysil, He seide, 'It is endid'; and bowide doun þe heed,
and sente out þe spirit.

Sermons.   Þe Passioun on Good Friday.

B. *Parallel Versions by Wyclif, 'Hereford', and Purvey.*

Surge, illuminare, Jerusalem.—YSAYE lx. 1.

I. *Wyclif.*

Ryse, and be þou liȝtned,
Jerusalem, for þi liȝt is comen, and glorie of þe Lord is
sprongen upon þee. For lo,
derknesse shal hile þe erþe,
and þicke myst shal hile þe
puplis.   But upon þee shal
þe Lord spryng, and in þee
shal his glorie be seen.   And
folk shulen wandre in þi
liȝt, and kyngis in shynyng
of þi birþe.   Lifte up al
aboute þin eyen and see;
al þes ben gederid, and ben
comen to þee; þi sones
shulen come fro ferr, and þi

'*Hereford.*'

Rys, be thou liȝtid, Jeru- 15
salem, for comen is thi liȝt,
and the glorie of the Lord
up on the is sprunge.   For
lo, dercnesses shul coveren
the erthe and mystinesse 20
puples; upon thee forsothe
shal springe the Lord, and
his glorie in thee shal be
seen.   And gon shul Gen-
tiles in thi liȝt, and kingus 25
in the shynyng of thi rising.
Rere in cumpas thin eȝen,
and see; alle these ben
gedered togidere, camen to
thee; thi sonis fro aferr 30

---

[1] modris *E.*   [2] Cleope *E.*

douȝtris shulen rise aside, and many cuntres shulen trowe in þee. Þanne þou shalt see and abounde, and 5 þin herte shal woundre and be largid, whan þe multitude of þe see shal be turned and þe strengþe of heþene men shal come to þee. Þe 10 flowinge of camels shal hile þee; men þat shulen ryde upon dromodes, men of Madian and of Effa, alle men of Saba shulen come, 15 bryngyng gold and encense, and tellinge heeryng to God.

Sermons. Þe Sonday Pistle Wiþinne Octave of Twelfþe Dai.

shul come, and thi doȝtris fro asyde shul rise. Thanne thou shalt seen, and have plenté; and merveilen, and ben spred abrod shal thin herte, whan convertid shal be to thee the multitude of the se, the strengthe of Jentiles shal come to thee; the flowyng of camels shal covere thee, dromedaries of Madian and Effa; alle fro Saba shul come, gold and encens bringende, and preising to the Lord tellende.

Cap. LX.   *The Profecie of Ysaye.*

Egressus Jesus ibat.—LUC. xix. 1.

II. *Wyclif.*

Jesus wente out, and wente unto Jericho. And lo! þer was a man þat hiȝte 20 Ȝachee, and he was prince of publicans, and he was a riche man. And he souȝte to see Jesus, and he miȝte not for þe puple, for he was 25 litil in stature. And he ran bifore and stiede into a sycomor tree for to see Jesus; for he was to passe þerbi. And whanne he cam 30 to the place, Jesus, lokynge up, saw him. And Jesus seide to him, 'Ȝachee, haste þee to com doun, for to-day Y moot dwelle in þin hous.'

Purvey.

And Jhesus goynge yn, walkide thorou Jericho. And lo! a man, Saché bi name, and this was a prince of pupplicans, and he *was* riche. And he souȝte to se Jhesu, who he was, and he myȝte not for the puple, for he was litil in stature. And he ran bifore, and stiȝede in to a sicomoure tree, to se hym; for he was to passe fro thennus. And Jhesus biheld up, whanne he cam to the place and saiȝ hym, and seide to hym, 'Saché, haste thee, and come down, for to dai Y mot dwelle in

And ʒachee hastide him, and cam doun and took Crist ful joyfulli. And alle þe men, whanne þei sawen, grucchiden and seiden þat he turnede to synful man. And ʒachee stood, and seide to þe Lord, ' Lo ! þe half of my goodis, Sire, Y ʒyve to pore men ; and ʒif Y have ouʒt bigiled ony, Y ʒelde aʒen þe forefold.' And Jesus seide to him, ' For to-day helþe is maad to þis hous, for he is Abraham's Sone. For mannis sone cam to seke and make saf þat was perishid.'

S.rmons. Þe Gospel on Dedicacioun Day of a Chirche.

thin hous.' And he hiʒynge cam doun, and ioiynge resseyuede hym. And whanne alle men sayn, thei grutchiden seiynge, For he 5 hadde turned to a synful man. But Saché stood, and seide to the Lord, 'Lo ! Lord, Y ʒyve the half of my good to pore men ; and if 10 Y have ony thing defraudid ony man, Y ʒelde foure so myche.' Jhesus seith to hym, ' For to dai heelthe is maad to this hous, for that 15 he is Abrahams sone ; for mannus sone cam to seke, and make saaf that thing that perischide.'

Luyk, Cap. XIX.

III. [DUYK ABYMALECH DESTROYS SHECHEM]

' *Hereford.*'

And Abymalech sat in Rana. Zebul forsothe Gaal and his felaws he putte out of the cyté, ne in he suffrede to dwelle. Thanne the day folowynge the puple ʒede out into the feeld ; the whiche whanne it was toold to Abymalech, he took his oost and dyvydide in three companyes, settinge busshementis in the feeldis. And seynge that the puple wente out of the cytee, he roos and felle into hem with his

Purvey.

And Abymalech sat in 20 Ranna. Sotheli Zebul puttide Gaal and hise felowïs out of the citee, and suffride not to dwelle therynne. Therfor in the dai suynge, 25 the puple ʒede out in to the feld. And whanne this thing was teld to Abymelech, he took his oost and departide into three cumpanyes, and 30 settide buyschementis in the feeldis. And he siʒ that the puple ʒede out of the citee ; and he roos and felde on

oost, aȝen fiȝtynge and bi-
seegynge the cytee. For-
sothe two companyes,
opynly rennynge hidir and
5 thidir bi the feeld, the
adversaryes pursueden.
Forsothe Abymalech al that
day overcam the cytee, the
which he took, slayn the
10 dwellers of it, and it de-
struyede, so that salt in it
he sprengide.

Judges ix. 41.

hem with his cumpeny, and
empugnyde and bisegide
the citee. Sothely tweie
cumpenyes ȝeden aboute
opynly bi the feeld and pursueden adversaries. Certis
Abymelech fauȝt aȝens the
citee in al that dai, which
he took, whanne the dwel-
leris weren slayn. And that
citee was destried so that
he spreynte abrood salt
therynne.

Judges ix. 41.

IV. [JESUS AND 'LITLE CHILDREN']

'Hereford.'

And thei offriden to him
litle children, that he
15 schulde touche hem; sotheli disciplis thretenyden
to men offringe. Whom
whanne Jhesus hadde seyn,
he baar hevye, *or unwor-*
20 *thili*, and seith to hem,
'Suffre ȝe litle children for
to come to me, and forbede
ȝe hem not, forsoth of suche
is the kyngdom of God.
25 Treuli I seie to ȝou, who
evere schal not receyve the
kyngdom of God as this
litle child, he schal not
entre in to it.' And he
30 biclippinge hem, and put-
tinge hondis upon hem,
blesside hem.

Mark, Cap. X.

Purvey.

And thei brouȝten to
hym litle children, that he
schulde touche hem; and
the disciplis threteneden
the men that brouȝten hem.
And whanne Jhesus hadde
seyn hem, he baar hevy and
seide to hem, 'Suffre ȝe litle
children to come to me, and
forbede ȝe hem not, for of
suche is the kyndom of God.
Treuli Y seie to ȝou, who
ever resseyveth not the
kyngdom of God as a litil
child, he schal not entre in
to it.' And he biclipide
hem, and leide hise hondis
on hem, and blisside hem.

Mark, Cap. X.

C. *Oo Confort is of Knyʒttis.*

Cristis armure is good to ech Cristen man to hav, for
it noieþ not hevely, neþer in pees ne in werre, and it
makiþ Cristen men hardi aʒens þe fend & alle hise lymes.
And herfore seiþ Crist to Hise: ' Þerfore drede ʒe hem
not ; ' for we have betere ground þan þei, and more helpe 5
þan þei have ; but oure helpe is spiritual, hid to þis world
and for ¹ þe toþer.

And þis lore is nedeful now in þis world, for Anticrist ;
for he haþ turned hise clerkes to coveitise and worldli
love, and so blindid þe peple and derkid þe lawe of Crist, 10
þat hise servantis ben þikke, and fewe ben on Cristis
side.   And algatis þei dispisen þat men shulden knowe
Cristis liif, for bi His liif and His loore shulde helpe rise
on His side, and prestis shulden shame of her lyves, and
speciali þes hiʒe prestis, for þei reversen Crist boþe in 15
word and dede.

And herfore oo greet Bishop of Engelond, as men
seien, is yvel paied þat Goddis lawe is writun in Englis
to lewide men ; and he pursueþ a preest, for he writiþ to
men ² þis Englishe, and somoniþ him and traveiliþ him, 20
þat it is hard to him to rowte.³   And þus he pursueþ
anoþer preest bi þe helpe of Phariseis, for he prechide
Cristis gospel freeli wiþouten fablis.   O men þat ben on
Cristis half, helpe ʒe now aʒens Anticrist ! for þe perilous
tyme is comen þat Crist and Poul telden bifore.   25

But oo confort is of knyʒttis, þat þei savoren myche þe
gospel and han wille to rede in Englishe þe Gospel of
Cristis liif.   For aftirward, if God wole, þis lordship shal
be taken from preestis ; and so þe staaff þat makiþ hem
hardi aʒens Crist and His lawe.   For þree sectis fiʒten 30
here aʒens Cristene mennis secte.   Þe firste is þe Pope
and cardinals, bi fals lawe þat þei han made ; þe secounde
is Emperours ⁴ bishopis, whiche dispisen Cristis lawe ; þe
þridde is þes Pharisees, possessioners and beggeris.   Alle
þes þree, Goddis enemyes, traveilen in ypocrisie, and in 35
worldli coveitise, and idilnesse in Goddis lawe.

¹ fro *E.*   ² to men *om. E.*   ⁸ route *E.*   ⁴ emperour *A.*

Crist helpe His Chirche from þes fendis, for þei fiȝten perilously.

Sermons. Þe Gospel of Many Martris.

D. The Case for Translation.

Ant heere þe freris wiþ þer fautours seyn þat it is heresye to write þus Goddis lawe in English, and make
5 it knowun to lewid men. And fourty signes þat þey bringen for to shewe an heretik ben not worþy to reherse, for nouȝt groundiþ hem but nygromansye.

It semyþ first þat þe wit of Goddis lawe shulde be tauȝt in þat tunge þat is more knowun, for þis wit is
10 Goddis word. Whanne Crist seiþ in þe Gospel þat boþe hevene and erþe shulen passe, but His wordis shulen not passe, He undirstondiþ bi His woordis His wit. And þus Goddis wit is Hooly Writ, þat may on no maner be fals. Also þe Hooly Gost ȝaf to apostlis wit at Wit Sunday
15 for to knowe al maner langagis, to teche þe puple Goddis lawe þerby; and so God wolde þat þe puple were tauȝt Goddis lawe in dyverse tungis. But what man, on Goddis half, shulde reverse Goddis ordenaunse and His wille?

And for þis cause Seynt Ierom travelide and translatide
20 þe Bible fro dyverse tungis into Lateyn, þat it myȝte be aftir translatid to oþere tungis. And þus Crist and His apostlis tauȝten þe puple in þat tunge þat was moost knowun to þe puple. Why shulden not men do nou so?

And herfore autours of þe newe law, þat weren apostlis
25 of Iesu Crist, writen þer Gospels in dyverse tungis þat weren more knowun to þe puple.

Also þe worþy reume of Fraunse, notwiþstondinge alle lettingis, haþ translatid þe Bible and þe Gospels, wiþ oþere trewe sentensis of doctours, out of Lateyn into
30 Freynsch. Why shulden not Engliȝschemen do so? As lordis of Englond han þe Bible in Freynsch, so it were not aȝenus resoun þat þey hadden þe same sentense in Engliȝsch; for þus Goddis lawe wolde be betere knowun, and more trowid, for onehed of wit, and more acord be
35 bitwixe reumes.

And herfore freris han tauȝt in Englond þe Paternoster in Engliȝsch tunge, as men seyen in þe pley of ȝork, and in many oþere cuntreys. Siþen þe Paternoster is part of Matheus Gospel, as clerkis knowen, why may not al be turnyd to Engliȝsch trewely, as is þis part? Specialy 5 siþen alle Cristen men, lerid and lewid, þat shulen be savyd, moten algatis sue Crist, and knowe His lore and His lif. But þe comyns of Engliȝschmen knowen it best in þer modir tunge; and þus it were al oon to lette siche knowing of þe Gospel and to lette Engliȝsch men to sue 10 Crist and come to hevene.

Wel y woot defaute may be in untrewe translating, as myȝten have be many defautis in turnyng fro Ebreu into Greu, and fro Greu into Lateyn, and from o langage into anoþer. But lyve men good lif, and studie many persones 15 Goddis lawe, and whanne chaungyng of wit is foundun, amende þey it as resoun wole.

Sum men seyn þat freris travelen, and þer fautours, in þis cause for þre chesouns, þat y wole not aferme, but God woot wher þey ben soþe. First þey wolden be seun 20 so nedeful to þe Engliȝschmen of oure reume þat singulerly in her wit layȝ þe wit of Goddis lawe, to telle þe puple Goddis lawe on what maner evere þey wolden. And þe secound cause herof is seyd to stonde in þis sentense: freris wolden lede þe puple in techinge hem Goddis lawe, 25 and þus þei wolden teche sum, and sum hide, and docke sum. For þanne defautis in þer lif shulden be lesse knowun to þe puple, and Goddis lawe shulde be untreweliere knowun boþe bi clerkis and bi comyns. Þe þridde cause þat men aspien stondiþ in þis, as þey seyn: alle þes 30 newe ordris dreden hem þat þer synne shulde be knowun, and hou þei ben not groundid in God to come into þe chirche; and þus þey wolden not for drede þat Goddis lawe were knowun in Engliȝsch; but þey myȝten putte heresye on men ȝif Engliȝsch toolde not what þey seyden. 35

God move lordis and bischops to stonde for knowing of His lawe!

de Officio Pastorali, Cap. XV.

E. *A Review of Early Bible Translations.*

Worschipful Bede, in his first boke De Gestis Angulorum, tellith that Seint Oswold, king of Northeumberland, axide of the Scottys an holi pischop Aydan to preche to his puple, and the Kynge of hymself interpreted
5 it on Englische to the puple. If this blessid dede be aloued to the Kynge of al Hooli Chirche, how not now auȝte it to be alowed a man to rede the Gospel on Englische and do theraftur ?

It was herde of a worthi man of Almaine that summe
10 tyme a Flemynge—his name was James Merland—translatid al the Bibel into Flemyche, for wiche dede he was somoned before the Pope of grete enmyté, and the boke was taken to examynacoun and trwly apreved. It was delivered to hym agene in conficioun to his enemyes.

15 Also venerabile Bede, lede by the spirit of God, translatid the Bibel, or a grete part of the Bibile, wos originals ben in many abbeis in Englond. Also Sistrence, in his fifte booke, the 24. Cap., seith the Evangelie of Jon was drawen into Englice be the forseide Bede ; wiche
20 Evangelie of Jon and other Gospellis ben ȝet in many placis, of so oolde Englische that unnethe can any man rede hem. For this Bede regnede an hooly doctur aftur the Incarnacioun sevene hundered ȝeer and xxxij.

Also a man of Loundoun—his name was Wyring—
25 hadde a Bible in Englische of northern speche, wiche was seen of many men, and it semed too houndred ȝeer olde.

Also Cistrence, in his sext bok, Cap. 1, seith that Alfrede the kynge ordined opone scolis of diverse artes
30 in Oxenforde. And he turnede the best lawes in to his modir tunge, and the Sawter also. And he regned aftur the Incarnacioun eiȝt hundered ȝeer and seventi thre.

.   .   .   .

Also a nobil, hooly man, Richerde Ermyte, drew on Englice the Sauter, with a glose of longe proces, and
35 lessouns of Dirige and many other tretis, by wiche many Engliche men hav ben gretli edified.

Also sire Wiliam Thorisby, ercebischop of Ʒork, did
do to drawe a tretys in Englisce be a worschipful clerk,
wos name was Gaytrik: in the wiche weren conteyned
the *Articulis of the Feith, Sevene Dedli Synnes*, the
Werkes of Mercy and the *Comaundements*; and sente 5
hem in smale pagynes to the comyn puple to lerne this
and to know this, of wiche ben ʒit manye a componye in
Englond.

But there ben summe that seien: 'If the Gospel were
on Engliche, men myʒten liʒtly erre thereinne.' But wel 10
touchith this holy man, Richa[r]d Hampol, such men,
expownyng this tixte: *Ne auferas de ore meo verbum
veritatis usquequaque.* Ther he seith thus: 'Ther ben
not fewe but many wolen sustene a worde of falsenes for
God, not willing to beleve to konynge and better than 15
thei ben.'

. . . .

Also it is knowun to many men that in the tyme of
King Richerd—whose soule God assoile—into a Parliment was put a bille, be assent of two erchebischopis
and of the clergie, to annulle the Bibel that tyme trans- 20
lated into Engliche, and also other bokis of the Gospel
translatid into Engliche. Which, whanne it was seyn of
Lordis and Comouns, the good Duke of Lancastre, Jon,—
wos soule God assoile, for his mercy—, answered therto
sharpely, seying this sentence: 'We wil not be the refuse 25
of alle men. For, sithen other naciouns han Goddis
lawe, wich is lawe of oure byleve, in ther owne modur
langage, we wolen have oure in Engliche, who that evere
it bigrucche.' And this he affermede with a grete
othe. 30

Also the Bischope of Caunturbiri, Thomas Arrundel,
that nowe is, seide a sermon in Westimistir, thereas
weren many hundred puple, at the biriyng of Quene Anne,
of wos soule God have mercy. And, in his comendynges
of hir, he seide it was more joie of hir than of any woman 35
that evere he knewe. For, notwithstanding, that sche
was an alien borne, sche hadde on Engliche al the foure
Gospeleris, with the docturis upon hem. And he seide

that sche had sent hem unto him. And he seide thei
weren goode and trewe, and comended hir in that sche
was so grete a lady and also an alien, and wolde so
lowliche studie in so vertuous bokis.

From Purvey's *Determination, c.* 1405.

F. *Extracts from Purvey's General Prologue.*

[SIMPLE MEN MAY STUDY HOLY WRIT]

5   Cristen men and wymmen, olde and ȝonge, shulden
studie fast in the Newe Testament, for it is of ful
autorité, and opyn to undirstonding of simple men, as to
poyntis that be moost nedeful to salvacioun. . . . He that
kepith mekenes and charité hath the trewe undirstondyng
10 and perfectioun of al Holi Writ, as Austyn previth in his
Sermoun of the PREYSING OF CHARITÉ. Þerfore no
simple man of wit be aferd unmesurabli to studie in the
text of Holy Writ, forwhi tho ben wordis of everlasting
lif, as Petir seide to Crist in the vj Chapitre of Jon.

The General Prologue to the Second Version of the Bible.

[THE BOOK OF ESTHER]

15   The book of Ester tellith first, how the qwene Vasti
was forsaken for hire pride, and was departid fro mariage
of King Assuerus, and hou Ester for hire meeknesse,
bewté and Goddis grace, was maad qwene in the stide of
Vasty. Also the trewe Mardoché, the fadir in lawe of
20 adopcioun of this womman Ester, tauȝte hire to love
God, and kepe his lawe, and sche was full meke and
obedient to Mardochee, ȝhe, whanne sche was qwene, as
to hir fadir in lawe.

Thanne Aaman of the kinrede of Agag, conspyred bi
25 sotil malice to distroie al the peple of Jewis, in the lond
of Assuerus, and hadde a graunte of the King at his
owne wille and the day of distroiyng and of sleeing of the
Jewis was pupplischid thourȝ al the rewme.

Thanne Mardochee and the Jewis diden greet penaunce,
30 and maden gret sorwe, and preieden God to helpe in that
gret nede. And Mardochee sente to Ester that sche

schulde do the same and goo to the King, in perel of
hire lijf, to axe grace of him, and revoking of lettris and
power grauntid to Aaman, the enemy of Jewis.

And aftir myche fasting, penaunce and preier, Estir
bitook hirself to Goddis disposicioun, and to perel of her 5
deth, and entride to the King, ȝhe, aȝens the lawe of the
lond, whanne sche was not clepid, to axe mercy and help
of the King for hirsilf and al hire puple. And God
turnede the feersnesse and cruelté of the King to mekenesse, mersy and benyngnité aȝens Ester and the peple 10
of Jewis. And thanne he revokide the power grauntid
to Aaman, and leet hange him as he purposide to have
hangid the trewe Mardochee, and ȝaf general power to
Jewis to slee alle hire enemyes in his empire. Aftir these
thingis the King enhanside Mardochee, and made him 15
grettist next the king, and ȝaf greet fraunchise and onour
to the Jewis.

This story of Ester schulde stire men to be trewe to
Gode and his lawe, and put away pride and envye, and
evere triste in God in alle perrels. And tirauntis schulden 20
be aferd to conspire aȝens Goddis servantis, leest God
take veniaunce on hem as he dide on this man Aaman
that conspiride the deeth and general distroiyng of
Jewis.

Ibidem.

[THE PSALTER]

The Sautir comprehendith al the Elde and Newe 25
Testament and techith pleynly the mysteries of the
Trinité, and of Cristis incarnacioun, passioun, rising
aȝen, stying in to hevene, and sending doun of the Holy
Gost, and preching of the Gospel, and the coming of
Antecrist, and the general dom of Crist, and the glorie of 30
chosen men to blisse, and the peynes of hem that
schulen be dampned in helle ; and ofte rehersith the
stories of the Elde Testament, and bringith in the
keping of Goddis heestis and love of enemyes.

Noo book in the Eld Testament is hardere to undir- 35
stonding to us Latyns, for oure lettre discordith myche

fro the Ebreu, and many doctouris taken litel heede to
the lettre, but al to the goostly undirstonding.   Wel
were him that koude wel undirstonde the Sautir, and
kepe it in his lyvyng, and seie it devoutly, and convicte
5 Jewis therbi ; for manye men that seyn it undevoutly,
and lyven out of charité, lyen foule on hemself to God,
and blasfemen Hym, whanne thei crien it ful loude to
mennis eeris in the chirche.   Therefore God ȝeve grace
to us to lyve wel in charité, and sey it devoutly, and
10 undirstonde it treuly, and to teche it opinly to Cristen
men and Jewis, and bringe hem therby to oure Cristen
feith and brennynge charité.

Ibidem.

[THE PROFITABLE SAYINGS OF PHILOSOPHERS SHOULD
BE ' CALENGID ' BY CHRISTIANS]

Also Hooly Scripture wlatith sofymys and seith : He
that spekith sofistically either by sofymys, schal be
15 hatful, and he schal be defrauded in ech thing, as the
wijse man seith in xxxvij Cap. of Ecclesiastici.   If
filosoferis, and moost the disciplis of Plato, seiden eny
treuthis and prophitable to oure feith, not only tho
treuthis owen not to be dred, but also tho schulen be
20 calengid into oure us eithir profijt, fro hem, as fro uniust
possessouris.

And as Jewis token bi autorité of God the gold and
silver and clothis of Egipcyans, so Cristene men owen to
take the trewe seyingis of filosueris for to worschippe oo
25 God, and of techingis of vertues, whiche treuthis the
filosueris founden not, but diggeden out of the metals of
Goddis purvyance, which is sched everywhere.

So dide Ciprian, the swettest doctour and most blessid
martir.   So diden Lactancius, Victorinus, and Illarie
30 and Greekis withoute noumbre.

Ibidem.

[AN ABOMINATION AT OXFORD UNIVERSITY]

But alas ! alas ! alas ! the moost abomynacoun that
ever was herd among Cristen clerkis is now purposid in

Yngelond, bi worldly clerkis and feyned religiouse, and in the cheef Universitee of oure reume, as manye trewe men tellen with greet weylyng. This orrible and develis cursednesse is purposid of Cristis enemyes and traytouris of alle Cristen puple : that no man schal lerne dyvynité 5 neither Hooly Writ, no but he that hath doon his fourme in art, that is, that hath comensid in art, and hath been regent tweyne ȝeer aftir. This wolde be ix. ȝeer either ten bifore that he lerne Hooly Writ, aftir that he can comunly wel his gramer, thouȝ he have a good witt, and 10 traveile ful soore, and have good fynding ix. either x ȝeer aftir his gramer. This semith uttirly the develis purpos, that fewe men either noon schulen lerne and kunne Goddis lawe.

Ibidem.

[THE RIGHT METHOD OF TRANSLATING THE SCRIPTURES]

Thouȝ covetouse clerkis ben woode by simonie, eresie, 15 and manye othere synnes, and dispisen and stoppen Holi Writ as myche as thei moun, ȝit the lewid puple crieth aftir Holi Writ, to kunne it, and kepe it, with greet cost and peril of here lif. For these resons and othere, with comune charité to save alle men in oure rewme whiche 20 God wole have savid, a symple creature hath translatid the Bible out of Latyn into Englisch.

First, this symple creature hadde myche travaile, with diverse felawis and helperis, to gedere manie elde Biblis and othere doctouris and comune glosis, and to make oo 25 Latyn Bible sumdel trewe ; and thanne to studie it of the newe, the text with the glose, and othere doctouris, as he miȝte gete, and speciali Lire on the Elde Testament, that helpide ful myche in this werk ; the thridde tyme to counseile with elde gramariens and elde dyvynis 30 of harde wordis and harde sentencis, hou tho miȝten best be undurstonden and translatid ; the iiij. tyme to translate as cleerli as he coude to the sentence, and to have manie gode felawis and kunnynge at the correcting of the translacioun. 35

First it is to knowe, that the best translating is out of
Latyn into English, to translate aftir the sentence, and
not oneli aftir the wordis, so that the sentence be as opin
either openere in English as in Latyn, and go not fer fro
5 the lettre ; and if the lettre mai not be suid in the translating, let the sentence evere be hool and open, for the
wordis owen to serve to the entent and sentence, and
ellis the wordis ben superflu either false.

In translating into English, manie resolucions moun
10 make the sentence open, as an ablative case absolute
may be resolvid into these thre wordis, with covenable
verbe, *the while, for, if*—as gramariens seyn.   As thus :
the maistir redinge, I stonde may be resolvid thus : *While
the maistir redith, I stonde*, either *If the maistir redith*,
15 either *For the maistir* etc.   And sumtyme it wolde
acorde wel with the sentence to be resolvid into *whanne*
either into *aftirward*.   Thus :—*Whanne the maister red,
I stood*, either *Aftir the maistir red, I stood*.   And sumtyme it may wel be resolvid into a verbe of the same
20 tens, as othere ben in the same resoun, and into this
word *et*, that is, *and* in English.   And thus : *Arescenti-
bus hominibus prae timore* : that is, *And men shulen
wexe drie for drede*.

Also a participle of a present tens, either preterit, of
25 active vois, eithir passif, mai be resolvid into a verbe of
the same tens and a coniunccioun copulatif.   As thus :
—*dicens*, that is, *seiynge*, mai be resolvid thus, *and seith*,
either *that seith*.   And this wole in manie placis make
the sentence open where to Englisshe it aftir the word
30 wolde be derk and douteful. . . .

At the begynning I purposide with Goddis helpe to
make the sentence as trewe and open in English as it is
in Latyn, either more trewe and more open than it is in
Latyn.   And I preie for charité and for comoun profyt
35 of Cristene soulis that if ony wiys man fynde ony defaute
of the truthe of translacioun, let him sette in the trewe
sentence and opin of Holi Writ ; but loke that he
examyne truli his Latyn Bible, for no doute he shall
fynde ful manye Biblis in Latyn ful false, if he loke

manie, nameli newe.   And the comune Latyn Biblis han
more nede to be correctid, as manie as I have seen in my
lif, þan hath the English Bible late translatid ; and where
the Ebreu, bi witnesse of Jerom, of Lire, and othere
expositouris, discordith fro oure Latyn Biblis, I have set 5
in the margyn, bi maner of a glose, what the Ebru hath,
and how it is undurstondun in sum place.   And I dide
this most in the Sauter, that of alle oure bokis discordith
most fro Ebru. . . .

Lord God ! sithen at the bigynnyng of feith so manie 10
men translatiden into Latyn, and to greet profyt of Latyn
men, lat oo symple creature of God translate into English for profyt of English men ; for if worldli clerkis
loken wel here croniclis and bokis, thei shulden fynde
that Bede translatide the Bible and expounide it myche 15
in Saxon, that was English either comoun langage of
this lond in his tyme.   And not oneli Bede, but also
King Alured that foundide Oxenford, translatide in hise
laste daies the bigynning of the Sauter into Saxon, and
wolde more if he hadde lyved lengere.   20

Also Frenshemen, Beemers and Britons han the Bible,
and othere bokis of devocioun and exposicioun translatid in here modir langage.   Whi shulden not Englishmen have the same in here modir langage, I can no wite,
nobut for falsenesse and necgligence of clerkis, either for 25
oure puple is not worthi to have so greet grace and ȝifte
of God in peyne of here olde synnes.

But in translating of wordes equivok, that is, that hath
manie significacions undur oo lettre, mai liȝtli be peril.
For Austyn seith in the *ij Book of Cristene Teching* that 30
if equivok wordis be not translatid into the sense either
undurstonding of the autour, it is errour ; as in that place
of the Salme : *The feet of hem ben swifte to shede out
blood.*   The Greek word is equivok to *sharp* and *swift* ;
and he that translatide *sharp feet* erride ; and a book 35
that hath *sharp feet* is fals and mut be amendid ; as that
sentence *Unkynde ȝonge trees shulen not ȝeve depe rootis*
owith to be thus : *Plauntingis of avoutrie shulen not ȝeve
depe rootis.*   Austyn seith this there.

Therefore a translatour hath greet nede to studie wel
the sentence both bifore and aftir, and loke that suche
equivok wordis acorde with the sentence.   And he hath
nede to lyve a clene lif, and be ful devout in preiers, and
5 have not his wit ocupied about worldli thingis, that the
Holi Spiryt, autour of wisdom and kunnyng and truthe,
dresse him in his werk and suffre him not for to erre.

Also this word *ex* signifieth sumtyme *of*, and sumtyme it signifieth *bi*, as Jerom seith.   And this word
10 *enim* signifieth comynly *forsothe*, and, as Jerom seith, it
signifieth *cause thus, forwhi*.   And this word *secundum*
is taken for *aftir*, as manie men seyn, and comynli ; but
it signifieth wel *bi* eithir *up* ; thus *bi ʒoure word* either
up ʒoure word.   Manie such adverbis, coniuncciouns and
15 preposiciouns ben set ofte oon for another, and at fre
chois of autouris sumtyme ; and now tho shulen be taken
as it acordith best to the sentence.

By this maner, with good lyvyng and greet travel,
men moun come to trewe and cleer translating, and a
20 trewe undurstonding of Hoii Writ, seme it nevere so hard
at the bigynnyng.

God graunte to us alle grace to kunne wel and kepe
wel Holi Writ, and suffre ioiefulli sum peyne for it at the
laste.   Amen.

Ibidem.

III

POOR PRIESTS

Christus, deus noster, caput universalis ecclesie. fuit pro tempore huius peregrinacionis homo pauperrimus.

Conclusiones Triginta Tres.

Þis schulde Cristen men defende as þe feiþ of Crist, þat þe most holy werke and most duwe to prelatis, were to sowe Cristis seed by charité among þe peple. 5

Þe Seven Werkys of Mercy Gostly.

Primum, autem, istorum [sacerdotum] est Christi evangelii praedicatio, cum Christus, Marci ultimo, pro memoriali perpetuo sacerdotibus hanc injunxit.

de Ecclesia.

With reference to the origin of the Poor Priests, Workman gives the following interesting account :[1] 10

'The translation of the Bible and the publication of English tracts formed part of a larger purpose. Before either had been commenced Wyclif had devised another means for spreading his teaching. In his early days he had allied himself with the friars. He now copied the methods of St. Francis. From Oxford, as from 15 Assisi two centuries before, Wyclif, like Wesley four centuries later, sent out as early, probably, as the year 1377—certainly before the Peasants' Revolt, in which they were accused of playing a part—his order of " Poor Priests " or " itinerant preachers " who in the highways and byways, and by the village-greens and grave- 20 yards, sometimes even in the churches, should denounce abuses, proclaim the true doctrine of the Eucharist and teach the right thinking from which, as he deemed, right living would follow. It was for these " Poor Priests " that Wyclif prepared his tracts and skeletons of sermons, and undertook his paraphrase of the Bible.' 25

Though Wyclif was no doubt influenced by the example of St. Francis, he grounded himself characteristically on the teaching of the Gospels. The *Mission of the Seventy* was his real model for imitation.[2] He tended ever more and more to regard the licence of Christ as sufficient authority for the right 30

---

[1] H. B. W. ii. 201.   [2] See Extract A.

to preach. It is very interesting to observe how he arrived at this position. In medieval church theory the main function of a bishop was to preach himself, and to license auxiliary preachers. The bishops of Wyclif's day failed to do this
5 sufficiently for the adequate promulgation of the Gospel. Wyclif therefore declared that if the bishops fell short of grace, in this respect, recourse must be had direct to the chief bishop, namely, Christ, who of Himself would grant the necessary power and authority. This typically scholastic line of thought
10 is well illustrated by the following sentence from *Þe Pater Noster*: 'Praye we Jesus Crist, byschepe of oure soule, þat he ordeyne prechours in þe peple to warne hem of synne and telle hem þe truþe of God '.[1]

A. *A Rule of Life for Poor Priests.*

Designavit Dominus Jesus.—Luc. x. 1.

Þis gospel telliþ how Crist sente lesse disciplis to preche
15 to þe peple, and ordeyne for þe apostlis ; and þes wordis helpen moche for prechinge of simple preestis, for grete apostlis figuren bishopis, and lesse disciplis lesse preestis. But þese *disciplis weren two and seventy* in noumbre ; and so many, as men seien, weren langagis aftir making
20 of Babiloyne; and alle Cristis disciplis traveiliden to bringe to oon men of þe Chirche, so þat þer shulde be oon heerde and oon flok. Þis noumbre of Cristis disciplis *sente he, two and two bifore his face, into ech place þat he was to come to,* for to preche and to teche, as weren citees
25 and comune places.
And here moun Cristene men se þe falshede of þese freris, how þei letten symple prestis to preche þe gospel to þe folk. For as þei feynen falsely, noon of Cristis disciplis hadde leve to preche til þat Petir hadde ȝovun
30 him leve, and bi þis same skile, noo preest shulde preche to þe peple, but if he hadde leve of þe bishop or leve of þe pope. Þis gospel telliþ þe falsnesse of þes freris lesynge, for Crist sente þese disciplis to preche comunly to þe peple, wiþouten lettre or axinge of leve of Seint

[1] *S.E.W.* iii. 106.

Petir; and as Petir shulde not graunte þis leve in Cristis
presence, so preestis in Cristis presence have leve of Crist,
whanne þei ben preestis, to preche treuli þe gospel.
And if þei prechen þus treuli þe gospel as Crist biddiþ
hem, Crist is amyddis hem, and þe peple þat þei techen. 5
And alȝif prelatis shulden examyne prestis þat prechen
þus, neþeles it were more nede to examyne þes freris, þat
feynen hem to be preestis, for þei comen in of worse
ground, and ben more suspect of heresie.

Lord! what resoun shulde dryve herto, to lette trewe 10
preestis to preche þe gospel freeli, wiþouten ony let, or
ony fablis or flaterynge, and ȝyve leve to þese freris to
preche fablis and heresies, and aftirward to spoile þe
peple, and selle hem her false sermouns. Certis þe peple
shulde not suffre siche falshede of Antecrist. Also Poul, 15
Cristis apostle, techiþ in bokes of oure bileve, how God
wolde þat he prechide to þe peple wiþouten sich axing;
for fro þe tyme þat he was convertid, þree ȝeer after, he
preechide fast, and axide noo leve of Petir herto, for he
hadde leve of Jesus Crist. Siche novelries of pseudo 20
freris shulden prelatis and alle men aȝen stonden, lest her
falshede growide more and largerly[1] envenymede þe
Chirche. Þus shulden preestis preche þe peple freeli
Cristis gospel, and leve freris fablis and her begginge, for
þanne þei preche wiþ Cristis leve; and herof shulden 25
prelatis be feyn, siþ þei synnen moche on oþer sidis, but
if þei ben Antecristis preestis and shapen to quenche
Cristis lawe. But þe peple comunli trowide in Crist and
lovede Him, and þus þei obeschen[2] to þis tyme, boþe to
Crist and His lawe. 30

And Crist shewide þe cause and þe nede of þis prechinge, *for He seide, Ripe corn is moche, and fewe workmen
aboute it.* But for þis work is medeful, and Crist sove-
reynli performyde it, þerfore He techiþ His disciplis, to
preie þe lord of þis ripe corn to sende hise workmen þerto. 35
And here Crist techiþ opinli þat men shulden not bie þis
office, ne take no mede of þe peple to traveile þus in
Cristis name, for þanne þei puttiden upon Crist þat He

---

[1] largerely *E*.   [2] *So* *Ė*; *A* has oblishen.

sillide prechyng of His word, and ȝaf leve to do symonye ;
and boþe þes ben blasfemyes. But Crist stiride His men
to go, and telliþ[1] hem þe peril bifore, but He moveþ hem
privyly for greet mede to traveile þus ; *Go ȝe*, seiþ Crist,
5 *for Y sende ȝou as lambren among wolves.* And so we
have mandement of Crist, and autorité to go, and foorme
of þis perilous goinge, þat makiþ it more medeful. But
Crist ȝyveþ His prechours[2] foorme how þei shal lyve in
þis work ; *Nyle ȝe, He seiþ, bere sachil ne scrippe, ne hosis,*
10 *ne shoon, ne greete men bi þe weie,* ne do þing þat
shulde lette þis work. If ony siche helpe to þis work,
Crist wolde not þat þei leften it. And þus seiþ Crist þat,
*In to what hous ȝe entren, ȝe shal first seie, Pees be to þis
hous ; and if þere be child of pees, ȝoure pees shal reste*
15 *upon him, and ellis it shal turne aȝen to ȝou,* and so ȝoure
work shal not be idil. But if ypocritis worchen here, al
ȝif þei seien sich wordis, þe housis and þe peple ben
worse, þat þese false men comen among ; for Crist doiþ
þese vertues, in whos name þese prechours speken, and if
20 þei ben þe fendis lymes, comunly þei moven to synne.
But Crist wolde not þat Hise workmen wenten aboute
wiþouten fruyt, and þerfore He biddiþ hem *dwelle in þe
same hous* upon resoun ; but þei shulden be not idil þere,
ne curious in mete and drynke, but þe peple shulde gladly
25 fede hem, and þei shulden homly take þat þei founden,
and þei shulden take no newe reule bi which þe peple
were chargid. And neiþer part shulde grutche here to do
þus as Crist techiþ, for it shulde turne wiþoute charge to
mede of boþe partis ; and good lyf of sich workmen
30 shulden move þe peple to do hem good, and devocioun of
þe peple should preie hem to take her goodis. But
gredynesse and avarice letten here þes two partis ; and al
if boþe þes synnes letten moche fro Cristis work, neþeles
coveitise of preestis is more perilous in þis caas ; for
35 avarice of þe peple mai be helpid on many maners, oþer
to turne to oþer peple, or to traveile as Poul dide, or to
suffre wilfulli hunger, and þrist if it falle ; but coveitise of

---

[1] *So E; A has* telle.   [2] preciouse *E.*

wickide preestis blemyshiþ hem and þe peple, for comunly
þei shapen her wordis aftir þe ende þat þei coveiten.

And here þenken many men þat siche prechours
shulden be war þat þey come not wiþ myche peple ne
many hors to preche þus, but be paied of comun diete, 5
and þerwiþ redi to traveile, for þei shulden be noo cause
of synne, neþer of hem ne of þe peple. And here it
semeþ to many men þat þese newe ordris of freris shulden
eiþer leve her multitude, or traveile wiþ her hondis, and
if þei diden boþe þes two discretely, it were þe betere. 10
Ne take þei not of Cristis lyf to traveile not, as Crist did
not, for neiþer þey can ne moun be occupied ellis as Crist
was; but raþer þei shulden take of Poul and oþer apostlis
for to traveile, and leve her newe tradiciouns, as Petir
dide, wiþ oþer apostlis, and profitiden more þan þes men 15
done.   We shulden þenke how Petir lyvede whanne
Cornelious sente after him, how symply he was fed and
herborid, and how he answeride; but now freris reversen
Petir and multiplien newe lawes[1] and persones of þeir
ordris, havynge more þan Petir hadde. And herwiþ þei 20
seien to men þat þei passen bishopis and popis, and certis
þei seien here þe soþe, if þei menen passinge in synne, for
unleveful excesse is passinge to þes freris. And so as þei
varien in abitis, so þei ben speckid in her ordris, for as þe
sect of Sarasynes,[2] þei han sum good and sum yvele.   25

Sermons.   On Dai of oon Evangelist.

B. *The Poverty of Christ and His Disciples.*

In þe lif of Crist and His gospel, þat is His testament,
wiþ lif and techyng of His postlis, oure clerkis schullen not
fynde but povert, mekenesse, gostly traveile, and dispisyng
of worldly men for reprovyng of here synnes, and grete
reward in Hevene for here goode lif and trewe techyng, 30
and wilful sofforyng of deþ. Þerfore Jesus Crist was pore
in His lif, þat He hadde no house of His owene bi worldly
title to reste His heed þerinne, as He Hymself seiþ in þe
gospel. And Seynt Petir was so pore þat he hadde

<hr />

[1] *So E*; lawyes *A*.   [2] Sarascenes, *E*.

neiþer silver ne gold to ʒeve a pore crokid man, as Petir
witnesseþ in þe bok of Apostlis Dedis. Seynt Poul was
so pore of worldly goodis þat he traveilede wiþ his hondis
for his liflode and his felowis, and suffride moche perse-
5 cucion, and wakyng of gret þouʒt for alle chirches in
Cristendom, as he hymself witnessiþ in many placis of
holy writt. And Seynt Bernard writiþ to þe pope, þat in
þis worldly aray, and plenté of londis and gold and silver,
he is successour of Constantyn þe emperour, and not of
10 Jesus Crist and His disciplis. And Jesus confermyng þis
testament seide to His apostlis after His risyng fro deþ
to life, My Fadir sente me and I sende ʒow,—þat is, to
traveile, persecucion, and povert and hunger and martirdom in þis world, and not to worldly [pompe] as clerkis
15 usen now. Bi þis it semeþ, þat alle þes worldly clerkis
havyng seculer lordischipe, wiþ aray of worldly vanyté,
ben hugely cursed of God and man, for þei doun aʒenst
þe riʒtful testament of Crist and His postlis.

Þe Grete Sentence of Curs Expouned.

C. *Persecution of Poor Priests.*

Þe fourþ word þat Crist seiþ conteyneþ þre pursuingis;
20 'ʒe shulen be blessid,' seiþ Crist, ' whanne men shulen hate
ʒou, and whanne þei shulen departe ʒou, and after repreve
ʒou.'
Cristis servantis on many maneris ben departid here.
Worldeli men fleen hem and leven hem by hemsilf; þei
25 ben cursid of Anticrist, and put out of chirchis, and þei
ben partid in prisouns fro oþer men of þe world. And in
alle þes statis þei suffren reproves, and if þei ben certeyn
bi lore of her bileve þat þei suffren in all þis fro cause of
her God, þei moun be blessid and joiful for hope of þe
30 ende, as a syk man gladli wole suffre peyne whanne he
hopiþ þerbi to come aftir to hele. And joie þat seintis
shulen have whanne þei suffren þus is a manere of blisse
þat þei han here, for it is more joie þan all þese worldli
lustis.
35 And, as Crist telliþ, þese þat stonden in Cristis cause,

han her names cast out as cursid men and heretikes, for her enemyes ben so blynde and so depe in her synne þat þei clepen good yvel, and yvel good. But woo be to suche.

And Crist biddiþ his servantis *to joie þat dai in her* [5] *herte, and shewe a glad countynaunce,* to men þat ben about hem, *for certis her mede is moche in þe blisse of hevene.* And þis word counfortiþ symple men, þat ben clepid eretikes and enemyes to þe Chirch for þei tellen Goddis lawe. For þei ben somynned and reprovyd many [10] weies, and after put in prison, and brend [1] or kild as worse þan þeves. And maistris of þis pursuyng ben preestis more and less, and moost pryvy freris wiþ lesingis þat þei feynen; as Crist was pursued wiþ Caiaphas and oþer preestis, but privyli wiþ Pharisees þat weren Hise falseste [2] [15] enemyes. And þis gospel is confort to alle þat ben þus pursued.

But certis, as tradiciouns maid biside Goddes lawe of preestis and of Scribis and of Phariseis, blyndiden hem in Goddis lawe and made it dispisid, so it is now of [20] Goddis lawe by newe mennis lawis, as decretals and decres. And þe Sixte, wiþ Clementyns, done myche harm to Goddis lawe and enfeblen bileve. And þus done þes newe reulis of þese þree ordris, as þei harmen rewmes and cuntreis þat þei dwellen inne. But remedie aȝens þis [25] is used of many men to dispise all þese lawis whanne þei ben aleggid, and seien unto men þat aleggen hem þat falsehede is more suspect for witnesse of siche lawis, siþ Goddis lawe telliþ al truþe þat is nedeful to men.

In þis laste pursuying of our modyr, þat is greet and [30] perilous, haþ Anticrist moche part aȝens Jesus Crist, and feyneþ bi ipocrisie þat he haþ þe riȝt part. And defaute of bileve is ground of all þis errour.

Sermons. In Feestis of many Martiris.

---

[1] brent *E*.   [2] falseest *E*.

D. *The Armour of the Christian against Persecution is Patience.*

Crist telliþ Hise disciplis how *þei shulen be hatid of alle worldli men, for þe name of Him*; and þus ben men hated now bi lesengis of freris, for þei holdun þe gospel and lawis of Crist. But Crist comforteþ Hise and telleþ hem
5 þat no part of her bodi shal perishe at þe daie of dome; *so þat an heere of her heed shal not þanne perishe.* And armer to fiȝte wiþ in Cristen[1] men is pacience, for wiþ þis fouȝte Crist, and alle Hise gloriouse lymes; and in þis pacience bihetiþ Crist to Hise þat þei shulen hav her
10 soulis in pees, as Crist hadde His soule.

And here moven many men, siþ Cristes lawe is opyn, and His part is knowun good, and Anticristis wickid, and many devoute men holden wiþ Crist, what moveþ Cristene men to move hem not to fiȝtinge? For siþ þe
15 fend haþ but þree partis for his side, Cristene men myȝte soon meve to fle þes þree partis. For popis and bishopis and prestis of her sort, and þese new religiouse, possessioneris and beggeris, and seculer men þat ben disseyved wiþ hem, ben þe moste enemyes to Crist and his lawe.
20 Whi wolen not holi seculers risen aȝens þese þree, siþ þei moven seculers to fiȝte aȝens her enemyes?

Here men þenken þat Cristene men shulden algatis loven pees, and not procure to fiȝte; for Crist is a pesible kyng, and He seiþ in His Gospel þat in oure greet pacience
25 we shulen have oure victorie; and Crist shal fiȝte for us. But many men þenken þat seculer men shulden helpe here, not to fiȝte aȝens Cristis enemyes, but wiþdrawe her conceil and consent fro þes þree folk; and þis dede were sure before God and man.

Sermons. Þe Gospel of many Martris.

[1] *So E*; *A has* Criste.

E. *Lincolniensis.*

> Lincolniensis generaliter describit sic claustralem egres-
>   sum de claustro et sic fratrem; talis, inquit, est
>   cadaver mortuum de sepulcro egressum, pannis
>   funebribus involutum, a diabolo inter homines agi-
>   tatum.   5

Þere is, he seis, a deed caryone cropun of his sepulcre,
wrapped wiþ clothes of deul, and dryven wiþ þo devel for
to drecche men. Do we gode whil þat we have tyme, for
Judas slepes not nyght ne day, bot studyes by alle his
cautels hou þat he may slee Crist in His lymes. Bot his 10
malice and his faderes is knowen by his werkes; alþof
Crist lete hom noye His servauntis. Bot sith bothe mede
and synne stondes in wille, men may witte by his werkes
whos clerke he is. Sith Crist and Anticrist contrarien
togedir, and freris pursuen moste men þat tellen hem hor 15
sothes, þei schewen hom Anticrist clerkes, contrarie to
Crist. For Crist was more innocent þen any freris ben,
and suffred more reproves of His gode dedes, and ȝitte He
suffred most mekely, and cast Hym not to vengeaunce.
If þo freris do þo reverse, þei are Anticrist clerkes; and 20
for drede þat hor ypocrisye schulde be knowen to þe
puple,—and ypocrisie is noght but if hit be hid,—þei are
wode when þei are reproved oght of hor vices; as a horce
unrubbed, þat haves a sore back, wynses when he is oght
touched or rubbed on his rugge. And so shulde men 25
rubbe oute þe defautes of freris, and thriste oute þo quyter
of hor olde synnes, for þus dide Crist wiþ þo Pharisees.

And one þing I telle hom, þat hor neue ordir dos hom
to soule heele more harme þen gode. For al þo holynesse þat þei do to þe Chirche her moder myght þei do 30
wiþoute suche weddynge to hor sygnes; for so did Crist
and His apostels, lyvynge wiþ þo puple. And þerfore fle
ypocrisye, and be scolere of treuthe; and ouþer seme
þat þou art, or be þat þou semes. Owþer Gods lawe is
fals, or þe reume of Englonde schal scharply be puny- 35
schid for prisonynge of pore prestis. And when þo

grounde is sought oute, þo cause of hor punyschynge
stondes in two poyntes; ouþer þat Anticrist schulde
schame of hor lif, and hor wordes contrarye [1] to hym, or
for þei grauntid opunly þo feythe of þo Gospel, as þei
5 grucched in jugement, þat þo bred of þo auter is verrey
Gods body, as þo gospel seis and comyne feithe holdes.
And sothly a Sarasene or a hethen prelate wolden not
þus punysche Cristis prests for grauntyng of þo Gospel.
And one þing I sey boldely, certen of þo Gospel ; þat alle
10 þo freris of þis lond, or oþer blasphemes, connot disprove
þis faythe þat we telle.

And þof alle Cristen men schulden be on Cristis side,
and reverse Anticrist wiþ alle his disciplis, nereþoles
knyghtes schulde more scharply stonde in þis cause, for
15 by titel of þis servise þei holden of Crist, and kepen þo
ordire of knyght, in more perfeccioun þen þo ordire of
freris or of munkes. Þerfore þo Gospel approves hit by
Seynt Jon Baptist. And suche a covent of freris, or of
munkes ouþer, was never in Cristendome as Mauris and
20 his felowes ; and hit is likely þat al þis private religioun
makes not such a legioun of seyntes in Heven.

On þis schulden knyghtes þenke, and do servise to
Crist, for þere are none feller fendes þen are wickkid
prestis, as schewes Cayphas and Scaryot, and mony
25 soche oþer. Alle Cristen men schulden þenke on þis
faythe of þe Gospel, hou Crist schal cum at þe day of
dome, and reprove dampned men for hor unkyndenesse,
and when He was in prison þei visited Hym not. Gedir
we our wittes, and knowe we wisely þat hit is more [to]
30 assent to unskilful prisonynge, þen for to absent us fro
visitynge of prisouns. And one þing is knowun in Cristen
mennis byleve, þat whoso wiþdrawes his helpe fro cause
of Crist, he consentis to þo synne þat he schulde destrye.
And so everiche Englische mon þat helpes not soche
35 persouns is reproved of Crist as a fals servaunt. Somme
schulden helpe by preyer, and somme by gode speche,
somme by worldly pousté, and somme by gode lyve.

---

[1] *MS.* contraryen : *so Arnold.*

And trowe not þat wikkednesse of freris or ignoraunce of prestis excuses not secular lordes to autorise hor dedes. As knyghtes and alle Cristen men schal be dampned of God bot if þei do servise þat þei owe to Hym, so prestes are dampnable, þat God schewes periles by whom He wil 5 punysche þo puple, for hydynge of hom, as þo prophete seis.

And þis worlde neded prophetis to speke and drede no mon. Amen.

IV

SERMONS

*To sum men it plesiþ for to telle þe talis þat þei fynden
in seintis lyves, or wiþouten Holi Writt; and sich þing
plesiþ ofte more þe peple. But we holden þis manere
good: to leeve sich wordis and triste in God, and telle
5 sureli His lawe, and speciali His gospellis. For we
trowen þat þei camen of Crist, and so God seiþ hem alle.*

Sermons. *Þe Gospel on þe Sixte Day after Cristmasse Dai.*

Preaching, to Wyclif, was the paramount duty of the priest.
To use his own phrase, it was the work 'most duwe to prelatis'[1] from the very fact of their priesthood. Wyclif's Latin
10 & English writings contain numerous references to this prime
function of the pastor. In a Latin sermon he declared:
'Primum atque precipuum opus pastoris est veritatis fidei
evangelizacio'; and in his *Opus Evangelicum*: 'Evangelizacio
talis verbi est preciosior quam ministracio alicuius ecclesiastici
15 sacramenti curati.'

Wyclif, however, restricted the charter of the preacher to the
expounding of Scripture. He had the utmost scorn for the
popular methods adopted by the friars, such as the relation of
fables and marvels or the employment of tags of rhyme. He
20 declared that the friars 'fordon prechinge of Crist and prechen
lesyngus and japes plesynge to þe peple . . . þei docken Goddis
word and tateren it bi þer rimes þat þe fourme þat Crist ȝaf it
is hidde by ypocrisie'.

Like the Puritans at a later date, he invested the words of
25 Scripture with the utmost authority. He realized that many
passages of the Bible are difficult to explain, but such diffi-
culties whetted his appetite, and he attempted to find in all
the words of Holy Writ a literal and a mystical meaning:
'First, I intend, in my Dominical Sermons to give the literal
30 meaning and then to explain the mystical and like Augustine
I will welcome the knotty points.'[2]

Wyclif favoured also the usual medieval fourfold interpreta-

---

[1] *Þe Seven Werkys of Mercy Gostly.*   [2] Preface to Latin Sermons.

tion of Scripture.   Commenting on the history of Ishmael and
Isaac he says :

> *Þes two children of Abraham* [Ishmael and Isaac] *bitoken two*
> *lawes of God, and two children þat God haþ.   Þe first child shal*
> *be dampned, þe secounde shal be saved.   And so men seien comounly,* 5
> *þat Holy Writ haþ foure wittis.   Þe first witt is of þe storye, or*
> *even as þe wordis shulden tokne.   Þe secounde witt is allegoryke,*
> *þat figuriþ þing þat men shulden trowe ;   as þes two sones of*
> *Abraham figuren þes two þingis.   Þe þridde witt is tropologik,*
> *þat bitokeneþ witt of vertues.   Þe fourþe witt is anagogyke, þat* 10
> *bitokeneþ þing to hope in blisse.*[1]

He is careful to point out that the preacher must proceed to
these secondary meanings with great caution : 'Non debet mora-
lizari ad sensus contrarios.'   When all is said the 'literal witt'
is the 'sweetest, wisest, and most precious'[2].   15

For whom were these sermons intended ? Apparently for his
'Poor Priests'.   This is evident from the concluding paragraph
in each of the first four of the *Evangelica Dominicalia* : e.g.

> *Sermon I. 'In þis Gospel may preestis telle of fals pride of*
> *riche men, and of lustful lyf of myȝty men of þis worlde, and of* 20
> *longe peynes of Helle, and joyful blisse in Hevene and þus lengþe*
> *her sermoun as þe tyme axiþ.'*
> *Sermon III. 'We may touche in þis Gospel what spediþ men*
> *and what þing lettiþ men for to be saved.'*

The style of the majority of these sermons is excellent.   Let 25
the reader take the opening paragraph of our first example.
He will find that in it the clauses are well balanced, the movement is quietly rhythmical, the vocabulary is simple but not
poor, the thought is sufficiently grave and cogent.   The manner
of writing is similar to that in the best paragraphs of *Þe Chirche* 30
and hir Membris.   It is beyond the reach of Purvey and is
totally different from that of Hereford.

A. *Þe Sixte Sondai Gospel after Eestir.*

Cum venerit Paraclitus—JOHN XV. 26.

[THE MISSION OF THE COMFORTER]

Crist telliþ His disciplis of comyng of þe Confortour, þe
which is þe Holy Goost, and what lyf þei shal after lede.

[1] Sermons. *Þe Fourþe Sondai in Lente.*   [2] *Sermo XII.*

And ech man shulde cunne here þis lore, for þan he may
be soulis leche, and wite, bi siȝnes of his life, wher his
soule be seke or hoole.   Lord ! siþ a fisician lerneþ dili-
gentli his siȝnes, in veyne, in pows, and oþer þingis,
5 wher a mannis bodi be hool ; how myche more shulde
he knowe sich siȝnes þat tellen helþe of mannis soule, and
how he haþ him to God.   Alȝif siche þingis ben pryvé
and passen worldly witt   of men, neþeles þe Holy
Goost telliþ men sum of siche siȝnes, and makiþ hem
10 more certeyne þan men can juge of bodily helþe.   And,
for we shulden kyndely desire for to knowe þe soulis
state, þerfore þe Holy Goost, þat techiþ us to knowe þes
siȝnes, is clepid a confourtour of men, passinge oþer
confortours.   And as a mannis soule is beter þan þe bodi,
15 and endeles good passiþ temporal good, so þis knowynge
of þe soule passiþ oþer mannis cunnynge.

Crist seiþ þus to His disciplïs, *Whan þis confortour shal
come þat Y shal sende ȝou of þe Fadir, Goost of treuþe þat
comeþ forþ of him, he shal also bere witnesse of me ; and
20 ȝe shal also bere witnesse, for ȝe ben wiþ me alwey fro
þe bigynnynge* of my prechinge.   But here may Grekes
be moved to trowe þat þe Holy Goost comeþ not forþ
but of þe Fadir and not of Crist þat is His Sone ; for þe
toon seiþ Crist, and in þis gospel leveþ þe toþer.   And it
25 semeþ to sum men, ȝif þis were treuþe þat shulde be
trowid, God wolde liȝtly telle þis treuþe as He telliþ oþer
þat we trowen ; and ellis it were presumpcioun to charge
þe Chirche wiþ þis truþe, siþ neiþer autorité of God, ne
resoun, techiþ þat þis is soþ ; and al bileve nedeful to
30 men is tolde hem in þe lawe of God.

Here me þinkiþ þat Latynes synneden sum, what in
þis poynt, for many oþer pointis weren now more nedeful to þe Chirche ; as it were more nedeful to wite, where
al þis Chirche hange in power of þe Pope, as it is seid
35 comounly, and where men þat shal be savyd ben nedid
here to shryve hem to preestis, and þus of many degrees
þat þe Pope haþ liȝtly ordeyned.   But me þinkiþ þat it is
soþ þat þis Goost comeþ boþe of þe Fadir and of þe
Sone, and þes persones ben o cause of him ; and me

þinkiþ, to noon entent shulde Crist seye, He sendiþ þis
Goost, or þat þis Goost is His, but ȝif þis Goost come
of Him.

And to þis þat Grekes seien, þat Crist leveþ þis word,
certis so doiþ He many oþer for certein cause, and ȝit we 5
trowen hem; as Crist seiþ His lore is not His, for it is
principaly his Fadris; and ȝit we trowen þat it is His,
but þe welle is in his Fadir.　So we trowen þat þe wille
bi which þe Fadir loveþ þe Sone comeþ of witt þat is þe
Sone, but principaly of Goddis power.　And in þis word 10
Crist techiþ us to do algatis worship to God.　And þus
þes Grekes may not prove þat we trowen fals in þis
bileve, or þat Crist lefte þis treuþe, wiþouten cause to
telle it þus; for bi þis þat Crist seiþ, þe Holy Goost came
of his Fadir, and leveþ þus þe comynge of Him, He stoppiþ 15
þe pride of þe Chirche and techiþ men to worshipe God.
But whan He seiþ þat He sendiþ þe Holy Goost to His
disciplis, and alle þat his Fadir haþ ben His, He techiþ
clerely þat þis Goost comeþ of Him ; and oþer wise shulde
Crist not speke.　　　　　　　　　　　　　　　　　　　　　20

And þus Latyns ben to blame, for þei leven nedeful treuþe,
and depen hem in oþer treuþe, þat is now not so nedeful.
And þus seien sum men þat þe bishop of Rome, þat þei
clepen heed of þe Chirche, and þerto Pope and Cristis viker,
doiþ more harme to þe Chirche of Crist þan doiþ viker of 25
Thomas in Inde, or viker of Poul in Grees, or þe Soudan
of Babilon.　For þe rote of which he came, þat is
dowynge of þe Chirche and heying of þe emperoure, is
not ful holy ground, but envenymed wiþ synne.　But þis
venym first was litil, and hid by cautelis of þe fend, but 30
now it is growen to myche and to hard to amende.　Soþ
it is þat ech apostle was obedient to ech oþer, as Petre
obeishid unto Poul whan he reprovede hym ; and þus
þenken sum men þat þei shulden obeishe to þe Pope, but
no more þan Crist biddiþ, no more þan to oþer preestis, 35
but ȝif he teche bettre Goddis wille and more profitiþ [1] to
men ; and so of alle his ordenaunce, but ȝif it be groundid

---

[1] profite *E*.

in Goddis lawe, sette no more prys þerby þan bi lawe of þe
emperoure. Men shulden seie myche in þis matere, and
oþer men shulden do in dede; but men wolden holde
hem heretikes, as þe fendis lymes diden Crist. And so
5 þicke ben his membris þat who so holdiþ wiþ Cristis
lawe, he shal be schent many weyes and algatis wiþ
lesyngis.

And þis telliþ Crist bifore unto His postlis, to make
hem stronge and arme hem aȝens siche persecuciouns.
10 *Þes þingis, seiþ he, Y spake to you, þat ȝe be not sclaundrid.*
He is sclaundrid þat is lettid by word or by dede, so þat
his riȝt wille falle doun fro his witt; and so ȝif a man be
pursued and suffre it paciently, he is not sclaundrid, al
ȝif men synnen aȝens him. Þe first pursuyt aȝens Crist
15 shal be of false preestis, not al oonly lettyng þe membris
of Crist to reule þe puple in chirchis, as curatis shulden
do, but putte hem out of chirche as cursid men or heretikes. And herfore seiþ Crist þat þei shal make ȝou
wiþout synagogis. But ȝit shal more woodnesse come
20 after þis, for þei procuren þe puple, boþe more and lasse,
to kille Cristis disciplis for hope of grete mede. And herfore Crist seiþ certeyn of þis mater, *þat hour is come þat
ech man þat killiþ þus good men, shal juge him to do to
God medeful obedience.*

25 And to þis ende procuren freris, Antecristis disciplis,
þat wel nyȝe it is þus now among Cristene men. Sum
men be sumnyd to Rome and þere putt in prisoun, and
sum ben cryed as heretikes among þe comoun peple;
and over þis, as men seien, freris killen þer owen breþeren,
30 and procuren men of þe world to kille men þat seien hem
treuþe. And oo drede lettiþ hem þat þei stirte not to
more woodnesse, for þei defenden þat it is leveful and
medeful, preestis for to fiȝt in cause þat þei feynen
Goddis; and so ȝif þer parte be stronger þan seculers, þei
35 may move þes preestis to fiȝt aȝens þes gentilmen. And
as þei have robbid hem of temporal goodis, so þei wole
pryve hem of swerde as unable, and seie þat sich fiȝting
shulde best falle to preestis. Þus hadden preestis þis
swerd bifore þat Crist cam, and þei drowun so ferre out

of religioun of God til þat þei hadden kild Crist, Heed of
holy Chirche.

Alle men shulden be ware of cautelis of þe fend, for he
slepiþ not, castynge fals weies, and al þes done fendis
lymes; *for þei knowen not þe Fadir and his sone* bi pro- 5
pertees of hem.   Þe fend blyndiþ hem so in worldly purpos, þat þei knowen not strengþe of God ne wisdom of His
bidding; for feiþ failiþ unto hem þat þei loken not aferre,
but þing þat is nyȝe þer eye, as beestis wiþouten resoun.
Alle þis haþ Crist spoke to his disciplis þat whan tyme 10
comeþ of hem, þei shulden þan have mynde þat he haþ seid
hem þes perelis to come.   And þe Holy Goost moveþ
ever sum men to studie Goddis lawe and have mynde of
þis witt; and so love of Goddis lawe and sadde savoure
þerynne, is token to men þat þei ben Goddis children, but 15
ȝit of þer ende ben uncerteyn.

B. *Þe Gospel of oon Confessor and Bishop.*

Vigilate, quia nescitis qua hora.—MATT. XXIV. 42.

[THE DUTY OF WATCHFULNESS]

Þese gospellis ben passid þat fallen to þes martiris, and
now comen gospelis þat fallen to confessouris.   And so
þis gospel techiþ a wisdom of Crist, how men þat have
cure shulden kepe þer sheep; and þis lore perteyneþ to 20
moo þan to preestis, but þei shulden kepe passingli þe
lore þat Crist techiþ here.   Crist biddiþ first þat Hise
servantis *wake, for þei witen never whanne þe Lord is to*
come.   And it is knowen to men þat Crist spekiþ here of
wakinge fro synne, for þat is þe best wakynge, and þis 25
beste Lord spekiþ of beste þing; for as creaturis tellen a
man his God, so þingis of kynde tellen men how þei
shulden serve God.   It is knowen to clerkis þat man haþ
fyve wittis, and stopping of þese wittis bringiþ in sleep to
man; and þanne man is half deed and unable for to 30
worche or to defende himsilf aȝens enemys þat wolen
harmyn him.   Þese wittis ben clepid siȝte and heering,
smelling and taist, wiþ groping; and alle þes shulden be

fed wiþ God, þat mai never faile fro mannis witt. But
stopping of love wiþ worldli þingis lettiþ mannis heed to
perceyve God ; and so, as clerkis seien, þes fyve wittis
comen of a vertue wiþinne in þe heed, and ȝif a man bi
5 sleep be lettid in þis virtue, ouþer bi fumes, or drunkenes,
or oþer cause, þes fyve wittis ben stoppid and wanten
her worching.   And letting of þese fyve wittis is clepid
mannis sleep.

But al þat man haþ is ȝovun to him of God, for to
10 serve his God, ouþer worching or suffring ; and ȝif he leve
þis service, þanne he slepiþ goostli.   And wit wiþinne in
mannis heed, þat is God himself, mut move his out-wittis
to worche as þei shulden ; and so al þat lettiþ man to be
moved þus of God bringiþ in sleep of synne, and lettiþ
15 him to wake.   And so erþeli fumes comyng fro þe
stomak ben grete cause of þis sleep, and lettiþ helping
of God ; for God dwelliþ not wiþ man bisi aboute erþeli
þingis.   But worching of a mannis soule aboute siche
þingis makiþ worldli fumes lette [1] a mannis resoun to
20 knowe hevenli goodis, and wake wiþ hise wittis ; for sich
a man loveþ more goodis of þis world þanne he loveþ his
God, for on hem his wille is more sett.

And þerfore clepiþ Poul þese averouse men, serveris of
mawmettis, and brekeris of Goddis heestis ; and alle wittis
25 of sich men slepen fro Goddis service.   We shulden
wake to resoun, and knowe þat our siȝte is ȝovun us of
God, to serven Him and oure soules ; and ȝif we failen
hereof, for synne þat we ben inne, we misusen oure siȝte,
and slepen wiþ it.   Siȝte is ȝovun to man as hiest out-
30 witt, for to sue his profite, and flee þing þat harmeþ him ;
and þingis þat ben bifore him, þe which he shulde do,
shulde a man wel knowe, and take to him þe profitable.
And þus, as Crist techiþ, men synnen in siȝte of wymmen,
for he þat seeþ a woman for to coveite her, he haþ in þat
35 done lecherie in his herte.   For, as Crist techiþ, þe rote
of a mannis synne is wiþinne in his herte bifore þat it be
in dede, and herfore men shulden flee cause þat þus
bringiþ synne to mannis herte.

[1] and lettiþ *E.*

Þe synne of siȝt is not þus oonli in lecherie of fleish, but it is also in coveitise of worldli goodis ; as whanne þou seest erþeli þing, and coveitist to hav it, aȝens þe wille of þi God, þou synnest þanne in þi siȝte.   And þus seiþ Seint Joon, þat in coveitise of iȝen is understonden al 5 coveitise of oþer wittis aȝens resoun.   Ne a man synneþ not in siȝt, al oonli on þes two maneres, but whanne he is idil in his siȝt, and aspieþ not his profit ; as sum men loken to veyn plaies, and many siȝtis of worldli þingis, þe which profiten not to her soule, but raþer doiþ hem harm. 10 And siȝt is þe first witt stoppid whanne a man slepiþ. Soþeli we shulden ever loke upon God, as we mai here seen Him bi mirrour, in a derknes of þingis þat He haþ maad ; ȝhe, boþe niȝt and dai, slepinge and wakinge, shulde we þus þenke on God and His lawe.   15

Þe secounde uttir witt is heeringe of man, þat is brouȝt many weies in to sleping of synne.   For God haþ ȝovun us þis virtue for to heeren him, and so to heeren pees and charité þat He spekiþ in us ; but men ben now redi to heeren of unpees, batailis, and strives, and chidingis of 20 neiȝboris ; and cause of sich heeringe is assent to siche þingis, for litil worldli wynning and lesyng of pees. And bi sich heeringe men mai knowe whos children þei ben. We shulden witen þat heeryng was graunted to man for to cunne his bileve, as Seint Poul seiþ ; and so bileve is 25 of heering, and heering is by Cristis word.   And for þis, Crist wole þat men preche þe gospel ; and for þis haþ kynde ordeyned þat heering shulde be in a sercle, bifore men, and bihinde men, and on ech side of men, as bileve is of treuþis, bifore us, and bihinde us.   And to 30 oure bileve shulde we shape oure heering.

And þis is o defaute þat men have in heeringe, þat þei wolen gladli heere fablis, and falsehedis, and slaundris of her neiȝbouris, al ȝif þei knowen hem false.   But al ȝif sich telleris ben moche for to blame, neþeles sich heereris 35 ben hatid of God.   For kynde haþ ȝovun to men to heeren voicis in þe eire, and not in erþe bineþen us, where voices comen not ; in tokne þat we shulden ȝyve oure wittis to trowe þing þat mai be in eire, þat is

aboven us, which þing profitiþ to oure soule. And if we
heeren sich falsenes þat we wite profitiþ not, we shulden
not heeren but wiþ. peyne, and trowe not þerto, and
algatis fle sich men þat tellen sich talis; for God haþ
5 ʒovun us heeringe to heeren his workes, þat ben moo and
sutiler þan þis witt wole suffise to.

And herfore þe gospel telliþ how Crist dide a miracle,
and heelide a deef man and domb upon þis manere:
Crist toke him aside fro þe comune peple, and putte his
10 fyngris in his eeris, and wiþ His spitting touchide his
tonge, and ʒaf him þanne vertue to heeren and to speke.
God here techiþ man for to fle fablis þat ben in comune
peple, and take hede to Him. Þe sutil workes of God
ben Hise smale fyngris, þat men shulden heer and trowe,
15 and þerwiþ fede þer wittis, and wiþ sich savery treuþis
occupien her speechis. And þus mai we þenke how we
ben deffe and dumbe; but we shulden wiþ þes two wittis
wake to oure God, for He wole have rekenynge, boþe in
oure deþ and at þe daie of dome, how we have dispendid
20 vertues þat He haþ ʒovun us.

And siþ we witen not whanne þis rekenynge shal falle,
it is a greet wisdom to wake aʒens þis tyme; and herfore seiþ Crist, *Þis þing wite we wel, þat ʒif þe hosebonde
wiste whanne þe þeef were to come, certis he wolde wàke,*
25 *and suffre him not to myne his hous.* Þis þeef is þe fend,
joyned to man, to tempte him, and to harme him al þat
he can, and speciali in tyme þat þis man shulde die; for
if he take þeefli virtues fro þis man in hour of hise deeþ,
he doiþ þise þefte moost. And ʒif he have maistrie to sle
30 siche a man, he chesiþ sich a tyme whanne he is moost
unredi; and þanne he is ful bisie to bringe in þe worste
synne, for þanne his ful victorie is endid in þat man.

And here men douten comunli, what hour men shal
dien, wheþer God shal take hem in her beste tyme. But
35 here we shal wite, þat alle þo þat shal be saif waken in
hour of her deþ, and over comen þe fend, and suffren him
not þanne to undirmyne her hous. And so þes men dien,
whanne þei ben moost ripe. But ʒif þe fend lede hem
þanne as his owne servantis, and þei shal be dampned,

he waitiþ him a tyme whanne he trowiþ best to overcome þes men; and so þes men dien in her worste tyme, for
in tyme þat þei have þe synne þat evermore shal laste. And
þat is þe worste yvel, þat God mai suffre to be; for God
mote nedis punishe þis synne in helle wiþouten ende. 5
And for þis peril of þis þeef shulden men waken warli; but,
for þis harm of þis þeef is not but bi Goddis jugement,
þerfore seiþ Crist to warn alle men; *And þerfore be ȝe
redi, for in þat hour þat ȝe hopen not Crist is to come.*
For, as it is ofte seid, deeþ is þe þridde þing þat God 10
wole have unknowun to man, for he shulde ever be redi.

And, for ech man shulde governe alle his wittis, and
make hem serve to hise profit, as a man doiþ his meyné,
þerfore seiþ Crist þus: *Who, trowest þou, is a trewe servant, þat þe Lord haþ put to be upon his meyné, þat he* 15
ȝyve hem mete in good tyme to ete? Þis Lord is God
Himsilf, and we ben His servantis; þis meyné of þis Lord
ben alle oure wittis, which we ȝeven mete for to serve
God, whanne we leden hem bi resoun to profite to oure
soule. *Blessid be þat servant, þat whanne his Lord is* 20
comen, he haþ foundun him doinge so unto þis meyné;
soþeli Y seie to ȝou, þat he shal putte him upon alle hise
goodis, and make him his eire. Þat man þat doiþ þus
shal come to Hevene, and þere shal he be Cristis eire, and
ful lord of Cristis heritage; and þis lordshipe shal serven 25
to alle Cristis children.

C. *Þe Gospel on Feestis of many Confessours.*

Misit Jesus duodecim discipulos.—MATT. X. 5.

[RULES FOR PRIESTS]

Þis gospel telliþ how preestis shulden traveile in
Goddis cause, and how kynde þat þei shulden be boþe to
God and to þe peple. For wordis seid to Cristis disciplis shulden teche us preestis how we shulden do, siþ 30
we shulden be vikeris of hem; and ellis Crist bindiþ us
bi no lore. And þus a prest dampneþ himsilf þat seiþ
þat Crist spekiþ not here to him; for he seiþ in a maner
þat he is þe fendis child. And for his unkyndnes Crist

wolde not bidde him do Goddis work, but do as yvel as
he mai; and Crist þerafter shal dampne him; and þis
man beriþ upon him mater of his dispeiring. And þis
shulde moove prestis alle to fille þe wordis þat Crist bad;
5 for if þei dispisen þes wordis, þei mai dispeire as fendis
children. And þus boþe bishopis and freris beren her
dispeir wiþ hem, and þis will not be shaken of, but ȝif
þei leven her olde synne, and suen þe love of Crist þat He
techiþ in þis gospel.

10 Þis gospel telliþ how, *Jesus sente hise twelve disciplis,
and comandide hem: Go ȝe not out* aȝens my bidding
in to weie of heþene men, and entre ȝe not into citees, þe
which ben *of Samaritans.* Þese wordis moten be wel
undirstondun to þe witt þat God spekiþ hem; for Crist
15 Himsilve wente ofte tymes to Gentilis and Samaritans;
and He biddiþ at His departing þat þei shulden teche alle
folk; and þus þes Gentile folk weren turned, many moo
þan weren of Jewis. And herfore seien holi men þat
Crist tauȝte ordre in preching, how men shulde first go
20 to her kyn, and first moove hem to turne to God; and
ȝif God telde hem unablité[1] of her kyn, þei shulden
speke to oþer. And to þis entente dide Crist, and tauȝte
Hise apostlis to do. And so men seien comunli þat Crist
here forbed goinge in to þe weie of Gentile folk; but he
25 forbed not to go to hem; but Crist biddiþ *raþer go to þe
sheep þat perischiden of þe hous of Israel.* And it semeþ
þat þes sheep ben þo men þat shal be saif; for all þes
ben of Goddis hous, and men þat seen God in Hevene.
And alle þes weren in point to perishe bifore Cristis
30 treuþe was teld to hem. To þes folk shulden men
preche; for Cristis word wole florishe in hem, and mede
and worship is in Hevene to men þat prechen to þis peple.
*Crist bad hem go and preche þis:—þat þe kingdom of
hevene shulde neiȝe.* And þis is soþ; for Crist shal come
35 to His laste jugement, and rekene sharpli wiþ Hise, boþ
wiþ servauntis good and yvele. And Crist is ofte clepid
in þe gospel þe kingedom of Hevene, for He is heed. And
þis bileve, among oþer, shulde meve men to turne to

[1] þe inablité *E.*

Crist. For love of þis gode Lord and drede of His ponishinge shulde be two sporis to Cristene men for to drawe in Cristis ȝok; but wanting of bileve makiþ many men dolle[1] in þis.

And fyve maneres enjoyneþ Crist to His prechours for 5 to kepe. First, þat *þei shal hele sike men*, oþer of bodili sykenesse, or þerwiþ of goostli sekenesse. Boþe þes hadde Cristis apostlis, but we have unneþe þe toon; for we have greet grace of God ȝif we heele men fro synne. And we failen in þis craft whanne we bosten of oure 10 power, and leven Cristis lore, or to lyve or to preche.

Þe secound manere þat we shulden have shulde be, *to reisen up deed men;* and þis mai be on two maneris. As it was seid of þe firste, algatis we shulden traveile to reise up men deed bi synne; for þis is more þan þe firste, 15 and eende wherfore þe firste is good. And ȝif we don oure diligence þat God haþ ȝovun us power to, we mai liȝtli do þes two; for synne is þicke sowen in londe.

Þe þridde cure þat we shulden do, we shulden *hele leprouse men.* And siþ lepre is heresie, a synne bi þe whiche men ben 20 defoulid, we have power to do þis wondir, ȝif we worchen after oure power; and oo lepre left unheelid mai enblemisshe many folk. And þus we shulden be diligent to worche þis wondir in þe Chirche; for o leprous mai foule a flok, and a flok mai foule a more. 25

Þe fourþe work þat preestis shulden do shulde be, þat *þei shulden caste out fendis.* And þis we done on betere manere ȝif we casten out synnes fro men; for ech synne haþ a fend, þat goiþ whanne þis synne goiþ. But þe fend on two maneres is in diverse men. In sum men he 30 is to tempte hem, al if he be not in her soule: In sum men he is incorporate, as in men þat have synne; and in þes soulis þe fend dwelliþ, as who shulde dwelle in his house.

Þe fifte manere þat prestis shulden have shulde be 35 þankful traveilinge; for ȝif þei wolen have þank of God, þei shulden here fle symonie, and neiþer sille her preching ne oþer workes þat þei done. And þis forgeten many

---

[1] dul *E.*

men, boþe more prestis and lesse; for popis wolen have
þe firste fruytis for benefices þat þei 3yven, and bishopis
an hundrid shillingis for halewynge of oo Chirche; and
lordis wolen have longe service for o Chirche þat þei
5 3yven, and þis is worþ 3eer bi 3eer moche rente or moche
moneie. And howevere we speken, God woot wel how
þis chaffaringe is maad, pryvyli or apertli; for God
knowiþ al kyn þingis, and God biddiþ us do þes dedis
and hope no3te here for hem; for 3if we hopen to be
10 here rewardid oure hope perishiþ to have blisse.

And wiþ þis synne ben freris bleckid þat shapen to
preche wynnyng here; and herfore þei prechen þe peple
fablis and falshede to plesen hem. And in tokene of þis
chaffare, þei beggen after þat þei have prechid; as who
15 seiþ : 3yve me þi moneie, þat Y am worþi bi my preching.
And þis chaffare is sellinge of preching, however þat it be
florishid. Soþeli preestis mai medefulli, after þer sermouns,
ete wiþ folk; but not calenge for her sermouns, neiþer
bi dette ne bi custome. And herfore seien many preestis,
20 þat no men þat have cure shal lyve but on Goddis part,
as on dymes and on offringis; and so bi clene titil of
almes shulden þei have goodis þat þei have. For þus
lyvede Crist, hi3est Pope. What art þou þat wole not
lyve þus? wolt þou be gretter þan Crist þat is Lord of al
25 þis world?

Also þis manere is more meedeful to men þat shulden
fynde þes preestis, and more meke and lesse worldli to
prestis þat shulden be susteyned. And so it is on boþ
sidis more vertuous þan þes rentis now. And þanne
30 God, wiþouten doute, biddiþ þat þis manere be kept.
Who drediþ þat ne it is more mede man to 3eve wel his
charité þan to 3yven his worldeli dette which he oweþ bi
worldli lawe? And who drediþ þat ne it is more meke
to be paied on Goddis part þan to calenge bi worldis
35 titil more þan Goddis lawe axiþ? For þis were neer to
Poulis reule, þat preestis shulden be paied of foode and
hiliyng wiþouten more worldli richesse; and þanne our
titil my3te be groundid; and oþer is feyned to þe fend.

Also men my3ten bi conscience 3yve good men, and

take fro truauntis[1] betere þan þei now done. And so
þis were Goddis wille, bi what resoun shulde he have
dymes and offringis of þe peple þat lyveþ in lustis and
in ydilnes, and profitiþ not to þis peple ? Certis þis were
a fendis lawe, to ȝyve Goddis part to sich men. And so 5
comunes weren excludid of false ȝyvynge to alyens ; as
to popis, and cardinals, and siche Antecristis disciplis.
Þei weren also excusid of ȝifte to persouns þat ben lordis
clerkis, þat lyven unclerkliche ; and þei weren excludid
wel of þes chirches þat ben aproprid to ȝyve Goddis part 10
to men which ben of þe fendis covent.

And cursinge noieþ not to man, but ȝif he lyve aȝens
resoun.   Freris wolen have anoþer titil, and plete and
fiȝte for siche goodis ; but þis is Goddis lawe, however þe
fend termyne.   And þus curatis shulden not selle no kyn 15
service þat þei done ; but do freeli, and taken aȝen almes
þat men wolen ȝyve hem ; and never more curse, ne plete
for sich almes of þe peple, but flee sich lawis þat techen
þis, as þei weren lawis of Anticrist.   And þus preestis
shulden lyve clenli bi Goddis lawe, as þei diden first. 20
And þus men shulden wiþdrawen her hond fro freris þat
beggen whanne þei have prechid ; for þei ben coupable
bi consente þat ȝeven hem on þis manere.   For al þis
chaunging shulde be free, þat man shulde do bi Goddis
titil.   25

And þus seiþ þe gospel here, *Siþ we token freeli of
God we shulden freeli ȝyve to men,* for hope of more mede
in Hevene.   But here the peple shulde be tauȝt how þei
shulden freeli ȝyve þingis þat ben nedeful to preestis,
for tyme þat þei shulden serve hem; for þus ȝeveþ God 30
to his servauntis þing nedeful to his service, and man
ȝeveþ to his bodi þing nedeful to serve him.   And herfore Poul seiþ it is litil ȝif we taken þing nedeful to us.
But first, er men done symony, þei shulden travaile wiþ
her hondis, or go to anoþer peple, or raþer sterve in her 35
bodi.   But þis wolde falle late or never, but ȝif oure
synne be in cause,   And þus men þenken þat prestis mai
take almes of her parishis, and go to scole, and gadere

[1] tirauntis *E.*

hem lore to teche hem efte þe wey to Hevene ; but þis is
fer fro dwelling of lordis,[1] or from oþer unhoneste liif, or
from wendinge to Rome to gete a fattere benefice.
Myche þing shulden men knowe here þat is hid bi þe
5 fend, and lettiþ service of Cristis Chirche þat He ordeynede
to be done.

D. *Þe Gospel on þe Trinité Sonedai.*

Erat homo ex Phariseeis Nychodeme.—JOHN III. I.

[THE DOCTRINE OF THE TRINITY.]

Þis gospel undir a story telliþ of þe Trinité, and boþe þes
ben harde, as comounly is Jones gospel. Þe storye telliþ
þat þer was a man of Pharisees þat hiȝte Nichodeme, and
10 *was prince of þe Jewis ; he cam to Jesus on a nyȝt and seide*
þus to him ; Rabi we witen wel þat þou art come fro
God ; and raby is as myche as maister in Englishe. And
Nichodeme tolde þe cause whi he trowide þis, *for no*
man may make, he seide, *þes signes þat þou makist, but ȝif*
15 *God be wiþ him,* and so he comeþ fro God. *And Jesus*
answeride Nychodeme, and seide þus *to him*: Bi my
double kynde Y seie to þee, *but ȝif a man be born aȝen,*
he may not se Goddis rewme. And þes wordis weren
woundirful to Nichodeme, *and perfore he axide where a*
20 *man myȝte be bore whan he were an old man, wher he*
myȝte crepe in to his moder wombe for tyme þat he was
olde *and be born aȝen.*

Þis Nichodeme cam in þe nyȝt, þat figuride his ignoraunce, but to þe literal witt, he dredde him for his
25 breþeren, to come apertly in þe day, and speke wiþ Jesus
Crist ; and boþe þes undirstondingis shope þe Holy
Goost. And so þis goostly birþe þat Nichodeme mut first
have bitokeneþ þe Fadir of Hevene þat bryngeþ forþ two
oþer persones ; and so Nichodeme to litil knewe þis per-
30 sone of God, and for þis unknowinge he axide þis questioun. For he seide not þat Crist was kyndely Goddis
Sone, ne þat He was Goddis word and so God him silfe ;

[1] wiþ lordis *E.*

and so þis Nichodeme hadde nede to be cristened in feiþ,
and so Crist lovede his persone, alȝif He hatide his ordre,
for Crist savyde his persone and distryede his ordre.
And þus Crist lovede Poul, þat seiþ he was a Pharisee ;
but þe more part of Pharisees weren fals and heretikes. 5
And þis nativité shewiþ Crist in þes wordis ; *Forsoþ, forsoþ, Y seie to þee, but ȝif man be born of water and þe
Holy Goost he may not entre in to Goddis rewme.* And
þus by þis baptym, þis water and þe Holy Goost, Crist
tolde him þe Trinité ȝif he koud conseyve it. Þis baptym 10
seiþ þe Trinité, in whos name it is mad ; þis water is þe
waishinge þat ranne of Cristis herte ; and so baptym and
water and þe Holy Goost tellen Nichodeme þe Trinitee,
and þerwiþ þe sacrament, for Crist is compendious in
spekynge of His wordis. 15

But Crist makiþ distynccioun of two manere of birþis,
and seiþ þat *þing born of fleishe is fleish* in his kynde,
and þing þat is born of spirit is spirit on sum manere ;
and *þerfore, wounder þou not þat Y seide to þee, ȝe moten
be born aȝen,* and bi Goost made children of holy Chirche, 20
and so in spirit maad Goddis children, and so His spouse
shal be your moder. Þis gendrure of þis Goost is boþe
free and wilful, and herfor Crist seiþ to Nichodeme, þat
þe spirit breþiþ wher he wole, and þou herest his vois bi
which he moveþ þee. And on þis maner þe Spirit of 25
oure Lord haþ fillid þis world wiþ witt of oure feiþ, and
þat þing þat holdiþ alle haþ science of vois. And herfore at Wit-Sonday whan þis Goost apperide was a greet
soun, and tungis of fier, to telle þat men shulden speke on
hiȝt [1] to þer breþeren, and þei shulden have charité, þe 30
which seiþ þe Holy Goost. And alle ȝif we knowen þe
vois of þis Goost, neþeles we witen not whennes þat it
comeþ ne whidir þat it goiþ, to men þat ben biside us ;
for we knowen not þe ordenaunce of God, whi he enspireþ
þes men, and to what ende, or wheþer he shal save þis 35
man or wende awey from him. *And so ech man þat is born
of þis spirit* is unknowun to oþer by many hid resoun,

---

[1] heyȝt *E.*

and so ech man is sumwhat knowun and sumwhat unknowun for wisdome of þis spirit.

But *Nichodeme answerede and seide here to Jesus,
How may þes þingis be done? And Crist seide to him ;*
5 In þe lond of Israel ben manye blynde maisters, *for þou
art maister in Israel, and ʒit þou unknowist þes þingis :*
and so it is noo wounder ʒif þis lond be mysled, for ʒif þe
blynde leden þe blynde, þei fallen boþe into þe lake.
And neþeles Y teche hem as myche as þei ben worþi ;
10 and so seiþ Crist to Nichodeme, *Soþely, soþely, Y seie to
þee,* defaute is not in me, in teching of þes puple, but in
untrewe hardnesse of it; for, *þing þat we knowun we
tellen to hem,* and *þat we have sene* in Godhede, *we wit-
nessen, and ʒe taken not oure witnesse,* for ʒoure unkynde
15 hardnesse. And þerfore ʒe knowen not þe gendrure of
þe firste persone. *ʒif Y seide to ʒou erþely þingis and ʒe
trowen hem not, how, ʒif Y seide to you hevenly þingis, shal
ʒe trowen hem ?* Crist tolde here of bodily birþe, and
ofte tymes of erþely treuþe, but þei trowiden Him not for
20 þer fole hard herte ; but neþeles Crist telliþ þis man know-
inge of þe secounde persone, and in an article of bileve,
þat is, His ascensioun ; and *no man, seiþ Crist, steieþ in to
hevene but he þat cam doun fro hevene, mannis sone þat
is in hevene.* And in þes wordis myʒt Nichodeme undir-
25 stonde boþe þe godhede of Crist and þerto His manhede,
and so shulde he knowe wel þe secounde persone of God.
By þat þat Crist steied þus, and þus is mannis sone, miʒt
he knowe His manhede bifore oþer manhedis ; for alʒit
oþer men steieden a litil in þis eire, neþeles no man steieþ
30 in to Hevene þus but Crist. And so noon oþer man
comeþ to Hevene but ʒif he be Cristis membre, and be
drawun bi þe Trinité in to þis hey place.

And þus seiþ Crist soþ, þat no man steieþ in to Hevene,
but Him silf aloone ; and seiþ þere ben foure manere of
35 bryngingis forþ of man, and þe fourþe and þe laste,
apropred unto Crist, is þat man comeþ clene of womman
wiþout man. Crist clepiþ Him wel here a sone of man-
kynde ; and þus bi þes two wordis myʒt he knowe Cristis
manhede. And by oþer two wordis myʒt he knowe

Cristis godhede; first by þat he seiþ þat þis man cam
doun bifore fro Hevene, and þis myȝt nevere be but ȝif
Crist were God or He were man. Þe secounde word
þat shewiþ þe godhede of þis persone, is, þat Crist seiþ
þat He is mannis sone þat is in Hevene, ȝhe, after þat He 5
bycam man; for þus is Crist two kyndes godhede for
evermore, and evermore in Hevene drawynge to Him
whom Him likeþ. And þus Crist techiþ wel ynouȝ to
knowe þe secounde person, boþ in godhede and in manhede, as myche as he shulde þan knowe Him.   10

But to telle þe þridde persone, in pointis of bileve,
Crist telliþ to Nichodeme, *As Moyses heied þe addre in
desert* to hele þe puple by lokynge on him, *so mut mannis
sone be hyed* in þe cros, *þat ech man þat trowiþ in him,
perishe not* in helle, *but have lyf wiþouten eende*, þat is 15
blisse of Hevene. Here mut we knowe þe storye of þe
olde lawe hou þe puple was hirt by stynging of addres,
and Moses preied God to telle him sum medecyne; and
God bade him take an addre of bras, and hong hym hye
on a tree to þe puple to loke on, and he þat lokid on þis 20
addre shulde be helid of þis yvel. And al þis was figure
of hanging of Crist, for Crist was in forme of addris of
venym, but he hadde no venym in his owene persone, as
þe addre of bras hadde no venym in hym. But as riȝt
lokynge on þis addre of bras savyde þe puple fro venym 25
of serpentis, so riȝt lokynge bi ful bileve in Crist saveþ
his puple fro synne of þe fendis. And þe fende was þe
first addre þat ever noyed man, and Crist was hongid in
tre, as þis addre hongide in tree.

But it were to wite over, hou þis story perteyneþ to þe 30
Holy Goost, siþ al þis was done in Crist; but we shal wel
wite þat ech of þes þre persones is in ech oþer, as ech
bitokeneþ oþer. And siþ þat Crist seiþ þat no man haþ
more love þan for to put his lyf for his frendis, þis blesside
hanginge of Crist in þe crosse is þat hye charité þat 35
God lovede man inne, and þis charité is þe Holy Goost;
and þus was Nichodeme tauȝt þe feiþ of þe Trinité, and
in þis feiþ many oþer articlis, and þus is þis gospel
approprid to þis feste. Þere ben many witnessis and

resouns to þe Trinité, but þis manere of lore is more
plentevouse and more profitable to men; and herfore
Crist seiþ it þus; and þus eche man shulde reule al his lyf
after þis holy Trinité, for ellis he must faile.   Loke first
5 þat he be groundid in stable bigynning, and siþ þat he
procede in gracious mene, and siþ þat he ende in fulnesse
of charité, and þan his lyfe is ensaumplid aftir þe Trinité.

V

CHURCH AND STATE

God mut nedis be cheef Lord of alle creaturis.

de Papa.

No drede, boþe lordis and reumes my3ten wel con-streyne prestis to holde þe povert þat Crist ordeynede.

Ibidem.

Wyclif set forth his views on Church and State in a series of elaborate Latin treatises: *de Dominio Divino, de Civili* [5] *Dominio, de Ecclesia*, and *de Officio Regis*. Some of the main positions advanced in these works were concisely stated in two short Latin writings—the *Libellus*, preserved by Netter,[1] and *Conclusiones Triginta Tres*.[2]

He placed God (or Christ in God) at the head of Church [10] and State. God is the supreme lord of all earthly creatures: 'Ergo super omnem creaturam . . . habet Creator dominium.'[3] Of God, the overlord, each individual is the tenant-in-chief and holds possession of his 'goods' [bona] in so far as he is in a state of grace. 'Whoever exists in a state of grace has, for [15] his lifetime, right over all "the goods" of God.' Conversely, those who do not possess the grace of God are not his legitimate tenants. But with regard to clerics another law applies. Clerics must never be 'possessioners', for the reason that Christ, during his earthly pilgrimage, was the poorest of men:[4] [20] 'All priests of Christ, Pope, cardinals, bishops, abbots, &c., are bound to follow Christ in evangelical poverty.'[5] Further, a priest may not exercise civil rule[6] and may only have the 'use of things' as alms.[7] It follows, therefore, that temporal lords should not endow the church with goods, and that the [25] king may deprive ecclesiastics of the temporalities of which they stand possessed.

---

[1] *Fasc. Ziz.* 245–57.   [2] *Op. Min.* 19–73.
[3] *de Dominio Divino*, p. 11.
[4] *Conclusiones*, p. 19.   [5] Ibid., p. 20.
[6] *Ibid.*, p. 21.
[7] Ex mero titulo meritorie elemosyne, ibid., p. 23.

Further, it is lawful for laymen to judge prelates[1] and the duty of the king to defend the law of the Gospel.[2] The latter idea is carried further in *de Officio Regis* where the king is almost made head of the national church and is given power to
5 see that the bishops teach true theology. Such a doctrine approaches the position taken up by Henry VIII.

In an age in which the civil service was almost entirely filled by clerics Wyclif held that: 'Neither the King nor any other secular lord should employ a priest or curate in secular busi-
10 ness.'[3]

It must not be supposed that he was the first to propound these opinions. Marsiglio of Padua, 'of damned memory', was rightly singled out as the precursor of Wyclif by Gregory XI, when, in 1377, he dispatched his bulls against the Reformer.
15 Wyclif, however, had probably not read Marsiglio's famous *Defensor Pacis* in which an attempt is made to limit the power of the Church in favour of secular authority. But he acknowledged his debt to Richard Fitzralph, Archbishop of Armagh, from whose *de Pauperie Salvatoris* he derived the groundwork
20 of his doctrine of 'dominion'. Grosseteste, the reforming Bishop of Lincoln, also anticipated Wyclif in his attack on pluralities. But a more important predecessor was William of Ockham, 'Doctor Invincibilis', a greater schoolman than Wyclif himself. Ockham, as a Spiritual Franciscan, stressed
25 two of Wyclif's main ideas, viz. (1) the importance of poverty as a necessary condition of the priestly office, and (2) the desirability of the limitation of the jurisdiction of the Church in worldly matters.

Wyclif owed much to previous thinkers; but it is his special
30 distinction that he massed together their partial ideas.[4] His mind was equal to the task of surveying the whole structure of Church and State. His nature was strong, sincere, and fearless. His glance was wide and keen. As a result, the criticism which he brought to bear on the Roman Church of his day was
35 at once penetrating, powerful, and comprehensive.

---

[1] *Conclusiones*, p. 30. Cf. Ecclesiasticus, immo Romanus Pontifex, potest legitime a subiectis corripi, et ad utilitatem ecclesie, tam a clericis, quam a laicis, accusari.

[2] Ibid., p. 71.   [3] Ibid., p. 48.

[4] Marsiglio's work is not included in this statement. The *Defensor Pacis* is a masterly performance in its own field.

A. *Dominion by Grace.*

I

So eche man in his degree is boundoun to serve God.
And ȝif he wante þis service, he is no lord of goodis bi no
trewe title.   For he þat stondiþ in grace is verrey lord of
þingis ; and whoevere failiþ by defaute of grace, he failiþ
riȝt title of þing þat he occupieþ, and unabliþ himsilf to 5
have þe goodis of God.

Þe Ten Comaundementis.

II

Here we schal suppose as Cristen mennes bileve, þat
God is cheef lord of eche þing of þis world.   And so, al
ȝif kyngis and oþere han free lordschipe, neþeles God is
more free lord of þat same þing, ne it is nouȝt leeful to 10
seculere lordis, to alyenen his lordschipe wiþouten leeve
of God ; as in mannes lordschipe a litil lord haþ no leeve
to alienen his heritage but bi leve of þe cheif lord, and
þis lawe haþ more resoun in þe lordschipe of God.

Here may we se, siþ lordis of þis world hadde noȝt 15
leeve of God þus to dowe his clerkis, here fool ȝifte
schulde noȝt stonde bi skile, siþ God may noȝt be contrarie to him silf.   But God ofte tyme in his two Testa-
mentis forbediþ his clerkis to be þus dowid ; and so þis
gile, þat cam bi cautel of þe fend, schulde be now broken 20
for defaute of ground.

Ne grucche noȝt herfore þat God is cheif lord, for it
falliþ to his Godhed to be lord of eche þing, and more
curteys lord may no man have, ne more profitable lawis
to lede a man by resoun.   For þis lord suffriþ hee noȝt to 25
leese good but bi resoun, ne he axiþ no rente but for þin
owne profite.

. . . .

Þis dowynge aȝens Goddis lawe doiþ harme to lordis
and clerkis and comunys, boþe bodily harme and harme 30
to here soulis ; and negligent of lordis in amendement
hereof is a manere of consence and greggiþ here synne.

And it harmeþ here elderis þat bigan þis errour, ne good
doþ it noon; but moveþ lordis to pride þat here kyn haþ
þus foundid housis of religioun.

And siþ God in His lawe cursiþ men þat breken it, it
5 semeþ þat boþe ben cursid, lordis and clerkis, and herfore
confessouris and alle þat ben on Goddis halfe schulde
move and meynteyne þis lawe of oure God. And siþþe
þe moste unfredom is unfredom of synne, for þat makiþ
a man servaunt to nouȝt and servant of þe fend, and
10 dampneþ him in helle, coveytise of fredom schulde move
men herto, and so synne bi his manere bryngiþ his doere
into þe same myre þat he eschewiþ.

. . . .

But here we schal supposen as Cristen mennes bileve,
þat no mennes lawis ne chartirs maad of men han
15 strengþe but in as myche as Goddis lawe confermeþ
hem; for what is ony chartre or lawe worþ but ȝif God
conferme it by His lawe? And so þis grete chartre
wolde move by Goddis wytt, þat kyngis and here
rewmes schulde meynteyne þe Chirche by þe ordey-
20 naunce of God, and distroie þe contrarie.

And ȝif we taken hede, boþe kyngis and rewmes, bi
here opyn oþis, schulden take awey þes rentis þat þe fend
haþ dowid wiþ clerkis aȝens Jhesu Crist. And so to
chalenge of þe kyng to maynteyne alle here chartres and
25 alle here newe lawis þat þei han founden were to chalenge þe kyng as þe fendis servaunt; and þere were overe
myche dispit to here lyge lord.

And ȝif þou seie þat cursyngis purchased of þe Pope
and oþere felle sensuris, þundured overe til Englond,
30 schulde fere ouere rewme to do siche þingis, here we
schal suppose oure bileve þat no mannes cursynge haþ
ony strengþe but in as myche as God Himsilf cursiþ.

Of Dominion.

B. *Divine and Royal Prerogative.*

[THE RULE OF JESUS CHRIST SURPASSES ALL OTHER
RULES]

Plese it to oure most noble and most worþi King
Richard, kyng boþe of Englond and of Fraunce, and to
þe noble Duk of Lancastre, and to oþere grete men of þe
rewme, boþe to seculers and men of holi Chirche, þat ben
gaderid in þe Parlement, to here, assent, and meyntene 5
þe fewe articlis or poyntis þat ben seet wiþinne þis writing, and proved boþe by auctorité and resoun ; þat
Cristen feiþ and Cristene religioun ben encreessed, meyn-
teyned, and made stable.

Þe first article is þis ; þat alle persones of what kynne 10
privat sectis, or singuler religioun, maad of sinful men,
may freely, wiþouten eny lettinge or bodili peyne, leve
þat privat reule or neue religioun founden of sinful men,
and stably holde þe reule of Jesus Crist, taken and ȝoven
by Crist to his apostelis, as far more perfit þan any sich 15
newe religion founden of sinful men.

Þe resoun of þis axinge is shewyd þus. Þe reule of
Jesus Crist ȝoven to apostlis, and kept of hem aftir
Cristis ascencioun, is most perfit to be kept for staat of
lyvinge in þis world ; and eche reule of what kynne 20
privat secte, or singuler religioun maad of sinneful men,
is lesse perfit þan þe reule ȝoven of Crist of His endeles
wisdom, and His endeles charitee to mankinde.

[THE KING IS THE CHIEF LORD OF CLERGY AND
LAITY]

Þe secounde poynt or article ys þis ; þat þo men þat
unresonably and wrongfully han dampned [þe kyng] 25
and al his counsail, be amendid of so gret errour, and þat
here errour may be publisshid to men dwellinge in þe
reume.

Þe resoun of þis axinge ys shewyd þus. Noþing oweþ
to be dampned as errour and fals, but ȝif it savour errour 30
or unriȝtwisnesse aȝens Goddis lawe. But neiþer þe kyng

ne his counsayl deede unriʒtfully, for as muche as he took
awey þe possessiouns of summe prelatis þat trespaceden,
whoos contrarie freres han determined opinly.   Þerfore
resonably men shulden assente to þis axing.   For summe
5 freris writen þus in Coventré, among articlis þat þei
dampneden as heresye and error, þat it is errour to saye
þat seculer lordis may levefully and medefully taken
awey temporal goodis, ʒoven to men of þe Chirche.   But
siþ oure kyng haþ don so, and oþere kynges his prede-
10 cessoures han don so manie tymes, by laweful cause, as
perteynynge to here regalie, and of comun lawe, by
counsail of pieres of þe rewme, it sueþ þat not oonly
oure kyng now present haþ errid, but also his prede-
cessours, and generally al his counseillores, as lords and
15 prelatis, and alle men of þe Parlement counceilinge þerto.

For þe chief lordshipe in þis lond of alle temporalties,
boþe of seculer men and religious, perteyneþ to þe kyng
of his general governynge.   For ellis he were not kyng
of alle Englond, but of a litel part þerof.   Þerfore þe men
20 þat bysyen hem to take awey þys lordshipe fro þe kyng,
as don freris and here fautours, in þis poynt ben sharper
enemys and traitours þan Frensshe men and alle oþere
naciouns.

Also it perteyneþ to þe kyng, þe while a bishop or an
25 abbotis see is voyde, to have in his hond al here temporaltees, and at his owne wille to ʒeve hem to prelatis.
Þerfore þe kyng may take awey þes temporaltees from
prelatis, whan laweful cause exitiþ.

A Petition to the King and Parliament.

C. *The Clergy should be tried in Secular Courts.*

But aʒens þis blaberen Antecristis clerkis and aleggen
30 Goddis lawe, but to false sentense, þat seculer men
schulde noʒt iuge of clerkis, how evere þei don ; for þei
han propre iuges, as popis and bischopis and oþere iugis
undir hem.   And herto þei leggen but lewydly Goddis
lawe . . .
35   Sum tyme iugement God grauntid to kyngis, as Daviþ

and Salamon and many oþere kyngis. And ȝif þou seie
þat popis lawe spekiþ oþer wise of iugement, have þe
popis lawe more suspette, siþ Goddis lawe spekiþ þus,
and þus Crist biddiþ þe Iewis to iuge of Him riȝt iugement. Lord, wheþer þes clerkis ben more hiȝe overe 5
seculeris þan was our Lord Ihesu Crist overe þes falce
Iewis? for trewe men ben certeyn þat Crist bad hem
noȝt iuge of Him but ȝif it were leeful to lewid men to
iuge of clerkis. And so it were al on to denye siche
iugement and denye regalye þat falliþ to þe kyng.   10

Lord, wheþer þe lawe of Ynglond schal be now distried
bi fablis of heretikis contrarie to Goddis lawe?

Of Dominion.

VI

WYCLIF AND THE MEDIEVAL CHURCH

And it semeþ to sum men, ʒif þis were treuþe þat
shulde be trowid, God wolde liʒtly telle þis treuþe as He
telliþ oþer þat we trowen ; and ellis it were presumpcioun
to charge þe Chirche wiþ þis truþe, siþ neiþer autorité of
5 *God, ne resoun, techiþ þat þis is soþ ; and al bileve nedeful*
to men is tolde hem in þe lawe of God.

Sermons. Þe Sixte Sondai Gospel After Eestir.

A. In early manhood Wyclif accepted the orthodox, medieval
idea that there should be one head of the Church Militant on
earth—the Pope. The character and career of Urban V (1362–
10 70) did nothing to shake his belief. But the conduct of
Gregory XI (1370–8) and of Urban VI (1378–89) caused him
the greatest misgiving. Until 1378, however, Wyclif contented
himself with censure of the character and actions of the Pope
as an individual, but the Schism of 1378 and the subsequent
15 strife of Pope and Antipope caused him to subject the Papacy
itself to a searching inquiry.[1] He reached the conclusion that
the Gospel does not ordain one Pope ; that Peter was not
above the other apostles nor the Pope above other bishops.

In his later years Wyclif denied the impeccability and
20 infallibility of the Pope and used against him the doctrine of
Predestination. The Pope, he said, might be destined for
Hell. How dare such an one arrogate to himself the power to
bind and to loose ? In *Þe Chirche and hir Membris*[2] he defi-
nitely rejected the Papacy and defined the Church as the body
25 of 'trewe men' elected to bliss, whose sole Head is Christ.
'And ʒif þou seie þat Cristis Chirche mut have an heed here in
erþe, soiþ it is, for Crist is Heed, þat muste be here wiþ His
Chirche unto þe day of dome.'

B. In 1377 Gregory XI launched against Wyclif a series of
30 bulls and also cited him to Rome. The Reformer excused
himself in a Latin letter to the Pope (1378).[3] Our extract is

---

[1] See *de Potestate Pape* (1379) and the shorter *de Ordine Christiano.*

[2] See pp. 120, 123.

[3] Assigned by Netter of Walden (*Fasc. Ziz.*, p. 341) to 1384. Loserth

a free translation made possibly by Nicholas Hereford, as the dialect employed resembles that of *Lincolniensis* and the *Seven Deadly Sins*.

F. Wyclif's root objection to *Monasteries and Colleges* was that they served as 'castels' in which God's word was shut up and kept from the people.   The Church of Christ should not 5 be enclosed 'in coolde stones' but should manifest itself 'fre and large under the cope of Hevene'.   Priests should exercise their primary function, namely, pastoral care.   They should not lurk in cloisters 'doump of lore'.

G. Wyclif's belief as to the nature of the Host approached 10 most nearly to that which, since Luther's day, has been designated *Consubstantiation*.   He held that the substance of the bread and its 'accidents' (i.e. its qualities—size, colour, &c.) remain after the act of consecration but that the body of Christ is present also, hidden in the elements.[1]   He did not, 15 therefore, accept the orthodox idea of 'cessation of substance', i.e. that the substance of the bread disappears but the 'accidents' remain.   He poured scorn incessantly on those who held the foolish 'heresy' of 'accidents wiþouten subgett'.

In his latest years Wyclif grew impatient with subtle argu- 20 ments as to the nature of the Host.   His position, in effect, was : 'Let us accept the unexplained phrases of Scripture and receive this sacrament to freshen within our hearts the image of Christ.'   *To þis entent men taken now þis sacrament, so þat bi takynge hereof þer mynde be freschid in hem to þenken on* 25 *kyndenes of Crist to maken hem clene in soule.*

H. Wyclif preserved his veneration for the Virgin Mary throughout his life.   This is attested by many passages in his Sermons.   But he never countenanced the extreme forms of Mariolatry which prevailed in the Middle Ages.   Christ re- 30 mained to him the supreme object of worship.   Indeed the Virgin Mary received from him such a special meed of praise simply because, more than others, she heard and kept Christ's teaching.   'And herfore God ordeynede hir to be maistiresse

pointed out that since Wyclif had taken up a hostile position in regard to Urban VI in *de Potestate Pape* (1379) the following sentence 'could not possibly have been written in 1379 much less 1384': 'cum autem Deus dederit pape nostro instinctus iustos evangelicos, rogare debemus quod instinctus illi non per subdolum consilium extinguantur.'

[1] This he was bound to accept as a strict 'Bible-man' for Christ had said : 'This is my body.'

to His apostlis, for she fel not fro þe feith, ne fro þe wordis of Hir Sone, but kepte hem wel in her herte, and caste wel what þei menten.'[1]

The *Ave Maria* here printed is taken from the *Lay Folks' Catechism*.[2]

L. *Predestination.* In Wyclif's view the true Church Militant consists of the body of the Elect. No man, however, not even the Pope, knows whether he is destined to be saved. To be *in* the Church is not necessarily to be *of* the Church. It follows, therefore, that salvation does not depend on connexion with the visible Church or upon the mediation of the priesthood. 'Wyclif's doctrine involves the universal priesthood of the predestinate and his free, immediate access to God in Christ'.[3]

A. *Pope or Antichrist?*

3if þis þing and many siche ben soþe of þe Pope of Rome, he is very Anticrist and not Cristis viker.

de Papa.

God seiþ bi Ieremye þat He wakide eerly to His puple and criede His lawe bi His prophetis, þat weren martrid in Goddis cause and for profit of His Chirche, boþe for clerkis, lordis and comyns. But God seiþ by Salomon þat His wisdom cryeþ in streetis but men despisen His counsel and wolen not lyve by His lore, and þerfore God shal ley3e in þe tyme þat þey shulen perische; þanne þei shulen crie to Hym and He shal not here and spede hem.

Þus God moveþ many men in tyme of grace to telle His lawe; and 3it Anticrist dispisiþ it and lordis ben necgligent in þer help. And for prestis faylen on þer syde, as oþere men don, summe prestis þenken þat þey shulden crye and telle Goddis lawe to þe puple; for it may falle þat þey boþe shulen perische for þer necgligense.

Ground of Cristen mennus bileve seiþ þat Crist is God

[1] Sermons. *On Assumpcioun Evyn.* *S. E. W.* i. 380.
[2] See note, p. 165.   [3] H. B. W. ii. 12.

and man, and was porerste man of lif and mekerste and
moost vertuous. Cristen men taken over þat Petre was
Cristis viker, and suyde Hym in maner of lif and tauȝte
þe Chirche bi His lore. Þe fend hadde envye to Crist
and oþere men þat suyden Hym, and temptide prestis to 5
worldly lordchipis as he temptide Crist in His Person,
and as he liȝede in þis temptyng and seyde þat he wolde
ȝyve to Crist alle þe reumes of þe world so þat He wolde
loute hym, so bi craft of his lesyngis he haþ getun lordchip to clerkis; so þat now myche of þis world holdiþ on 10
Anticristis syde; as many seyen þat þe Pope shulde bi
vertu of Cristis lif be seculer lord of al þis world, and bi
his leeve kyngis ben lordis.

 .   .   .   .

   And for þe Pope is holdun moost and next viker of
Iesu Crist, þerfore þe fend in þe Pope haþ gederid many 15
worldly poyntes boþe of lordchip and worldly lif, and
castiþ to disseyve þe Chirche by hym. For manye taken
as bileve þat he may not do amys, but what þing þat he
grauntiþ or seiþ, Crist mut conferme it; and bi þis cautel
of þe fend ben many men dampnyd to helle. And 20
ground of al þis disseyt is lesing contrarye to treuþe; for
as þe fend disseyvede Eve bi lesing þat she shulde not
dye, whanne God hadde seyd þat she shulde dye what
day þat she eet of þe appul, so þe fend disseyveþ þe
Chirche bi oon opyn lesing, þat Crist was heere worldly 25
lord most hye of alle oþere, and so shulde his viker be
þat is clepid þe Pope of Rome. . . .

de Papa.

[CHRIST AND THE POPE: A CONTRAST]

   It were to wite over hou God shewiþ love to His
Chirche bi dyvysioun of þes Popis þat is nou late fallun.
Oure bileve techiþ bi Poul þat alle þingis fallen to good 30
to Goddis children þat dreden Hym, and þus shulden
Cristenmen take hem. Þe firste bok of Goddis lawe telliþ
hou God manaasside þe fend: 'Y shal putte enemyté',
seiþ God, 'bitwixe þee and womman, and bitwixe þy seed
and heere seed, and she shal al to-squatte þyn heed.' 35

And so taken sum men, þat hooly preyer of þe Chirche maad to Crist and His modir moveþ Hym to sende þis grace doun to departe þe heed of Anticrist, so þat his falsed be more knowun. And it semeþ to hem þat þe
5 Pope is Anticrist heere in erþe, for he is aȝenus Crist boþe in lif and in lore.

Crist was most pore man fro His birþe to His deþ, and lefte worldly riches and beggyng, aftir þe staat of innocense ; but Anticrist aȝenus þis, fro þe tyme þat he
10 be maad Pope til þe tyme þat he be deed heere, coveytiþ to be worldly riche, and castiþ bi manye shrewid weyes hou þat he may þus be riche.

Crist was moost meke man and bad lerne þis of Hym ; but men seyen þat þe Pope is moost proud man of erþe,
15 and makiþ lordis to kysse his feet where Crist wayschide His postlis feet.

Crist was moost homely man in lif, in dede and in word ; men seyen þat þis Pope is not nexst to Crist in þis, for where Crist wente on His feet boþe to citees and
20 litil tounnes, þey seyen þis Pope wole be closid in a castel wiþ greet aray.

Where Crist cam to Ioon Baptist to be baptisid of hym, þe Pope sendiþ aftir men to come to hym where evere he be ; ȝe, ȝif Crist have sumnyd hem for to come
25 not to hym.

Crist bicliptide ȝonge and pore in tokene of His home-lynesse ; men seyen þat þe Pope wole biclippe worldly worchip, and not trewe men for Goddis sake lest he unworchipe hym silf.
30 Crist was bisy to preche þe gospel not for His worldly worchip ne wynning ; men seyen þat þe Pope leeveþ þis, but he wole gladly make a lawe and make þis lawe in more worchip and more drede þan Cristis lawe.

Crist lovede so myche His floc þat He puttide His lif
35 for hem, and sufferide sharp peyne and deþ for to brynge hem to blis ; men seyen þat þe Pope loveþ so myche worchip of þe world, þat he wole feyne asoyling to men to go streyȝt to Hevene, so þat þey do a travel þat sounneþ to his worldly worchip. And so his foly may

be cause of deþ of many þousynd men boþe in body and
in soule. But hou sueþ he Crist in þis?

Crist was so pacient and so myche sufferide His oune
wrong, þat He preyede for His enemyes and tauȝte His
postlis to take no veniaunse ; men seyen ʃat þe Pope of 5
Rome wole be vengid on alle maners, boþe bi sleyng and
bi cursing and oþere peynes þat he feyneþ.

Crist tauȝte men to lyve wel bi His oune lif and His
wordis, for what He tauȝte He dide in dede, and bad
men trowe to His werkis ; men seyen þat þe Pope goiþ 10
al bi contrarye weye to þis, for his lif is not ensaumple to
oþere men hou þey shulden lyve, for no man shulde lyve
lik to hym, as he feyneþ bi his hye staat.

Crist in ech His dede and His word souȝte þe glory of
God, and sufferide many reproves in His manheed for þis 15
ende ; men seyen þat þe Pope aȝenward sekiþ his oune
glory on alle weyes, ȝe, ȝif Goddis worchip be lost. And
þus he feyneþ many ungroundid gabbingis. And ȝif þis
þing and many siche ben soþe of þe Pope of Rome, he is
very Anticrist and not Cristis viker heere. 20

Ibidem.

[THE POMP OF POPES AND CARDINALS]

Þer ben groundis þe which Crist kepte contrarie to
keping of prelatis nou. For Crist tauȝte þat hoolynesse
shulde be hid in mennus hertis and not shewid to þe
puple in sensible signes wiþoute fruyt ; for þanne men
hopiden reward of God and axiden not glory of þis 25
world. But nou it is turnyd upsedoun fro religioun ʃat
Crist ordeynede, for nou he is neþer Pope ne prelat, but
ȝif he have a worldly meyné þat shewe his hyenesse to
þe world, as he were a seculer lord. And bi þis gile haþ
þe fend brouȝt in þat more prestis shulden have worldly 30
glorye. And þis makiþ þe Pope and bischops to axe
richessis to þer staat ; for, as þei seyen, þer staat wolde
perische but ȝif siche richesse shewide it out.

First þes prelatis blasfemen in Crist and in His hooly
apostlis. For bileve techiþ us þat Crist was bischop of 35
mennus soulis, betere bi a þousynd part þan any siþ þe

Chirche was dowyd. And so weren Cristis apostlis betere
þan ony Pope of Rome. For þis name is newe foundun
and it bitokeniþ *wundirful*; for summe þenken it greet
wundir þat worldly glory and hoolynesse shulden be
5 knyttid in o persone. Siþ Crist forsok it in word and
dede, and bi His lore His apostlis, lord, why shulden not
prelatis do nou so?

And by þis cause haþ þe fend brouʒt yn þat religioun
of þes newe ordris shal be shewid in sensible signes, as
10 habitis, and bikenes, and hye housis ; and herfore haþ þe
fend brouʒt in þat cumpany of many lumpis shal be
ioyned to o persone for worldly worchip of þer staat.
Þus þer ben many cardenals and many men knytted to
hem ; myche meyné to a bischop and manye persones in
15 an ordre. And al is charge to comyn men and strengþe
to þe fendis part. Crist ordeynede þat His apostlis fro
tyme þat He steyede to Hevene shulden be scaterid in
many cuntreys and conquere wickid men to Crist. Wel
y rede þat Seynt Petre dwelte in a corieris hous, but y
20 rede not of cardenal ne page þat he hadde wiþ hym.
And ʒit þis apostle cam to Cornely and convertide hym
wiþ oþere. And þus may Cristen men lerne boþe of
Crist and His apostles þat religioun of Crist is not in
siche worldly signes.

25 And so men moten oþer denye bileve, or seye þat
Cristis religioun stondiþ not in siche signes as nou þe
Chirche is chargid wiþ. Soþ it is þat seculer prinsis and
worldly lordis moten have siche worldly signes, for þey
shulden teche to drede God by austerneté and worldly
30 drede. But it is aʒenus Cristis wille þat prestis meddle
þes two togidere, for þey shulden teche by mekenesse
and paciense, as Crist dide. . . .

Crist as a goode maystir hadde twelve apostlis to
teche hem ; Anticrist ordeyneþ many twelve to lyve
35 worldly and charge þe Chirche. Crist koude ensaumple
kynghod and presthod in her groundis, but prestis þat
comen after Crist ben not able to do so. And þus þey
passen þer maystir, Crist, boþe in presthod and in
knyʒthod.

And þus ȝif Popis wolden have cardenals, þey shulden chese gode men and pore, and loke þat þey chargide not þe Chirche bi costly array and idilnesse. But nou men seyen þat cardenals ben brouȝt yn bi Anticrist to bargeyne by symonye and by oþere disseytis bigile men, and þus 5 as þe Pope is wundirful, so Cardenals ben an herre to þe fendis hous.

And oþere ground han þey noon, but for Anticrist wole þus.

Ibidem.

[ABSOLUTION AND INDULGENCES GRANTED BY THE POPE ARE USELESS]

Ȝit Anticrist argueþ þat it is nedeful to þe Chirche þat 10 þe Pope and his cardenals and oþre prelatis reule it. For who shulde ellis assoyle men and graunte hem so large indulgensis boþe of peyne and of synne, have þei nevere so longe synned? And oþere privylegies of þe Pope may not be teld of erþly men.   15

In þis mater han Cristenmen seyd prively as þey dursten, þat it were good men to be war lest Anticrist disseyve hem. . . . And þus men seyen bi Cristis lore þat Anticrist faillip first whanne he seiþ þat it is nedeful þat þe Pope and cardenals reule Cristis Chirche. For 20 whanne Cristis Chirche þrof, weren no siche Pope and cardenals. And siþen þes prelatis weren comun yn reg- nede Anticrist wiþ synne.

And anentis assoyling, bileve techiþ Cristenmen þat Iesu Crist mut nedis assoyle ȝif ony man shule be 25 assoylid, and Anticrist may not for shame denye opynly þis bileve. But he seiþ þat Crist mut nedis assente wiþ hym in asoyling and he groundiþ þis bi þe Gospel, but it is shame to reherse it. Soþ it is Crist grauntide to Petre þat what þing he asoylide on erþe shulde be assoylid in 30 Hevene and so it is of bynding. But þis was lymytid to Petre and hise þat suyden þe steppis þat Petre wente, and whanne þer soyling and þer bynding acordide wiþ God in Hevene. But nou it is no bileve þat þes gon Petris steppis and suen Crist þe streiȝt weye þat shulde lede herdis to 35

Hevene. And also it is no bileve þat what tyme þat þes prelatis feynen hem to asoyle, þey acorden wiþ Crist above; and so it is no bileve þat þei acorden evere wiþ Crist. . . .

5 It is no poynt of bileve þat þe Pope evere more in graunting of þes indulgensis acordiþ wiþ Goddis wille; as it is no bileve þat so longe shal þis worlde stonde, as þe Pope grauntiþ indulgensis. But bileve techiþ Cristenmen þat indulgensis shulen no lengere laste; and þus it is no
10 bileve ʒif þe Pope, for bidding of a kyng, grauntiþ so large indulgensis þat a man may in a masse tyme where evere he heriþ þis masse gete twenti þousynd ʒeer of pardoun, and þat wole passe alle þe tyme þat soulis shulen dwelle in purgatorye; and þus he shal not dwelle
15 in peyne bi þe graunt of þe Pope.

Manye siche þingis ben writun þat ben nouʒt of bileve and þerfore it is perelous to trowe hem as bileve. *We bileven on Cristis lawe þat ʒif man synnede nevere so longe, and were nevere asoylid of Pope ne of his prest*
20 *undir hym, ʒif he wolde forsake his synne and be contrit for formere synne and ende his lif on þis maner, God wolde forʒyve hym his synne.*

Ibidem.

B. *Letter to Pope Urban VI.*

I have joy fully to telle to alle treue men þo bileve þat I holde, and algatis to þo Pope; for I suppose þat if my
25 fayth be riʒtful and gyven of God, þo Pope wil gladly conferme hit; and if my fayth be errour, þo Pope wil wisely amende hit.

I suppose over þis, þat þo Gospel of Crist be hert of þo corps of Gods lawe;[1] for I byleve þat Jesus Crist, þat
30 gaf in his owne persoun þis Gospel, is verrey God and verrey mon, and be þis hert passes alle oþer lawes.

I suppose over þis þat þo Pope be moste oblischid to þo keping of þo Gospel among alle men þat lyven here;

---

[1] þe herte of Goddis lawe *Q.*

for þo Pope is hyeste vicar þat Crist has here in erthe.
For morenesse of Cristis vicar is not mesurid by worldly
morenesse, bot bi þis, þat þis vicar sues more Crist by
virtuous lyvyng; for þus techis þo Gospel, þat þis is þo
sentence of Crist.   5

And of þis Gospel I take as byleve, þat Crist, for tyme
þat He walkid here, was moste pore mon of alle, boþe in
spirit and in havyng; for Crist seis þat He had noȝt for
to reste His hed on. And Poule seis þat he was made
nedy for our love. And more pore myȝt no mon be, 10
nouþer bodily ne in spirit. And þus Crist putte fro Hym
al maner of worldly lordschip. For þo gospel of Jon
telliþ þat when þei wold have made Crist kyng, He fled
and hid Hym fro hem, for He wold non such worldly
hynesse.   15

And over þis I take as byleve, þat no mon schuld sue
þo Pope, ne no seynt þat now is in Heven, bot in als
myche as he sues Crist. For Jon and James errid when
þei coveytid worldly hynesse; and Petir and Poule
synned also when þei denyed and blasphemed in Crist; 20
bot men schuld not sue hom in þis, for þen þei wente fro
Jesus Crist. And[1] þis I take as hoolsome counseil, þat
þo Pope leeve his worldly lordschip to wordly lordis, as
Crist gaf hom,—and move spedely alle his clerkis to do
so. For þus did Crist, and tauȝt þus his disciplis, til þo 25
fende had blyndid þis world. And hit semes to sum men,
þat clerkis þat dwellen lastandly in þis error ageyns Gods
lawe, and flees to sue Crist in þis, ben open heretikes, and
hor fautours ben partyneris.

And if I erre in þis sentense, I wil mekely be amendid, 30
ȝhe, by þo deth, if hit be skilful, for þat I hope were gude
to me. And if I myȝt travel in myn owne persoun, I
wold wiþ gode wille go to þo Pope. Bot God[2] has nedid
me to þo contrarye, and tauȝt me more obeche to God
þen to mon. And I suppose of oure Pope þat he wil not 35
be Anticrist, and reversen Crist in þis wirkynge, to þo
contrarie of Cristis wille; for if he summone ageyns

[1] and *Q*.   [2] *supplied from Q*; *om. W*.

resoun, by him or by any of his, and pursue þis unskilful
summonyng, he is an open Anticrist.

And merciful entent excusid not Peter, þat ne Crist
cleped hym Sathanas.   So blynde entent and wicked
5 counseil excuses not þo Pope here ; bot if he aske of
trew prestis þat þei travel more þan þei may, he is not
excusid by resoun of God þat ne he is Anticrist.   For
oure byleve techis us, þat oure blessid God suffris us not
to be temptid more þan we may ; how schulde a mon
10 aske such servyce ?   And þerfore preye we to God for
oure Pope Urban þo Sex, þat his olde holy entent be not
quenchid by his enemyes.   And Crist, þat may not lye,
seis þat þo enemyes of a mon ben specialy his homely
meyneȝ ; and þis is soth of men and fendis.

C. *Simony.*

15 Also, alle symonyentis þat bien or sillen spiritual
þingis for temperal þingis unlefful, ben cursed solempneli,
boþe bi Goddis lawe and mannis.   But þre degres ben in
symonyentis.   Summe ben symonyentis in ordre, summe
symonyentis in beneficis, and summe symonyentis in
20 sacramentis.

Of symonyentis in holy ordre ben þre degres. Summe
come to ordre of presthod, dekenhede, or oþere ordris
hiere or lowere, by ȝevynge of money.   And þes ben no
prestis ne dekenes but han only þe name. . . . Summe
25 by symonye comen to siche ordre for preiere of lordis, or
oþere worldli frendis, not bi clene entent and worþinesse
of kunnynge and lyvynge, but only bi favour of men.
And þes [ben] in þe cursed heresie of symonye. . . . Þe
þridde tyme, summe comen to ordris by symonye, bi
30 servyce to lordis or prelatis or oþer officeris, servynge
longe tyme to men for þis ende. . . . And þes fallen in
þe same dampnacioun wiþ þe firste, for it is al on to ȝyve
money and to serve þus for holy ordris, before or after.

Þe fourþe tyme, summe comen to holy ordris not for
35 devocion and love of God, but for to lyve in worldly
lordischip and have welfare of mete and drynk, and gay

cloþis, and ese, and rejoischen hem þerinne, and bisien
hem not aboute Goddis lawe ne holy lif, but in lecherie
and vanyté and ydelnesse and worldly myrþe.   And in
þe riȝtful dom of God þei ben symonyentis as was Simon
Magus.   For þei sillen to fendis of helle here soule, here 5
body, and tyme, and catel, for to have and use unworþily
þe holy ordre of presthod.

On þre maneres ben men symonyentis in beneficis, bi
ȝifte of money to þe patroun for presentacioun, or to
prelat for collacion, or ȝevyng institucion, or induction, or 10
bi brocage maade to mene persones for to have ony
beneficis of þe Chirche.   And þis is cursed heresie, for it
presumeþ to sille þe Holy Gost, as þe lawe witnessiþ ; siþ
it presumeþ to sille þe ȝiftis of þe Holy Gost, þat schulden
be ȝoven frely to alle men, as Crist biddiþ.   15

On þe secunde manere don many men symonye, whanne
þei serve lordis or prelatis undwe servyces longe tyme, for
to have a benefice in þe ende of here servyce.   And herefore þei biheten to serve lordis and prelatis in worldly
office on here owene cost, and dwellen in here courtis 20
absent fro here chirchis.   And þis is cursed marchaundise
wiþ temperal servyce and benefices of þe Chirche.   And
oure Lord Jesus drof alle siche out of þe temple, in token
þat þei ben not approved of Him in þe Chirche, but
schullen be dreven to helle bi jugement of God, ȝif þei 25
lasten in þis synne to here deþ.   And þerfore seiþ Seynt
Gregory and þe lawe, þat þei þat don siche symonye
schullen be dampnyd in everelestynge fier of helle, but
ȝif þei resygnen here benefices, and in tyme of deþ ben
founden in scharpe penaunce.   30

On þe þridde manere don men symonye bi tunge, þat
neiþer ȝeven gold ne servyce to lordis, ne prelatis, ne
mene persones, but bi flateryng and preier of myȝty men
comen to benefices.

.   .   .   .

What man comeþ now to ony fat benefice or prelacie 35
wiþouten ȝifte of money or servyce, or flateryng and preier
boþe of himself and oþere grete men of þe world ?   For
now many lordis axen moche for presentacion, and longe

worldly servyce of þes clerkis, bifore here benefices and
aftir; and of privy ȝiftis and preieris is noon ende in
mannus witt. Who getiþ ony fat benefice of þe Bischop
of Rome wiþouten siche flateryng and preier, and gold
5 for his dede lede, and þe first fruytis, and omage, and
swerynge, oþer þan Crist and his apostlis diden?

. . . .

Ȝit on þes þre maners don men symonye in sacramentis, as ordris, masse synging, confession and alle þe
sevene sacramentis of Holy Chirche.
10 A! Lord, hou moche is oure kyng and oure rewme
holpen bi massis and preieris of symonyentis and heretikis, ful of pride coveitise and envye? Þat haten so
moche pore prestis, techynge Cristis lif and þe Gospel
to meyntene holy life of Cristene peple and þe kynges
15 regalie, þat þei cursen hem and prisonen hem wiþouten
answere.

Þe Grete Sentence of Curs Expouned.

D. *Friars.*

[FALSE FRIARS HINDER TRUE PREACHING]

Heere breken out þes freris ordris, for al ȝif þei han no
worldly lordchip as han prestis þat ben dowid, ȝit þei
spuylen men of moeblis and wasten hem in noumbre and
20 housis; and þis excees is more synne þan synne of þe
fend in o persone.

And þus þey turnen þe ende of þer prechyng for to gete
hem siche godis. And þis entent mut nedis make falsed
in maner of þer preching, for þei shapen þer sermouns
25 more to gete hem good þan to profite to þe Chirche.
And as þe firste wile of þe fend bigan soone in Silvestris
tyme, so þis second wile bigan in grounding of þes newe
ordris.

. . . .

Þe fourþe cause [þat lettiþ trewe prechyng] is bringing
30 in of false freris bi many cuntreys; for, as it is seid

bifore, þei letten trewe prechiñg to renne and maken
curatis bi many weyes to leeve þis most worþy offiss.
First þey robben hem many weyes and maken hem bisy
for lyve, for þey depraven hem to þer parischens bi
floriȝshid wordis þat þey bringen yn. And no drede þey 5
shapen þer sermouns bi dyvysiouns and oþere iapis þat
þey maken moost plese þe puple. And þus þey erren in
bileve and maken þe puple to trowe to hem þat sermouns
ben nouȝt but in þer foorme and þus þei stoppen symple
curatis þat þei doren not preche to þe puple. And þis 10
defaute of preching of Crist is more þan defaute in
hereris.

And so as Crist seiþ in þe Gospel, boþe Sodom and
Gomor shulen be lesse punyshid at domes day þan þes
newe sectis brouȝt yn ; for þey synneden in mannus seed, 15
but þes synnen in seed of God, þat is Goddis word, þat
prestis shulden preche to turne þe lewid puple to God.

And as it is seyd bifore, þe puple is smyttid bi þis
synne, for þe puple assentiþ to hem bi iapis and wilis þat
þey tellen hem. Þe puple shulde not trowe to þe prechour 20
whatever he seye in þis staat, but ȝif his word be groundid
in God as Goddis lawe or suynge þer of. For þis staat
is not covenable to telle iapis ne bourdis to men, but þat
þat wole trewely fede þer soule, as is þe Gospel and oþer
Goddis lawe. And þis bourding or oþere iapis shulde 25
make þes freris suspect heere and make hem wante
worldly wynning, for þey ben worþy myche more peyne.
But lewidnesse of þe puple makiþ hem nurshe þer mooste
enemyes.

And God make þis enmyté knowun. For þis is þe 30
laste and þe moste fendis cautel ; but good wille and
trewe speche of Goddis lawe shulde make hem knowun.
For failing of Goddis word and coveytise of mennus good
shewen opinli to men whoos children þat þey ben. Lord,
siþen pariȝshens shulden take þe preching of þer oune 35
curat and þe mynistring þat he shulde do, for þat shulde
suffise to þat puple, why shulden not men fle fro false
prophetis, as Crist biddiþ in þe Gospel ?

But bullis of þe court of Rome blynden many men

heere, for it semeþ þe hed of errour and propre nest of
Anticrist.

de Officio Pastorali, Cap. XXVI.

E. *Tithes.*

Of þis it semyþ to many men þat neþer persoun ne
prelate shulde wringe out þe godis of his sugettis bi
5 cursis ne worldly ple.   For þey ben pure almes as we
supposen, on which almes shulde renne no ple ; for þei
shulden be willeful and ȝovyn wiþoute resoun of mannus
dette.

Also Crist and His apostlis neþer cursiden ne pletiden
10 for þer dette and þey shulden be ensaumple to us.   Why
shulden we curse or plete for hem ?   And in tokene
hereof God telde in His newe lawe litil or nouȝt of ȝyvyng
of dymes.

And it semiþ to trewe men þat God wolde þat dymes
15 weren partid bitwixe prestis and oþere pore men þat
weren feble, lame or blynd.   And þerfore telliþ Luk in
his gospel hou Crist cam þoruȝ Samary wiþ His disciplis
and þey wolden neþer ȝyve fode ne herbore for Hym and
Hise.   And Ioon and Iames axiden of Crist þat fier
20 shulde come doun fro Hevene and destrie hem, as Ely
dide.   But Crist answeride to þes apostlis and tauȝte
þat He wolde not curse þus : ' Ȝee witen not ', seiþ Crist,
' whoos spiritis ȝee ben, and hou Y love mekenesse and
paciense, for mannus Sone cam not into þis world to lese
25 mennus soulis but to save hem.'   And iurisdiccioun of
Crist was largere and freere þan þe Popis.

Siþen Crist wolde not curse for þes wrongis and þei
weren more þan oure wrongis, bi what lawe shulden we
have title to curse þus for oure lesse wrongis ?   No drede
30 Crist hadde more riȝt to þes dymes þan ony Cristenman
may have to dymes or to offeringis or to ony good by
mannus lawe.   And siþen Crist tauȝte in þis dede not to
plete for his dette, why shulden not prestis sue Crist
heere siþen Cristis dedis ben myrour to hem ?

35   And ȝif þey taken of þe olde lawe þat dymes ben due
unto prestis, myche more in þe newe lawe whan prestis

ben more worþy bi Crist. Soþ it is þat dymes weren due
to prestis in þe olde lawe but þey weren holdun to do
aȝen sleyng of beestis and hard servyss. But God forbede þat oure prelatis oblische hem to travele þus, for
þanne þei abiden aȝenus bileve, sleyng of Crist þat was 5
þanne figurid.

Also no man shulde plete an oþer, and algatis þe curat
his sheep, but for charité to þe pleted man ; siþen Poul
seiþ þat alle oure dedis shulden be done in charité, ȝe þat
shulde strecche to oure enemyes. And ȝif þou seyst þat 10
charité moveþ þee to plete þus for dymes, forȝyve þou
hem as Crist dide, for þat is more liȝt and of more love.
And ȝif a man plete in Goddis cause and alegge þat þou
hast synned in doyng of þyn herdis offiss, in þingis þat þou
shuldist ȝyve þi sheep, no drede þou maist not answere 15
heere ne iustefie þy part bi Goddis lawe.

And þus in þe newe lawe siþen prestis bigunnen to
plete þus, þei han lefte to do þer offiss, as þei leften in þe
olde lawe. And so instode of siche plees þe curat shulde
move his sheep bi paciense and oþere vertues and trewe 20
travel in his offiss. And ȝif þis wole not move þe puple
to ȝyve hym þingis þat ben nedeful, turne þis prelat to
oþer puple ; for so dide Crist and God faillip not. Or
ellis lyve he on his bodily travel or oþere mennus almes
as Poul dide. 25

Of þis ground may men se over, þat ȝif an hye prelat
charge a persoun to ȝyve hym godis þat is not groundid
bi lawe of God for to ȝyve, þys persoun shulde not ȝyve
þes godis, neþer for cursing ne oþere censuris ; for a man
shulde not assente to synne for noþing as it is seyd. . . . 30
And it is all oon to an hye prelat to curse þis persoun for
þis cause and to seye : ' Robbe þou pore men and take of
hem so myche good, and Y shall mayntene þi robbery ;
and ellis Y shal curse þee in þyn hed and suspende þee
and þe puple þat þey here not Goddis servyss.' . . . 35

Bischops and archidekenes wiþ þer officials and denes
shulden not amersy pore men ; for þis is worse þan comyn
robberye, siþen ipocrisie is feyned over wrong-taking of
þes godis.

A prest shulde raþere .leeve þis offiss and suffere deþ
or he assentide by ony maner of consentis to siche piling
of pore men.

de Officio Pastorali, Caps. VI and VII.

F. *Monasteries and Colleges.*

Ʒit argueþ Anticrist þat bi þis fel foly perpetual almes
5 in abbeys and in collegies shulde be destried : but where
were more synne ? And siþ it is greet meede to do
almes for a tyme, it were myche more meede to contynue
perpetual almes ; and þus charteres of lordis and kyngis
of þer perpetual almes shulden be destried, and gostly
10 help þat sueþ þerof. And no drede þe Pope is ground of
alle siche perpetual alms.

Heere han trewe men ofte seyd þat it were myche
betere þat men lyveden opyn lif þan in siche nestis of þe
fend ; for siche abbeys and collegies ben hordis of synne
15 to herbore hym.

And herfore seiþ Crist in þe Gospel þat men shulden
not be bisi to þe morowe; but Anticrist haþ hardy maner
to his castel for many ʒeere. And þus þat Crist durst
not do, ne his apostlis aftir Hym, Anticrist dare blyndly
20 do in holding of siche castels. And þis is a fendis cautel
þat he haþ brouʒt yn of newe. . . .

And þus siche nestis shulden not be callid perpetual
almes of worldly lordis, but dennes of þeves and nestis
of serpentis, and homely housis of quyc devels. And
25 þei don harm to Cristis Chirche bi perpetualté in þer
synne. And oþer ground han no men for to founde siche ·
dennes, but þat Crist forfendide hem. And se þe cautel
of þe fend, hou quentely he haþ brouʒt þis yn. He
moveþ þes founderis to pride and seiþ þey ben comen of
30 grete men, þat han foundid perpetuel abbeys in so myche
multitude. Where is more Satanas pride aʒenus mekenesse of Iesu Crist ? For oure bileve techiþ us þat a man
doiþ no lengere merit þan þe while he lyveþ heere in erþe.
Hou shulde þis meede evere laste ? . . .

Se hou Anticrist and þes lordis stryven as fendis in þis

point. Anticrist seiþ þat al þis lordchip felde to hym bi
title of Crist, and so þes lordis ȝaven aȝen godis þat þey
hadden unjustly holdun, and so þei han no more meede
but maken aseeþ for þer formere synne. And þus it is
not perpetual almes but perpetual part of makinge 5
aseeþ. . . .

And to þe foorme of Anticristis skile. He and alle
hise kunnen not grounde þat þis was evere ony almes to
make þus siche Cayms castels. Soþely in þe olde lawe
was Salomons temple a figure of þe Chirche in þe newe 10
lawe, but not þat þe Chirche shulde be siche, but fre and
large undir þe cope of Hevene, and stonde in vertues of
mannus soule.

But Anticrist wole close it nou in coolde stones þat
moten perisshe.   15

de Papa, Cap. X.

Þer ben þre maner of collegies þat usen þis craft of
appropring. Þe firste ben cathedral chirchis þat han
provendris approprid to hem ; þe secounde ben chapels
of prinsis þat han chirchis more approprid ; þe þridde ben
collegies of studies þat usen þis same craft. Bi þes may 20
men knowe oþere þat han appropring of chirchis. For
alle accorden in þis, þat þey han almes of pariȝschens
and ȝit dwellen not on þe pariȝs as herdis for to teche
hem. . . .

Also almes shulde be fre and discreet as Goddis lawe 25
techiþ, for ellis it were not meedeful and God ȝave no
leeve to do it. What meede shal a pore man have þat
he sufferiþ aȝenus his wille his almes to be borun to Cayms
castels to fede a floc of Anticristis ? Certis þey don þes
pariȝschis no good ne to general Hooly Chirche, but ȝif 30
þey don good as þe fend þat reversiþ Goddis ordenaunse.

Men shulden seke grounde of siche collegies wheþer
God haþ ordeyned hem to be, and þe floc fed bi hem þat
ben so fer and so lewid. And þus þes novelries of col- 35
legies semen to tempte Crist as þe fend, for þey gon not
to Hevene bi greesis þat God haþ ordeyned to lede þidur,

but þey wolen fle bi þe fendis craft and leeve þe weye þat Crist haþ set.

Crist ordeynede þat his herdis shulden dwelle wisely upon his sheep, and teche hem boþe bi lif and word hou
5 þey shulden lyve to come to Hevene. But Anticrist castiþ anoþer gile, þat his herdis dwelle afer in castels and be doump of lore of lif and lore of word to helpe þer sheep.

de Officio Pastorali, Cap. IX.

G. *The Eucharist.*

Riȝt so þe sacrid oost is verry breed kyndeli, and
10 Goddis bodi figurali, riȝt as Crist himsilf seiþ.

Sermons. On Wednesday in þe Secunde Weke of Advent.

Non tamen audeo dicere quod corpus Christi sit essentialiter, substantialiter, corporaliter, vel identice ille panis. ... Credimus enim quod triplex est modus essendi corporis Christi in hostia consecrata, scilicet virtualis,
15 spiritualis, et sacramentalis.

' Confessio Magistri Johannis Wycclyff.'

Fasciculi Zizaniorum.

I. Here after þis witt men may large þis gospel, and trete what mater þat þei wenen shulde profite to þe puple ; but it is comounly told of þe sacrament of þe
20 auter, and how men shal disposen hem now to take þis sacrament. And it is seid comounly, þat as þes holy wymmen hadde lefte þer former synne, and taken þer freshe devocioun ; so men shulden come to þe chirche to take þis holy sacrament and þus come wiþ þes hooly
25 wymmen wiþ liȝt of þe sunne.

And þus men shulden cloþen hem wiþ þes þre vertues, bileve, hope, and charité, to resceyve þis sacrament. Bileve is first nedeful ; and algatis of þis breed, hou it is Goddis bodi by vertue of Cristis wordis. And so it is
30 kyndely breed, as Poul seiþ, but it is sacramentally verré Goddis bodi. And herfore seiþ Austyn, þat þing is breed þat þi iȝen tellen þee and þat þou seest wiþ hem. For it

was not trowid bifore þe fend was losid, þat þis worþi
sacrament was accident wiþouten suget. And ȝit dwellen
trewe men in þe old bileve, and laten freris foulen hem
silfe in þer newe heresie. For we trowen þat þere is
beter þing þan Goddis bodi, siþ þe Holy Trinité is in 5
eche place. But oure bileve is sette upon þis point;
what is þis sacrid hoost, and not what þing is þere.

Þe secound vertue þat shulde cloþe trewe men is þe
vertue of hope, þat is ful nedeful ; how men shulde hope
bi þer lyfe here, and first, wiþ þe grace of God, for to 10
come to Hevene. And to þis entent men taken now þis
sacrament, so þat bi takynge herof þer mynde be freschid
in hem to þenken on kyndenes of Crist to maken hem
clene in soule. And herfore seiþ Poul þat he þat wantiþ
þis ende, etiþ and drynkeiþ his judgement, for he jugiþ 15
not þe worþines of Goddis bodi, ne worshipiþ his ordenaunce.

Þe þridde vertue nedeful for to take þis sacrament is
vertue of charité ; for þat is ever nedeful, siþ no man
comeþ to Cristis fest but ȝif he have þis cloþing. And 20
þus, as Austyn declariþ, foure poyntis þat falliþ[1] to
makinge of breed techen us þis charité, and algatis to
have it now. For ellis we greggen[2] our synne in etynge
of þis breed. And ȝif we have þis cloþinge, takinge þis
mete in figure, it shal brynge us to Hevene, þere to ete 25
Goddis body goostly wiþouten ende ; and þat is mennis
blisse.

Sermons. Þe Gospel on Eestir Day.

II. [WYCLIF'S CONFESSIO.]

JOHANNES WYCLIFF.

I bileve[3], as Crist and his apostels have tauȝt us, þat
þo sacrament of þo auter, whyte and rounde, and like to
oþer bred, or oost sacred[4], is verrey Gods body in fourme 30
of bred ; and þof hit be broken in thre partyes, as þo
Kirke uses, or elles in a thousande, evere ilk one of þese

---

[1] fallen *E.*   [2] agreggen *E.*   [3] We beleve *HH.*
[4] and lyke tyl oure brede or ost unsacrede *HH.*

parties is þo same Gods body. And right as þo persoun
of Crist is. verrey God and mon—verrey godhed and
verrey monhed—right so holy Kirke, mony hundred
winters, haves trowed þo same sacrament is verrey Gods
5 body and verrey bred, as hit is fourme of Gods body and
fourme of bred, as teches Crist, and his apostels. And
þerfore Seint Poul nemmes hit nevere, bot when he calles
hit bred ; and he by oure bileve toke in þis his witte of
God. And þo argumentis [1] of heretikes ageyns þis sen-
10 tense are light for to assoyle to a Cristen mon.[2] And
right as hit is heresye* to trowe þat Crist is a spiryt and
no body, so hit is heresye * [3] to trowe þat þis sacrament is
Gods body and no bred ; for hit is bothe togedir.

Bot þo moste heresye þat God suffred cum [4] to His
15 Chirche, is to trowe þat þis sacrament is accydent wiþouten
subgett [5]; and may on no wyse be Gods body.[6] And if
þou sey, by his [7] skil holy Kirke hafs ben in erroure
mony hundred wynters, for Crist seis, by wittenesse of
Jerome, þat þis bred is my body, soth hit is, specialy
20 sithen þo fende was loused, þat was, by wittenesse of þo
áungel to Jon þo Evangeliste, aftir a þousande wynters
þat Crist was styed [8] to Heven. Bot hit is to suppose þat
mony seyntis, þat dyed in þo meene tyme, bifore hor
deth were purged of þis errour. Ow ! how gret diversyté
25 is bytwene us þat trowen þat þis sacrament is verrey bred
in his kynde, and bytwene heretikes þat tellen þat hit is
an accydent wiþouten sugett ! For bifore þat þo fende,
fadir of leesynges, was loused, was nevere þis gabbynge
contreved.[9] And how gret diversité is bitwene us þat
30 trowen þat þis sacrament in his kynde is verrey bred, and
sacramentaly Gods body, and bytwene heretikes þat
trowen and tellen þat þis sacrament may on no wyse be
Gods body ! For I dar surely sey, þat if þis were sothe,
Crist and His seyntis dyed heretikes, and þo more partye

---

[1] argument *HH*.   [2] lyth to a Cristeneman for to assolve *HH*.
[3] *HH omits the words between asterisks*.   [4] come *HH*.   [5] accident wiþ
a substans *HH*.   [6] *Here HH inserts the following sentence* : For Crist
sayde, be witnesse of Johan, þat þis brede is my body.   [7] þis *HH*.
[8] stevenyde *HH*.   [9] contryvede *HH*.

of holy Kirke byleved [1] nowe heresye. And herfore
devoute men supposen þat þis counseil of freris at [2]
Londoun was wiþ erthe dyn [3] for þei putt an heresye
upon Crist and seyntis in Heven ; wherfore þo erthe
trembled, faylande monnis voice, answerande [4] for God 5
as hit did in tyme of His passioun, when He was dampned
to bodily deth.

Crist and His modir, þat in grounde have destryed alle
heresies, kepe His Kirke in right byleve of þis sacrament.
And move we [5] kyng and his reume to aske scharply of 10
clerkes [6] þis office ; þat alle possessioners, on peyne of
leesynge of alle hor temporaltees, telle þo kyng and his
rewme, wiþ sufficiaunt groundynge, what is þis sacrament ; and alle þo ordiris of freris, in peyne of lesynge
of alle hor legeaunce, telle þo kynge and his reume wiþ 15
gode groundynge what is þis [7] sacrament. For I am
certen, for [8] þo thridde part of clergye þat deffendes þis
sentence [9] þat is here seyde, þat þai wil deffende hit on
peyne of losyng of hor lyve.[10] Amen.[11]

H. *The Virgin Mary.*

Men gretyþ comunly oure Lady Goddys Moder 20
and we suppose þat þis gretynge savys many a man.
For we take as beleve þat Sche ys blyssyd in Hevyn.
And Crist wyl do at Hyr prayynge among al oþyr
    seyntys ;
And þow we trow þat noþer Crist ne Sche
wil do for man but y^t be resonable, 25
and men þat ben worthy to be holpyn.
And so mow men triste to be holpyn fully in suche
    prayer.
In þre partyes comunlyche þis gretynge ys dyvydyd.
The furst part contenys þe wordys of Gabriel.
    Whan he seyde to þis Lady. 30
Heyl, ful of grace, God is with the.

---

[1] belevyth *HH*.   [2] and *HH*.   [3] berydene *HH*.   [4] ansueride *HH*.
[5] þe *HH*.   [6] his clerkus *HH*.   [7] þe *HH*.   [8] of *HH*.   [9] þise
doutes *HH*.   [10] on payne of her lyf *HH*.   [11] om. *HH*.

The secunde part of þis gretynge buth wordys
þat Elysabeth spake to Hyr whan sche sayde :
Blyssid be þou amonge wommen, and blyssid be þe
fruyt of þy wombe.
The þrydde part has two wordys clowtyd for devo-
cyoun, Maria and Iesus.

5 Furst men seyn Heyl Marie, þat Gabryel lefte in his
gretynge
to teche us þat he was homly and knowyn with þis
Lady.
And þerfore wold he not nempne þis name of Marie.
The secunde word ys Iesus, addyd to Elyȝabethis
wordys ;
and þis word lefte þe Gospel here, to teche þat Marye
hadde but on child.

10 And þis child was Iesus, þat is Saviour of man-kynde.
But þis fyl longe [aftyr] þat oure Lady was gret þus.
The furste word, þat is ave, reversys þe name of Eva
to teche us þat oure Lady contraryyd Eve in livynge.
For ryȝth as Adam and Eve were cause of dampnynge
of mankynde,

15 So Iesus and Marie ben cawse of mannys salvacioun.
The secunde word of þe angel seys oure Lady was
ful of grace.
And man may be ful of grace on thre maneris be
Godys lawe :
Furst of hymself as Crist was þe furst qwyk welle of
grace,
for of Hym spronge grace to alle men aftyr Hym.

20 Our Lady was ful of grace as a stronde ful of watyr
[And] gaf grace plenteous boþe to oþer men and
wommen.
Seynt Stevyn was ful of grace þat sufficyd to his lyf
for to bryng hym to blysse.
And so be many oþer seyntys. And so God ys with
alle creaturis ;
But specialy with þe chaumbyr of his manhed þat was
oure Lady Marie.

.   .   .   .

Trust we to þe wordys of þe Gospel and worschipe we
Marie with all our myȝt. Amen.

'Ave Maria.'

Lay Folks Catechism.

I. *Church Services.*

Also bi song þe fend lettiþ men to studie and preche þe
Gospel ; for siþ mannys wittis ben of certeyn mesure and
myȝt, þe more þat þei ben occupied aboute siche mannus 5
song, þe lesse moten þei be sette aboute Goddis lawe.
For þis stiriþ men to pride, and iolité, and oþere synnys,
and so unableþ hem many gatis to understonde and kepe
Holy Writt, þat techeþ mekenesse, mornynge for oure
synnys and oþere mennus, and stable lif, and charité. 10
And ȝit God in all þe lawe of grace chargiþ not siche
song, but devocion in herte, trewe techynge, and holy
spekynge in tonge, and goode werkis, and holy lastynge
in charité and mekenesse. But mannus foly and pride
stieþ up evere more and more in þis veyn novelrie. 15

First men ordeyned songe of mornynge whanne þei
weren in prison, for techynge of þe Gospel, as Ambrose,
as [1] men seyn, to putte awey ydelnesse, and to be not
unoccupied in goode manere for þe tyme. And þat
songe and *our*[e] [2] acordiþ not, for oure stiriþ to iolité and 20
pride, and here stiriþ to mornynge, and to dwelle lenger
in wordis of Goddis lawe. Þan were matynys, and masse,
and evensong, *placebo* and *dirige*, and comendacion, and
matynes of Oure Lady, ordeyned of synful men to be
songen wiþ heiȝe criynge, to lette men fro þe sentence 25
and understondynge of þat þat was þus songen, and to
maken men wery, and undisposid to studie Goddis lawe
for akyng of hedis. And of schort tyme þanne [weren]
more veyn iapis founden : deschaunt, countre note, and
orgon, and smale brekynge, þat stiriþ veyn men to 30
daunsynge more þan [to] mornynge ; and herefore ben
many proude lorelis founden and dowid wiþ temperal
and worldly lordischipis and gret cost. But þes foolis

[1] and *X.*   [2] oþer *X.*

schulden drede þe scharpe wordis of Austyn, þat seiþ :
' As oft as þe song likiþ me more þan doþ þe sentence þat
is songen, so oft I confesse þat I synne grevously.'

And ȝif þes knackeris excusen hem bi song in þe olde
5 lawe, seie þat Crist, þat best kepte þe olde lawe as it
schulde be aftirward, tauȝt not ne chargid us wiþ sich
bodely song, ne ony of His apostlis, but wiþ devocion in
herte, and holy lif, and trewe prechynge, and þat is
ynowþȝ and þe beste. But who schulde þanne charge us
10 wiþ more, overe þe fredom and liȝtnesse of Cristis lawe ?

And ȝif þei seyn þat angelis heryen God bi song in
Hevene, seie þat we kunnen not þat song ; but þei ben in
ful victorie of here enemys, and we ben in perilous
bataile,[1] and in þe valeye of wepynge and mornynge ; and
15 oure song lettiþ us fro betre occupacion, and stiriþ us to
many grete synnes, and to forȝete us self.

But oure flecshly peple haþ more lykynge in here
bodely eris in sich knackynge and taterynge, þan in
herynge of Goddis lawe, and spekynge of þe blisse of
20 Hevene ; for þei wolen hire proude prestis and oþere
lorelis þus to knacke notis for many markis and poundis.
But þei wolen not ȝeve here almes to prestis and children
to lerne and teche Goddis lawe. And þus, bi þis novelrie
of song, is Goddis lawe unstudied and not kepte, and
25 pride and oþere grete synnys meyntenyd.

And þes fonnyd lordis and peple gessen to have more
þank of God, and [to] worschipe Hym more, in haldynge
up of here owen novelries wiþ grete cost, þan in lernynge,
and techynge, and meyntenynge of his lawe, and his
30 servauntis, and his ordynaunce. But where is more
disceit in feiþ, hope and charité ? For whanne þer ben
fourty or fyfty in a queer, þre or foure proude lorellis
schullen knacke þe most devout servyce þat no man schal
here þe sentence, and alle oþere schullen be doumbe, and
35 loken on hem as foolis. And þanne strumpatis and þevys
preisen Sire Iacke, or Hobbe, and Williem þe proude
clerk, hou smale þei knacken here notis ; and seyn þat

---

[1] baitale *X*.

þei serven wel God and Holy Chirche, whanne þei dispisen God in his face, and letten oþere Cristene men of
here devocion and compunccion, and stiren hem to worldly
vanyté.   And þus trewe servyce of God is lettid, and þis
veyn knackynge for oure iolité and pride is preised 5
aboven þe mone.

Also þe Ordynalle of Salisbury lettiþ moche prechynge
of þe Gospel ; for folis chargen þat more þan þe maundementis of God, and to studie and teche Cristis Gospel.
For ȝif a man faile in his Ordynale, men holden þat grete 10
synne, and reproven hym þerof faste ; but ȝif a preste
breke þe hestis of God, men chargen þat litel or nouȝt.
And so ȝif prestis seyn here matynes, masse, and evensong aftir Salisbury usse, þei hemself and oþere men
demen it is ynowȝ, þouþ þei neiþer preche ne teche þe 15
hestis of God and þe Gospel.   And þus þei wenen þat it
is ynowȝ to fulfille synful mennus ordynaunce, and to
leve þe riȝtfulleste ordynaunce of God, þat He chargid
prestis to performe.

But, Lord ! what was prestis office ordeyned bi God 20
bifore þat Salisbury uss was maad of proude prestis,
coveitous and dronkelewe ?   Where God, þat dampneþ
alle ydelnesse, charg*id*[1] hem not at þe ful wiþ þe beste
occupacion for hemself and oþere men ?   Hou doren
synful folis chargen Cristis prestis wiþ so moche novelrie, 25
and evermore cloute more to, þat þei may not frely do
Goddis ordynaunce ?   For þe Iewis in þe olde lawe haden
not so manye serymonyes of sacrifices ordeyned bi God
as prestis han now riȝttis and reulis maade of synful men.
And ȝit þe olde lawe in þes charious customes mosten 30
nedes cesse for fredom of Cristis Gospel.   But þis fredom
is more don awei bi þis novelrie þan bi customes of þe
olde lawe.   And þus many grete axen where a prest may,
wiþouten dedly synne, seie his masse wiþouten matynys ;
and þei demen it dedly synne a prest to fulfille þe 35
ordynaunce of God in his fredom, wiþoute novelrie of
synful men, þat lettiþ prestis fro þe betre occupacion ; as

---

[1] chargen *X*.

ȝif þei demen it dedly synne to leve þe worse þing, and take þe betre, whanne þei may not do boþe togidre.

And þus, Lord! Þin owen ordynaunce þat Þou madist for Þi prestis is holden errour, and distroied for þe fonnyd
5 novelrie of synful foolis, and, in cas, of fendis in helle.

But here men moste be war þat under colour of þis fredom þei ben betre occupied in þe lawe of God to studie it and teche it, and not slouȝ ne ydel in overmoche sleep, and vanyté, and oþer synnes, for þat is þe fendis
10 panter.

See now þe blyndnesse of þes foolis. Þei seyn þat a prest may be excused fro seiynge of masse, þat God comaundid Himself to þe substance þerof, so þat he here on. But he schal not be excused but ȝif he seie matynes
15 and evensong himself, þat synful men han ordeyned ; and þus þei chargen more here owene fyndynge þan Cristis comaundement.

A Lord ! ȝif alle þe studie and traveile þat men han now abowte Salisbury uss, wiþ multitude *of* [1] newe costy
20 portos, antifeners, graielis, and alle oþere bokis, weren turned into makynge of biblis, and in studiynge and techynge þerof, hou moche schulde Goddis lawe be forþered, and knowen, and kept, and now in so moche it is hyndrid, unstudied, and unkept. Lord! hou schulden
25 riche men ben excused þat costen so moche in grete schapellis, and costy bokis of mannus ordynaunce, for fame and nobleie of þe world, and wolen not spende so moche aboute bokis of Goddis lawe, and for to studie hem and teche hem : siþ þis were wiþoute comparison
30 betre on alle siddis, and lyȝttere, and sykerere ?

But ȝit men þat knowen þe fredom of Goddis ordynaunce for prestis to be þe beste, wiþ grete sorow of herte seyn here matynes, masse, and evensong, whanne þei schulden ellis be betre occupied, last þei sclaundren þe
35 sike conscience of here breþeren, þat ȝit knowen not Goddis lawe. God brynge þes prestis to þe fredom to studie Holy Writt, and lyve þerafter, and teche it oþer

[1] & *X.*

men frely, and to preie as long and as moche as God
meveþ hem þerto, and ellis turne to oþere medeful werkis,
as Crist and His apostlis diden ; and þat þei ben not constreyned to blabre alle day wiþ tonge and grete criynge,
as pies and iaies, þing þat þei knowen not, and to peiere 5
here owen soule for defaute of wis devocion and charité !

Of Feigned Contemplative Life.

J. *Privy Confession is a ' Cast' of the Fiend.*

Two virtues ben in mannes soule by whiche a man
shuld be rewled ; hoolynesse in mannes wille, and good
kunnyng in his witt.   Hoolynesse shuld put out synne,
and good kunnyng shuld put out foly.   But as wille haþ 10
principalité to-fore witt of mannes soule, so hoolynesse
is more worþe þenne is kunnynge of synful man.   For
wickud aungels han myche kunnyng, but þei han nouȝt
of hoolynesse.   And ellis iche man were hoolier aftur þat
he is more kunnynge ; but Poule seiþ þat mannes kunnyng 15
bolniþ hym bi pride. . . .

To make hoolynesse in men is confessioun nedful ; and
þerfor shuld hooly Churche witt sumwhat of confession.
. . . Confessioun þat man makiþ of synne is made of man
in two maners.   Summe is mad oonly to God truly by 20
herte or mouþe.   And sum confessioun is made to man
and þat may be on many maneres—ouþer opynly and
generaly as men confesseden in þe oolde lawe, or prively
and rownyngly as men confessen nowe-a-daies. . . .

It were to wite over in þis mater, wheþer privé con- 25
fession, made to prestis, be nedeful to synful men, and
where þis confession is groundid.   And it semeþ þat it is
not nedful, but brouȝt in late be þe fend, for Crist, alwitty,
used it not, ne noon of Hise apostles aftur.   And if it
were nedful to man, Crist wolde have used it or tauȝt it. 30

And þus it semeþ to many men þat Antecrist haþ cast
þis cast to make alle men soget to þe Pope, and lede hem
aftur þat hym likiþ.   Lord, where is fredom of Crist
whenne men ben casten in siche bondage?   Crist made
Hise servauntis free but Antecrist haþ made hem bonde 35

aʒeyne. And certis þer is noo autorité þat gave him leve
to make men þus þrallis.

Of Confession.

K. *On Justification.*

Þe secounde pryvylege of Petre stondiþ in þis—þat
Crist shal ʒeve him þe keies of þe rewme of Hevene.

5   Þes two keies ben soþli seid witt and power, to teche
men þe weie to Hevene and to opene hem þe ʒatis. And
þes keies hadde Petre wiþ many oþer seintis, for alle men
þat comen to Hevene have þes keies of God. And so
we shal not undirstonde þat þes ben keies of metal, þat
10 oonli Petre beriþ, to opene Hevene ʒatis to men; but þei
ben lore and power, þat men have goostli of God.

And so þis laste word seid is nede to be undirstonden
wel þat, *What kyn þing þat Petre bindiþ upon erþe shal
be bounden in Hevene, and what kyn þing he unbindiþ*
15 *upon erþe shal be unbounden in Hevene.*

Þes wordis weren not oonli seid unto Petre but comunli
to þe apostlis, as þe Gospel telliþ after, and, in persones
of apostlis weren seid to prestis, and, as many men
þenken to alle Cristen men. For, if man have mercy on
20 his soule, and unbinde it, or binde it, God bi his jugement
in Hevene jugiþ þe soule sich. For ech man þat shal be
dampned is dampned for his owne gilt, and ech man þat
shal be saved is saved bi his owne merit.

Sermons. Þe Gospel on þe Chairinge of Seint Petre.

L. *Predestination.*

Loquebatur Jesus cum discipulis.—MATT. XXII. I.

Þis gospel telliþ in a parable what men shulde trowe
25 of þis Chirche fro hennes to þe dai of dome, as it is
touchid sumwhat bifore.

Jesus spake wiþ hise disciplis in parablis and seide þus.
Þe rewme of hevene is maad liche unto a man þat is
a kyng, þat made wedding to his sone; and sente his
30 *servauntis to clepe þes men þat weren beden to þe brydale ;*

and, for þei wolden not come, he sente oþir servauntis and
seide, Scie ȝe to men þat ben beden, Lo Y have made redy
my mete, my boles and my volatils[1] *ben kild, and al oþir*
þingis ben redy; come ȝe faste to þe feste. But þei
dispisiden his biddinge, and sum wente into his toun, and 5
sum into his chaffarynge, and token þis kyngis servauntis,
and punishiden wiþ conteke[2] *and killiden hem. And þe*
kyng, whan he say þis, was wrooþ, and sente his ostis, and
loste þes mansleeris, and brente hir citee; and seide þan
to his servauntis, Metis of þis bridale ben redy, but men 10
clepid were not worþi; þerfore go ȝe to eendis of wcies,
and whomever ȝe finde clepe ye to þe mete. And þes ser-
vauntis wenten out, and gedriden men al þat þei founden
boþe good and yvel, and þe bridale was fulfillid wiþ men
sittinge at þe mete; al ȝif þei weren not alle ful served. 15
Þe Kyng cam in to se his gistis, and saw þere oon wiþoute
bride clopis, and seide to him, Frend, how entredist þou
hider wiþouten bride clopis? and he was doumbe. And
þan þe lord bade hise servauntis to bynde him boþe hondis
and fete, and sende him into utter derknesse, þere shal be 20
wepyng and gnastinge of teeþ. For many ben clepid and
fewe ben chosen.

Þe kyndom of Hevene is þe Chirche, þat takiþ name
of þe Heed, as þe gospel spekiþ comounly; and so þis
rewme is liche a kyng; þat is þe Fadir in Trinité; and 25
þis kynge made a mariage to Crist þat is his sone, and to
þis Chirche þat is his spouse, and to damyselis þerof.
For, as Salomon seiþ, foure degrees ben in þis Chirche;
sum ben quenes, sum ben lemmannes, and sum damyselis;
but oone is spouse þat conteyneþ alle þes þree, and þat is 30
al holi Chirche. And þus þere ben many chirches, and
a newe Chirche wiþ Crist; ȝhe al þe Chirche of men and
aungels is newid bi þe Incarnacioun.

Þe servantis of þis spouse bidden men to þe feste, whan
þei moven men to come to blisse bi þer just lyfe; and 35
þes servantis weren prophetis and apostolis of Goddis
two lawes; but þei weren clepid specialy whan Cristis

---

[1] volatiles *E*.   [2] contec *E*

birþe was shewid hem, for as it was seid bifore, þan alle
þingis weren made redi ; and many men in boþe þes
tymes wolden not come þus to þis feste.

After þes servantis he sent oþir, as men þat nexte
5 sueden þe apostlis ; and bolis and volatils weren slayn,
and mete was redy to þis feste. Þe boles bitokenen þe
olde fadris, as patriarkes and David, for þei diden bataillis
of God, and turneden his enemyes wiþ her hornes, and
ʒit þei kepten ful bisili þe grete mandementis of God. Þe
10 volatils þat serven seyntis at þe secounde cours of þis
feste ben seintis of þe newe lawe þat wiþ þes mandementis kepten Cristis conseilis ; and ʒit men forsoken to
come notwiþstondinge sample of þes seintis.

And sum wenten aftir lordship of þis worlde, and sum
15 after chaffare of þis worldely richesse ; but sum slowen
Cristis servauntis, as emperours of Rome and preestis.
Þe king of hem was wrooþ herfore, and sente his oostis
out to Jerusalem and slow þes sleeris of Crist, and brent
þer citee, as Josephus telliþ. And þis dede done in
20 Jerusalem þe two and fourty ʒeer after þe deeþ of Crist
bitokeneþ þe vengeaunce of God for sleing of Cristis
membris.

And þus men þat stoonden bihynde, boþe in þe olde
lawe and in þe newe, weren unworþi to fille þe nombre
25 þat God ordeynede to be saved. And now in þes laste
daies God bade Hise servantis clepen men boþe good and
yvel in to þe Chirche þat weren out of þe riʒt weye, and
wenten bi weyes of errours þat weren hard for to wende ;
and so as Petir in his first fishinge toke two manere of
30 fishes, sum dwelliden in þe nette, and sum borsten þe
nette and wenten awey ; so here in þis Chirche ben sum
ordeyned to blisse and sum to peyne, al if þei lyven
justly for a tyme. And so men seien comounly þat þere
ben here two manere of chirches, holy Chirche or Chirche
35 of God, þat on no manere may be dampned, and þe
chirche of þe fend, þat for a time is good, and lastiþ not ;
and þis was nevere holy Chirche, ne part þerof.

But þe king aftir þis feste came in at þe dai of dome,
for God shewiþ Him þanne to alle, for he knowiþ alle

mennes lyf; and þes þat wolden not laste in grace weren not cloþid in bride cloþis; and alle þes ben o man þat hadde noo witt to answere God. But, for þis man wiþ parts of him profitide to Cristis Chirche, and was of þe same kynde wiþ Crist, Crist clepiþ him frend, as He dide 5 Judas; but alle þes men can not answere how þei entren in to þe Chirche, for it was told hem opynli þat þei ben traitours but if þei lasten, and ben more worþi to be dampned þan men þat nevere entriden þus. And so al siche men token peyne bi just jugement of God, þat þer 10 willis shulden be bounden and þer profitable werkes, and shulden be cast in to helle, where men shulden wepe and gnaste wiþ teeþ; wepynge shal be sensible sorowe, and gnastynge shal be wantinge of blisse.

Wherfore men shal moost grutche, siþ þei myȝt liȝtly 15 have come to blisse, and aftir þis þei shal have noo wille neiþer to desire ne to wirche wel, and þus many men ben clepid, but few ben chosen to blisse.

Sermons. Þe Twentiþe Sonday Gospel Aftir Trinité.

VII

SOCIAL AFFAIRS

Sum state is here good for o man, and sum is good for anoþer; and God moveþ a man to his best state ʒif he lette not bi his synne.

Five Questions on Love.

A. Wyclif was no social revolutionary. He upheld the power
5 of king and secular lords and firmly believed in the manorial
system at its best. 'Oh! how happy and fertile would England
be if every parish church had as of yore a saintly rector residing
with his family, if every manor had a just lord residing with his
wife and children, then there would not be so much arable
10 land lying fallow and so great a dearth of cattle. The realm
would have abundance of every sort of wealth as well as serfs
and artizans.'[1]

But he fully realized the financial and civil disadvantages
under which the poor laboured. This is shown by the tract
15 *Of Servauntis and Lordis* which was probably written soon
after the Peasants' Revolt of the summer of 1381. Wyclif
appears in it as the champion of poor men who have been
starved or unjustly treated, but he exhorts them to obey their
masters and to do their work faithfully and well. His attitude
20 to the Peasants' Revolt can be discovered quite clearly in
de Blasphemia, written in 1382. There he points to the
wealth of the clergy as the root cause of the rising. In his
opinion the temporal possessions in the hands of the Church
really belonged to the poor. 'There is no doubt', he says,
25 'that this is the reason for all the dissension and dissatisfaction
in the kingdom.' In Cap. xiii of the same work he argues
that all cause of dissension would be removed if the king took
away temporal possessions from monks, friars, and clerics
generally, and with these relieved the poor.
30 Wyclif approved of service but not of servitude. In oppos-
ing serfdom he broke with the orthodox opinion of his time.
St. Thomas Aquinas, for instance, argued that slavery was
expedient and natural to men who had 'fallen' from Paradise.

---

[1] *de Civili Dominio*, ii. 14.

Here, as elsewhere Wyclif attained freedom from contemporary limitations of outlook by his frank acceptance of Christ's example and the words of Scripture. "Can a human being be sold 'for a mere song [vili pretio]', he asks, "for whose redemption Christ laid down his life?"[1]   Also he quotes the 5 words of Jeremiah : 'The word . . . came unto Jeremiah from the Lord . . . that every man should let his manservant, and every man his maidservant, go free.'[2]

B. See Gen. Introd., p. xxiv.

C and D. Wyclif's views on marriage and family-life, though 10 distinctly Puritan in character, were, for his particular epoch, sane and healthy. Most Church writers placed women and marriage on a very low plane. As the Wife of Bath complained :

> For trusteth wel, it is an impossible
> That any clerk wol speke good of wyves.   15

He was at one with his contemporaries in ranking marriage lower than celibacy, but he considered it as the natural state for the majority of human beings. In one of his English Sermons he goes so far as to point out that Christ approved of the marriage of priests : 'Here may men douten, and trete of þe 20 staat and liif of preestis ; how þei ben dowid and wyflees aȝens Goddis autorité ; for Crist forfendid dowyng boþe in hym and his apostlis, and approvede wedding in apostlis and many oþer. And þis [i. e. celibacy] is þe caste of þe fend, to kyndle fyr in heerdis.'[3]   25

A.

[THE DUTY OF SERVANTS]

First, servantis schullen trewely and gladly serve to here lordis or maistris and not be fals ne idel ne grucch- ynge ne hevey in here servyce-doynge, but holde hem paied of þe staat of servauntis, in which God haþ ordeyned hem for here beste to holde hem in mekenesse aȝenst 30 pride, and besi traveile aȝenst ydelnesse and slouþe. For Seint Poul biddiþ þat ȝif þou be clepid a servaunt, recke

---

[1] *de Civili Dominio*, i. 241.
[2] Jer. xxxiv. 8. 9. Wyclif, of course, quotes the Vulgate.
[3] Sermons. *þe Gospel of Mydsomer Evyn. S. E. W.* i. 364

þou not þer-of; þat is to seie, be not grucchynge ne hevy
þerfore. . . .

But here þe fend moveþ summe men to seie þat
Cristene men schullen not be servauntis or þrallis to
5 heþene lordis, siþ þei ben false to God and lasse worþy
þan Cristene men; neither to Cristene lordis, for þei ben
breþeren in kynde, and Ihū Crist bou3te Cristene men on
þe crois and made hem fre ; but a3enst þis heresie Poul
writiþ þus in Goddis lawe: ' What kynne servauntis ben
10 under 3ook of servage deme þei here lordis worþi alle
manere honour or worschipe, þat þe name and techynge
of þe Lord be not blasphemid.'

' But þo servauntis þat han trewe or Cristene lordis,
dispise þei not to serve hem for þat þei ben breþeren both
15 in kynde and in feiþ, but more serve þei for þe lordis ben
Cristene and lovyd.'

[POOR PRIESTS NOT SOCIALISTS]

But 3it summe men þat ben out of charité sclaundren
pore prestis wiþ þis errour, þat servauntis or tenauntis
may lawefully wiþholde rentis and servyce fro here lordis
20 whanne lordis ben opynly wickid in here lyvynge.   And
þei maken þis false lesyngis upon pore prestis to make
lordis to hate hem, and not to meyntene treuþe of Goddis
lawe þat þei techen opynly for worschipe of God and
profit of þe reume and stablynge of þe kyngis pouer and
25 distroynge of synne. For þes pore prestis distroien most
bi Goddis lawe rebelté of servauntis a3enst lordis, and
charge servauntis to be su3et þou3 lordis ben tirauntis, for
Seynt Petir techiþ þus: ' Be ye servantis suget to lordis
in alle manere of drede, not only to goode lordis and
30 bonere, but also to tirauntis, or siche þat drawen fro
Goddis scole.' . . .

And þis is a feyned word of Anticristis clerkis þat, 3if
sugetis may leffully wiþdrawe tiþes and offryngis fro
curatis þat openly lyven in lecherie and don not here
35 office, þan servauntis and tenauntis may wiþdrawe here
servyce and rentis fro here lordis þat lyven opynly a
cursed lif.

[THE DUTY OF LORDS]

See we now how lordis schulden lyve in here astaat.
First þei schulden knowe Goddis lawe and studie it and
meynteyne it, and distroie wrong and meyntene pore men
in here riȝt to lyve in reste, pees and charité, and suffre
no men under colour of hem to do extorcions, bete men, 5
and holde pore men out of riȝt bi strengþe of lordischipis.

Also God himself seiþ bi Ieromye þat he schal take
vengaunce on hem þat demeden not riȝtfully þe cause of
widwe, þe cause of fadirles and modirles, and þe cause of
pore men. Also God Hymself seiþ by Ysaie, þat princes 10
schullen cesse to don evele and lerne to do well and seke
dom, and helpe men oppressid wrongly, and ȝeve dom to
fadirles and modirles, and meyntene þe widwe.

[WRONGS DONE BY LORDS TO POOR MEN]

Lordis many tymes don wrongis to pore men bi
extorscions and unresonable mercymentis and unreson- 15
able taxis, and taken pore mennus goodis, and paien not
þerfore but white stickis, and dispisen hem and manassen
hem, and sumtyme beten hem whanne þei axen here peye.
And þus lordis devouren pore mennus goodis in glotonye
and wast and pride, and þei perischen for myschief, and 20
hungur and þrist and colde, and þere children also ; and
ȝif here rente be not redily paied here bestis ben stressid
and þei pursued wiþouten mercy, þouȝ þei be nevere so
pore and nedi and overchargid wiþ age, febilnesse, and
loos of catel and wiþ many children. 25

And ȝit lordis wolen not mekely here a pore mannus
cause and helpe hym in his riȝte, but suffre sisouris of
contré to distroie hem ; but raþere [þei] wyþholden pore
men here hire, for whiche þei han spendid here fleisch
and here blood. And so in a manere þei eten and 30
drynken pore mennus fleisch and blood and ben manquelleris, as God pleyneþ bi his prophetis. Wherefore
God seiþ bi þe prophete Ysaie, þat siche lordis ben
felawis of þevys and here hondis ben ful of blood ; and
þerfore whanne þei preien many preieris bi mouþ and 35

holden up here hondis, God wole not here hem ne resceyve
here offringis þat ben wrongfully geten of pore mennus
goodis bi extorcions and raveyne and robberie.

[UNJUST LAWYERS AND MERCHANTS]

And ʒit men of lawe þat schulden distroie siche fals-
5 nesse bi here offices and don eche man riʒt and reson,
meyntenen wrong for money and fees and robis, and
forbaren pore men fro here riʒt, þat it is betre to hem to
pursue not for here riʒt, be it nevere so opyn, þan to
pursue and lese more catel for disceitis of delaies and
10 cavellacions and evele wilis þat þei usen ; and þus wrong
is meyntened and trewþe and riʒt outlawid in many
statis.

Also stryves, contekis and debatis ben used in oure
lond, for lordis stryven wiþ here tenauntis to brynge hem
15 in þraldom more þan þei schulden bi reson and charité ;
and þei grucchen aʒen, and cursen and warien nyʒt and
day, and grete men of þis world debaten, and meyntenen
debatis at lovedaies ; and who so may be strengere wil
have his wille don, be it wrong be it riʒt, and ellis make
20 debate among many hundrid and þousand men and
sumtyme many countres, and by sich debatynge many
men holden grete houses and grete araies and grete costis.

In men of lawe regneþ moche gile, for þei meyntenen
falsnes for wynnynge and maken lordis to meyntene
25 wrongis and don wrongis, whanne lordis hopen to do riʒt
and plese God, and bi here coveitise and falsenesse þei
purchasen londis and rentis ynowe and don many extor-
sions and beren don þe riʒt boþe of pore and riche, and
ʒit þei maken it so holy in signes outward, as ʒif þei
30 weren angelis of Hevene, to colour here falsenesse and
blynde þe peple þerby.

In marchauntis regneþ gile in ful grete plenté, for þei
sweren falsly be alle grete membris of Crist and bi
Allemyʒty God in Trinyté þat here chaffere cost so
35 moche and is so trewe and profitable, to bigile þe peple
and to teche ʒonge prentis þis cursed craft, and preisen
hym most þat most bigileth þe peple.

[CONCLUSION OF THE WHOLE MATTER]

Lordis schullen traveile als faste to kunne Holi Writt and do treuþe and equité and meyntene riȝt of pore men, and reste and pees, as pore men ben bisi to labore for here owene liflode and to paye here rentis to lordis.

Of Servants and Lords.

B. *Guilds and their Shortcomings.*

Also alle newe fraternytes or gildis maad of men semen 5 openly to renne in þis curs. For þei conspiren many false errours aȝenst ȝe comyn fraternyté of Crist, þat alle Cristene[1] men token in here cristendom, and aȝenst comyn charité and comyn profit of Cristene men. And þerto þei conspiren to bere up eche oþer, ȝe, in wrong, and 10 oppresse oþere men in here riȝt bi here witt and power. And alle þe goodnes þat is in þes gildes eche man owiþ for to do bi comyn fraternyté of Cristendom, bi Goddis comaundement. And þei bryngen in moche pride, vanyté and wast, cost, and triste in mennus helpe more þan in 15 Goddis; and þus þei bryngen in moche evyl, and no good, more þan God comaunded frist; but þei letten moche unyté, pees and charité of Cristene peple, and meyntenen errour of wrong and gret discencion, and moche symonye, and letten pore mennus almes and 20 liflode þat lyn bedrede blynd and feble. Also men of sutel craft, as fre masons and oþere, semen openly cursed bi þis sentence. For þei conspiren togidere þat no man of here craft schal take lesse on a day þat þei setten, þouȝ he schulde bi good conscience take moche lesse, and þat 25 noon of hem schal make sade trewe werk to lette oþere mennus wynnyng of þe craft, and þat non of hem schal do ouȝt but only hewe stone, þouȝ he myȝt profit his maistir twenti pound bi o daies werk bi leggyng on a wal, wiþouten harm or penyng himself. See hou þis wickid 30 peple conspireþ aȝenst treuþe and charité, and comyn profit of þe lond, and ponyschiþ hem þat helpen frely here neiȝeboris.

[1] *corrected*; Criste *X.*

Also it semeþ þat marchauntis, groceris, and vitileris
rennen in þe same curs fully. For þei conspiren wickidly
togedre þat noon of hem schal bie over a certeyn pris,
þouӡ þe þing þat þei bien be moche more worþi, and þei
5 knowen wel þis ; and þat non of hem schal sille betere
chepe þan anoþer, þouӡ he may wel forþ it so, and it be
not so moche worþ as anoþer mannis chaffer ; þus he
schal be ponyschid sore ӡif he do trewe and good conscience.
10 Certis alle þis peple conspiriþ cursedly aӡenst treuþe,
charité, and comyn profit.

þe Grete Sentence of Curs Expouned.

C. *Marriage.*

See now how þis wedlok owiþ to be kept in boþ sides.
First þis wedlok shulde be maad wiþ ful consent of boþe
partis, principaly to þe worschipe of God, to lyve clenly
15 in þe ordre þat he made, and bringe forþ childre to fulfille
þe chosen noumbre of seyntis in blisse, and not to have
flescly lustis wiþoute reson and drede of God, as mulis
and hors and swyn þat han no undirstondynge. For þe
angel Raphael warned Tobie, þat þe fend haþ maistrie
20 upon siche men þat ben weddid, to have þus lustis of
flesch as bestis wiþoute resoun and drede of God. Also
þis contract shulde not be maade bitwixe a ӡonge man
and an olde bareyne widewe, passid child-berynge, for
love of worldly muk, as men ful of coveitise usen sum-
25 tyme,—for þan comeþ soone debat and avoutrie and
enemyté, and wast of goodis, and sorowe and care ynowӡ.
Many hote and coragious men wolen not take a pore
gentil womman to his wif in Goddis lawe, and make here
a gentil womman, and save here owene soule, but lyven
30 in þe develis servyce al here lif, or þe more part ; and
defoulen many templis of God to gret peril of here soule,
and abiden to have a riche womman for muk, and þanne
wasten here goodis in harlotrie and nyse pride, in avoutrie
on gaie strumpatis, and evere lyven in wraþe and chyd-
35 ynge, and in bondage of synne to þe fendis of helle. Also

summe myꝫtty men marien here children, where þat here
herte consentiþ not wilfully, but feynen for drede.

    .   .   .   .   .

    See now how þe wif oweþ to be suget to þe housbonde,
and he owiþ to reule his wif, and how þei boþe owen to
reule here children in Goddis lawe. First Seynt Petir 5
biddiþ þat wifis be suget to here housbondis, in so moche
þat ꝫif ony bileve not bi word of prechynge, þat þei
ben wonnen[1] wiþoute word of prechynge bi þe holy
lyvnge of wymmen, whanne men biholden þe chast
lyvynge of wymmen. And þes wymmen schulden not 10
have wiþouten forþ tiffynge of her, ne garlondis of gold,
ne over precious or curious cloþinge, but þei schulden
have a clene soule, peisible and meke and bonere, þe
whiche is riche in þe siꝫtte of God. And sumtyme holy
wymmen, hopynge in God, honoureden hem in þis 15
manere, and weren suget to here owene housbondis, as
Sara, Abrahamys wif, obeischid to Abraham, clepynge
hym lord ; and wymmen wel doynge ben gostly douꝫtris
of Sarra. Alle þis seiþ Seynt Petir.

    Also Seynt Poul spekiþ þus of housbondis and wifis : 20
I wole þat men preie in eche place, liftynge up clene
hondis, þat is, clene werkis, wiþouten wraþþe and strif.
Also I wolle þat wymmen ben in covenable abite, wiþ
schamefastnesse and sobirnesse ournynge hem or makynge
fair, not in wriþen here, ne in gold, ne in margery stones, 25
or perlis, ne in precious cloþ, but þat þat bicomeþ
wymmen bihetynge pité, bi goode werkis. A womman
oweþ to lerne in silence, wiþ alle obedience and subjec-
cioun. But Poul seiþ : I suffre not a womman to teche,
þat is, openly in chirche, as Poul seiþ in a pistel to 30
Corynthis; and I suffre not a womman to have lordischipe
in here housbonde, but to be in silence or stillnesse.

Of Weddid Men and Wifis.

---

[1] *Arnold's correction* : *X has* wÿmmen.

D. *Parents and Children.*

Poul biddiþ þe fadir norische his children in þe lore and
chastisynge of God ; and God comaundiþ in þe olde lawe
þat þe fadris schulden telle to herre children Goddis hestis,
and þe woundris and myraclis þat He dide in þe lond of
5 Egipt, and in þe Rede See, and in þe watir of Jordan, and
in þe lond of biheste. And moche more ben fadir and moder
holden to teche here children þe bileve of þe Trinyté, and
of Jesus Crist, howe He is verray God wiþouten bigynnynge, and was maad man þorouþ moste brennynge
10 charité, to save mankynde bi stronge penaunce, hard
torment, ānd bittir deþ.

But summe techen here children jeestis of bataillis,
and fals cronyclis not nedful to here soulis. Summe
techen novelries of songis, to stire men to jolité and
15 harlotrie. Summe setten hem to nedeles craftis, for pride
and coveitise ; and summe suffren hem in ydelnesse and
losengerie, to breden forth strumpatis and þeves ; and
summe wiþ grett cost setten hem in lawe, for wynninge
and worldly worschipe, and here to costen hugely in
20 many weies. But in alle þis Goddis lawe is putt bihynde,
and þerof spekiþ unneþis ony man a good word, to magni-
fye God, and to save mennis soulis.

Sume techen here children to swere and stare and
fiȝtte, and schrewe alle men aboute, and of þis han gret
25 joie in here herte. But certis þei ben Sathanas techeris,
and procuratouris to lede hem to helle, bi here cursed
ensaumple and techynge, and norischynge and meyntenynge in synne ; and ben cruel sleeris of here owene
children, ȝe, more cruel þan þouȝ þei hackeden here
30 children as small as morselis to here poot or mouþ. For
bi þis cursid techynge, and endynge þerin, here children
bodies and soulis ben dampnyd wiþouten ende in helle.
And þouȝ here bodies weren þus hackid nevere so smale,
boþe bodi and soule schal be in blis of Hevene, so þat þei
35 kepen trewely Goddis comaundementis.

Of Weddid Men and Wifis.

E. *Drunkenness.*

Hit were to long to telle þo harmes þat comen of
dronkenesse, for soche men, as beestis, serven þen not
Crist,—for Crist is wisedome of þo Fader,—and þei faylen
þen in resoun, and ben þen as hors and mule þat wanten
undirstondyng. Lord, sith hit is schameful to be in state 5
of a beeste, myche more schulde hit be to passe beeste
in foly ; and so done þes dronken men for tyme þat þei
ben dronken. A mon schulde not by resoun, to wynne
al þis worlde, ne to wynne þo blis of Heven, chese to lese
his witte ; for þen hit did hym no gode, lordschip ne blis 10
of Heven; as men seen þat beestis coveyten not monnis
lordschip. Bot siþ men fallen by dronkenesse fro resoun
worse þen beestis, who schulde not by pure skile fle to be
dronken ? And by þis skile al synne schulde algatis be
fled, for synne makes a mon noght in þat þat he is synful. 15
And if þou sey þat hit spedes a mon to be dronken ones
in a moneth, for myche gode comes þerof,—suppose we
to phisisians þat þei taken soth. Bot wil I wot þat more
gode comes of mennis synne; bot schulden men synne
herfore ? sith þat Poule seis nay. If gode cum of synne 20
hit is a grace of God, and men schulden not putt hom in
þis caas to wynne al þis worlde, for in þis þei tempten
God, and witten not wheþer his rightwisenes wil profyte
mercyfuly to mon when he synnes þus. And if þou sey,
mon fallyng in dronkenesse ryses sone þerof, and better 25
is disposid for to do his werk, or what þat he schulde do,
here þou spekes as a foole, as alle proctoures of synne.
For þou woste nevere wheþer þou schalt dye in tyme of
þi dronkenesse, and nere make asethe to God for synne
þat þou fallis inne. Bot Gods lawe techis us to lyve evere 30
in þat state þat we be redy to Hym, what tyme þat He
calles us. And amonge oþer causes, herfore haves God
ordeyned þat tyme of deth be uncerteyne to men þat
dwellen here in erthe, for we schulden evere be redy
whenevere God calles us to ende in His servise, and take 35
of Him þo blis of Heven. Mony soche blyndenessis
colouren mennis synne and maken hom Gods foolis, for

iche synne comes of folye. If þo worlde holde men foolis
for þo luf of Crist, hit is a gode token in men þat lyve
wel, for we schulden take as bileve þat mon when he
synnes dos hym harme, to body and to soule, to þis lif
5 and to þat oþer.

The Seven Deadly Sins.

F. *Thieves and Sanctuary.*

Alle þeves and alle þat reseten[1] hem wyttyngly, and
alle consentours to hem in synne, ben cursed of God, and
foure tymes in þe ȝeer of men, in alle parische chirches.
First, alle clerkis of our lond semen cursed in þis poynt,
10 for in eche parische chirche a comyn þef and manslcere
schal be resseyved fourty daies at þe leste, and no lawe
passe on hym to make restitucion, þouȝ he be of power,
and to ponysche him justly for chastisyng of oþere
mysdoeris ; but after fourty daies he schal forswere þe
15 kyngis lond, and þanne many tymes he robbeþ more and
sleþ mo men, in trist of siche refute. And þis makiþ
many stronge þeves and cursed manquelleris in oure
lond ; and to meyntene þis resset and norischyng of þeves,
oure worldly clerkis wolen coste and traveile and lyye and
20 die ; and þerfore þei ben stronge schameles heretikis, to
meyntene þis opyn errour aȝenst Goddis lawe.

Also grete houses of religion, as Westmynstre, Beverlé,
and oþere, chalengen, usen, and meyntenen þis privylegie,
þat whatevere þef or felon come to þis holy hous of
25 religion, he schal dwelle þere alle his lif, and no man
enpeche hym, þouȝ he owe pore men moche good and
have ynouȝ to paye it. And þouȝ he robbe and sleé
every nyȝt many men out of þe fraunchise, and every day
come aȝen, he schal be meyntened þerto bi vertu of þis
30 opyn heresie. And þes feyned clerkis crien faste, þat þe
kyng and alle þe lordis ben bounden bi vertu of here oþ,
in whiche þei sweren to meyntene holy Chirche and riȝttis
þerof, for to meyntene þis open þefte aȝenst Goddis heste
and here owene oþ, in whiche þei sweren to doo riȝtwis-

---

[1] *So Arnold* : receseten *X.*

nesse to eche man and meytene eche man þerinne. And
þus þei maken holy Chirche and her lege lord þe kyng,
patrons of here þefte, under colour of holynesse and
devocion. But certis þes placis ben synagogis of Satanas,
dennes of þeves, and worse þan Sodom and Gomor, as þo 5
þat resceyven not Cristis word in þe gospel ; and þes ben
cursed ypocritis, and weiward traitours to God and here
lege lord þe kyng and alle Cristendom, and þei ben con-
fermed in þis heresie, þat þei wolen lyve and die þerfore.

Þe Grete Sentence of Curs Expouned.

G. *Five Questions on Love.*

A special frend in God axiþ bi charité þes fyve ques- 10
tiouns of a mek prest in God. First, what is love. Aftirward, where is love. Þe þridd tyme he axiþ hou God
schuld medefully be loved. Þe fourþe tyme he axiþ hou
a trewe man may knowe wheþer he love his God in þe
fourme þat God axiþ þat a man love Him. Þe fifþe tyme 15
he axiþ, in what staat of þis lif a man may best love his
God, and more medefully to come to Hevene. Alle þes
questiouns ben hard to telle hem trewly in Englisch, but
ȝit charité dryveþ men to telle hem sumwhat in Englische,
so þat men may beste wite bi þis Englisch what is Goddis 20
wille.

To þe firste questioun þat is axid seien men on þis
maner ; þat love is a maner of werk, þat comeþ of a
mannis wille to wole good to loved þing ; and so love is
in mannis herte, and [þer is] nan oþer maner in lovyng.[1] 25
But to þe þrid questioun answeriþ Crist in Jones gospel.
Crist seiþ,—He þat haþ my maundementis and kepiþ hem
in his lif, he is þat ilk þat loveþ me. And þus he makiþ
redy love to God, þat studieþ wel Godis lawe, as þe first
Psalme seiþ. As to þe fourþe questioun,—a man may 30
wite bi himsilf wher he þenkiþ on Goddis lawe and loveþ

---

[1] *Arnold prints (S.E.W.* iii. 183) *the MS. reading* : and man oþer maner
in lovyng. *The Latin version does not, as Arnold hoped, suggest a very
obvious emendation.*

it and kepiþ it, and þanne Crist seiþ þat he loveþ God.
As anentis þe fifþe questioun,—it is knowun bi Goddis
lawe, þat þer ben in þe Chirche þre statis þat God haþe
ordeyned; state of prestis, and state of knyʒtis, and þe
5 þridd is staat of comunys. And to þes þree ben þre oþere,
comyn and leeful bi Goddis lawe,—state of virgyns, and
state of wedloke, and þe state of widewis. State of virgyns
is þe hiest, bi witnesse of Crist and seyntis in Hevene.
Sum state is here good for o man, and sum is good for
10 anoþer; and God moveþ a man to his best state ʒif he
lette not bi his synne.

But foure statis, of þe emperour clerkis, of munkis, of
chanouns, and of freris, semyn perelous, and not ordeyned
of God, but suffrid for mannys synne. And þerfore men
15 schulden be war to take of þes foure statis, for oþer statis
þat God haþ ordeyned bringen men bettere to blis of
Hevene; and he is a miche fool þat leeveþ þe bettere and
chesiþ þe werse. And þus it helpiþ heere to Cristen men,
to studie þe gospel in þat tunge in whiche þei knowen
20 best Cristis sentense. For our bileve techiþ us þat ech
Cristen man is holdyn heere to sue Crist in maner of
lyvyng, sum ferrer and sum nerrer, aftir þat God ʒyveþ
him grace; and he þat sueþ Crist most nyʒe loveþ Him
most, and is most lovyd of God. And siþ lif and dedis of
25 Crist, and His lore, ben in þe gospel, it is opyn to profit
of men to studie þis bok, to love Crist.

But over þis axiþ þis frend of God, what wil Daviþ
hadde in þes two versis þat he seiþ in þe Sauter,—and þei
ben comynly known in Latyn,—O Lord, I confesse to þee
30 þat I am þi servaunt, in bodie, soule,—and I am son of
þin hand-mayden, for Y am trewe child of holy Chirche.
Þou hast brokun my bondis, of synne, and bondis bi
whiche my soule loveþ my flesche; to þee I schal sacre
an ost of heriyng. And þus Y schal clepe inne to me þe
35 name of þe Lord, to dwelle in me. And þes same wordis
maie martris seie, þat loven so miche Goddis lawe, þat þei
wole suffre peyne of deeþ, for love and mayntenyng of þis
lawe. And bettere cause of martirdom schewid God
never to plese Him. And siþ a man mut nedis die, and

Goddis lawe haþe nowe manye enemyes, a man schulde
wisely put him forþ to suffre now þus gloriously.

> War, man, lette not for synne,
> Prest, knyʒt, ʒemon, ne page,
> Ʒif ʒee wole of God have large wage:
> Amen, Amen, Amen.   5

VIII

MISCELLANEOUS

A. Wyclif's opinions on war are developed at considerable
length in Ch. XII. of *de Officio Regis*. He there puts forward
the view that war is contrary to the teaching of Christ, and that
the highest Christian ideal demands the complete cessation of
5 hostilities among nations. Arguing on a lower plane, he allows
that war may be waged for two reasons—for the love of God [1]
or from the desire to correct a people.[2] His followers, both in
his lifetime and afterwards, were determined opponents of war.
Hereford, for example, includes in his *Seven Deadly Sins* an
10 outspoken condemnation of war as anti-Christian. He pic-
turesquely remarks, ' Jesus Christ, duke of oure batel, taught us
lawe of pacience, and not to fight bodily '. ' At Domesday
schal men witte who feghts þus for charité ; for it semes no
charité to ride ageyne þin enemye wil armed wiþ a sharp
15 spere.' [3] William Swynderby, in a written defence handed to
Trefnant, Bishop of Hereford, 3 Oct. 1391, agrees with Wyclif
that neither the Pope nor any lesser priest should resort to the
use of the sword. ' For then I say, gif the pope holde men of
armes in mayntenynge of his temporal lordeschipe to venge
20 him on hem that gylten and offenden hym . . . not putynge his
swerde in his schethe, as God comaunded to Petre, he is
Antycrist.' [4]

B. Wyclif's philological guesses are given as an interesting
example of the unscientific nature of language-study in his
25 time.

C. This passage shows how Wyclif could turn a problem of
the schools, handed down from Greek philosophy,[5] into a piece
of Christian ethics. There is a more elaborate treatment of
the same theme in *de Civili Dominio*, Ch. XXIII–XXV. In
30 both places the problem is considered in connexion with
Christ's rebuke to Martha. In the Latin writing Wyclif adduces

---

[1] *de Officio Regis*, cap. XII. [2] *Ibid.*
[3] *S. E. W.* iii. 138. [4] Trefnant, *Registrum*, p. 269.
[5] The *locus classicus* of the discussion of the respective merits of the
active and speculative life is the *Tenth Book* of Aristotle's *Ethics* to which
Wyclif refers *Civ. Dom.* 164.

'Aristoteles, gentilis philosophus' as a witness of the superiority, of the contemplative life, but is careful to rest his own approval on the words of the 'Celestis philosophus' [Christ].[1]

A. *Men who go to War cannot rightly use the Paternoster.*

ȝif þou wilt axe in Cristis name, axe þe blisse þat evere shal laste. And siþ Crist is treuþe and resoun, loke þi 5 axinge be resonable, and þan maist þou be sure to have þe þing þou axist þus. . . . ȝif man axe þus in resoun þat he be worþi to have it, he shal have it wiþouten doute whan best tyme were þat he hadde it. And he shal have on þe best manere þe þing þat he axiþ þus.   10

And herfore þe seven axingis þat Crist techiþ in þe Pater Noster meneþ þis forme of axinge ; and alᵹatis to axe in charité. And þerfore men þat lyven in werre ben unable to have þer axinge : but þei axen þer owne dampnynge in þe fifte peticioun, for þer þei axen þat 15 God forᵹyve hem þer dettis þat þei owen to hym, riᵹt as þei forᵹyven men þat ben dettours unto hem. And here we shal undirstonde þat ech man is dettour to God, and ech man owiþ to eche oþer to do him good in charité. And so failynge to love God of al þin herte and alle þi 20 wille, þou rennest in grete dette boþe aᵹens God and man.

And so in þis fifte axing þes men þat werren now-a-daies, axen Him as þei wolden mene.—forᵹyve us for we ben even wiþ þee, or ellis take venjaunce in ire of us, as we taken vengeaunce of oure breþeren. And þis is noo 25 good praier, but more axinge of Goddis venjaunce ; and for þis cause many men ben unherd in þer praier, and turned in to more yvel for þere unskilful praier. And siche men weren better to leve þan to preien on sich maner. For many men preien for venjaunce and for 30 worldis prosperité, and in þe ire of God He ᵹyveþ hem þat þei axen ; but it were beter to hem to preye not þus, ne to have þes þingis.

Sermons. Þe Fyfþe Sondai Gospel After Eestir.

[1] *de Civ. Dom.* i. 163

B. *Philological Guesses.*

Þese disciplis weren two and seventy in noumbre ; and so many, as men seien, weren langagis aftir making of Babiloyne.

Sermons. On Dai of Oon Evangelist.

Þe firste word, þat is ' Ave ', reversiþ þe name of Eva,
5 to teche us þat oure Ladi contrariede Eve in lyvynge.

Ave Maria.

And þis bitokeneþ Genasareþ, þat is, an wounderful birþe, for þe birþe by whiche a man is borne of water and of þe Holy Goost is myche more wounderful þan mannis kyndely birþe.

Sermons. Þe Fyfþe Sondai Gospel After Trinité.

10 Also þe Hooly Gost ȝaf to apostlis wit at Wit Sunday for tó knowe al maner langagis, to teche þe puple Goddis lawe þerby.

de Officio Pastorali.

In þe eende of þe Pater Noster, Amen is the signet of þe Lordis praier, whiche word þe Ebru translatoure,
15 Aquyla interpretid, ' and þe Lord confermede '.

The Pater Noster.

For þis name [Pope] is newe foundun, and it bitokeniþ ' wundirful ' ; for summe þenken it greet wundir þat worldly glory and hoolynesse shulden be knyttid in o persone.

de Papa.

C. *The Active and Contemplative Life.*

20 Criste . . . tauȝte þe Chirche in þes wymmen, and spak in þes wordis : *Martha, Martha, þou art bisie and troublid aboute ful many þingis : but certis, o þing is nedeful,* and betere þan þes many þingis : *Marie haþ chosen þe beste part, þat shal not be taken from hir.*
25 It is seid comunli, þat þes two wymmen ben two lyves, actif and contemplatif ; þe first is Martha, and þe toþer

I 2

Marie. And actif liif axiþ in mesure bisynesse aboute
worldli þingis; and alȝif þis liif be good, þe toþer liif is
moche better.   And so, for men failen ofte in þis liif fro
love of God, Crist doubliþ þis word Martha, for two
passen fro unyté.   Crist telliþ how actif liif mut nede be 5
troublid for many þingis; but contemplatif liif stondiþ in
oo þing, þat is, God, and haþ no bisynes aboute þingis of
þis world. For as a man bisieþ him not how his shadewe
shall passe þe water, so men þat ben contemplatif bisie
hem not aboute worldli goodis, but þei trusten and hopen 10
in God þat alle þes þingis shall falle to hem.   And oonli
in swetnesse of God þei bisien hem and taken þe toþer in
mekenes and in poverté, as Crist haþ tauȝt in word and
dede.

But men supposen over þis, þat Crist approveþ here 15
þree lyves.   Þe first is good, as children lyven whanne
þei be cristened.   Þe secound lif is þe betere; and þis is
clepid actif liif whanne men travailen for worldli goodis
and kepen hem in riȝtwisnesse.   And þis is hard, but it
is possible; and alȝatis ȝif coveitise be left; for Crist 20
techiþ bi Matheu þat men shulden not be besie aboute
her fode and hilyng, but bisynesse shulde be for Hevene,
þat shulde be eende of mennis traveile.   And exces of
þes goodis lettiþ ofte tymes þis eende.   Þe þridde liif is
þe beste, as Crist seiþ þat may not lye.   And þis is sum- 25
what here in erþe but fulli in þe blisse of Hevene.

And here douten many men wheþir of þes two lyves is
betere.   But men þat holden[1] bileve of Crist witen þat
þis þridde liif is best; for Crist seiþ þus þat may not lye
and chees to lyve ever þis liif.   For alȝif Criste dide 30
erþeli workes, neþeles he dide on sich mesure þat his
soule was ever fed in contemplacioun of God.   And in
þis many apes weenen to sue Crist here and þei slippen
into þe fendis weies for defaute of Cristis lore.

Þree resouns ben comune þat þis þridde is þe beste liif. 35
Oon, for Crist þe beste maistir seiþ þus, and may not lye.
Also, þis lif mote nedis laste in blis of Hevene wiþouten

---

[1] biholden *A*.

ende ; but þes oþer two lyves moten nedis be endid here.
And so þis liif þat makiþ men betere, and more lastiþ
wiþ hem in joie, mote nede be betere þan þe toþer þat
algatis moot be taken from man ; and þis is þe resoun of
5 Crist in þe laste word of þis gospel.

Also, an eende þat kinde ordcyneþ to come to men, bi
certeyn meenes, is alȝatis betere þan þes meenes, þat
comen nevere but for þis eende ; as, siþ mannis liif is
eende of his eting and oþer dedis, þis liif is betere þan þis
10 eting, or ellis kynde ordeyned amys. And so, siþ þes two
firste lyves ben meenes to þis þridde liif, algatis þis þridde
is þe beste, þat God ordeyned to ende þes two. And in
no persone ne ony stat ben þes first [1] lyves for to preise,
but ȝif þei ben quykened bi þis þridde, þat shal laste evere
15 perfitli.

Sermons. Þe Gospel on Assumpcioun Dai.

----

[1] two first *E*

IX

THE CHURCH AND HER MEMBERS

Nam sancti doctores dicunt concorditer quod omnes
electi a principio mundi usque ad diem iudicii sunt una
persona que est mater ecclesia.

de Ecclesia 20.

' *Sir, Master John Wycliffe was holden of full many*
men, the greatest Clerk that they knew then living; and 5
therewith he was named a passing ruely man and an
innocent in his living: and herefore great many com-
moned oft with him, and they loved so much his learning
that they writ it, and busily enforced them to rule them-
selves thereafter. Therefore, Sir, this foresaid learning 10
of Master John Wycliffe is yet holden of full many men
and women, the most agreeable learning unto the living
and teaching of Christ and his Apostles, and most openly
shewing and declaring how the Church of Christ hath
been, and yet should be, ruled and governed. Therefore 15
so many men and women covet this learning, and purpose,
through God's grace, to conform their living like to this
learning of Wycliffe.'

And the Archbishop said, ' That learning that thou
callest Truth and Soothfastness is open slander to Holy 20
Church, as it is proved of Holy Church. For albeit that
Wycliffe your author was a great Clerk, and though that
many men held him a perfect liver: yet his doctrine is
not approved of Holy Church, but many Sentences of his
learning are damned as they are well worthy.' 25

The Examination of Sir William of Thorpe.

This treatise has been placed last as a summary of Wyclif's final
views. He deals in emphatic but, on the whole, temperately-
expressed language with the structure of the true Church, the
Eucharist, Predestination, Confession, Absolution, Papal censures, and those two favourite themes : the paramount authority 30
of Scripture and the wickedness of friars.

The opening of Cap. IX shows him appealing to the 'coming-on' of time to bring about the reforms which he had so much at heart. In his last years the Reformer realized that his proposals were premature; but he still hoped that the future
5 would effect what his own day had failed to achieve. This is one sign of his greatness.

From the literary standpoint, too, the treatise is noteworthy. On the whole it is superior in construction and form of expression to any of Wyclif's other writings. It contains some
10 excellent strokes of irony and some fine rhetorical flourishes. At the end of Cap. I, he dryly remarks: ' ȝif ony man be tauȝt of God þat he shal be saved in Hevene, noon or fewe men ben siche; and asaye hem bi hemsilf, for þei schulden have noon evidence to seie þat God haþ told hem þis.' This reminds one
15 of Chaucer:

> But natheles, this wot I wel also,
> That there nis noon that dwelleth in this contree,
> That either hath in helle or heven y-be,
> Ne may of hit non other weyes witen,
20 > But as he hath herd seyd, or founde hit writen;
> For by assay ther may no man hit preve.

The finest stroke of irony, however, occurs near the end of the treatise. Wyclif charges the friars with assuming the Godhead in their attempt to create a new universe, 'and þus auctours of
25 accidentis hyen hem above Crist as ȝif þei wolden maken a newe world. . . . But þes GODDIS varien.'

The concluding paragraphs of *Þe Chirche and hir Membris* are informed by Wyclif's realism. God, he says, has established the 'goodnesse of þingis'. He, alone, 'appropriþ unto Him
30 to weie þingis, how þei shulden be loved'. Men must not therefore attempt to change the Universe by theories of Transubstantiation and the like. The world of 'þingis' must be accepted as found in 'Goddis lawe'. This is the final and complete reality. 'Crist telliþ fulli in His lawe how men
35 shulden trowe to Him and Hise; and þus no þing untouchid in þis lawe shulde be dun or axid to do.' 'Love of Crist [must] move men to holde his boundis.' All 'novelries' are man-made and therefore imperfect. Reality as expressed in the Bible must be strictly served. 'Þus þe crafte of love of
40 þingis is moost nedeful to al oþer; for no man may come to blis but bi vertue of þis crafte.'

HERE BIGYNNEþ A TRETICE þAT TELLIþ KNOWLECHE
SUMWHAT OF þE CHIRCHE AND HIR MEMBRIS.

Cristis Chirche is his Spouse, þat haþ þree. partis. Þe
first part is in blis wiþ Crist, Heed of þe Chirche, and
conteneþ angels and blessid men þat now ben in Hevene.
Þe secounde part of þis Chirche ben seintis in purgatorie ;
and þes synnen not of þe newe, but purgen þer olde 5
synnes. And many errours fallen in preiyng for þes
seintis ; and siþ þei alle been deed in bodi, Cristis wordis
may be taken of hem,—sue we Crist, in oure lif, and *late
þe dede birie the dede.* Þe þridde part of the Chirche ben
trewe men þat here lyven, þat schulen be aftir saved in 10
Hevene, and lyven here Cristen mennis liif. Þe first
part is clepid overcomynge ; þe myddil is clepid slepyng ;
þe þridde is clepid fiȝtinge Chirche ; and alle þes maken
o Chirche. And Heed of þis Chirche is Crist, boþe God
and man ; and þis Chirche is modir to ech man þat shal 15
be saaf, and conteyneþ no membre but oonli men þat
shal be saved. For, as Crist vouchiþ-saaf to clepe þis
Chirche his spouse, so He clepiþ curside men fendis, as
was Scarioth.

And fer be it fro Cristene men to graunte þat Crist 20
haþ weddid þe fend ; sith Poul seiþ in oure bileve þat
Crist comouneþ not wiþ Belial. And here we takun as
bileve þat ech member of holi Chirche shal be saved wiþ
Crist, as ech membre of þe fend is dampned ; and so þe
while we fiȝten here and witen not where we schal be 25
saaf, we witen not where we ben membris of holi Chirche.
But as God wole of þre þingis, þat we knowun hem not
in certein, so he wole for greet cause þat we witen not
where we ben of þe Chirche. But as ech man shal hope
þat he schal be saaf in blisse, so he shulde suppose þat 30
he be lyme of holi Chirche ; and þus he shulde love holi
Chirche, and worschipe it as his modir.

And by þis hope, bineþe bileve, shulden be two synnes
fled ; pride of men and coveitise, bi title þat þei ben men
of holi Chirche. For no Pope þat now lyveþ woot where 35
he be of þe Chirche, or where he be a lym of the fend, to

be dampned wiþ Lucifer. And þus it is a blynd folie þat
men shulden fiȝte for þe Pope more þan þei fiȝten for
bileve ; for many siche fiȝten for þe fend. And take we
þis as bileve, or treuþe þat is next bileve, þat no man þat
5 lyveþ here woot wheþer he shal be saved or dampned, al
ȝif he hope byneþe bileve þat he shal be saved in Heven.
Ȝif ony man be tauȝt of God þat he shal be saved in
Hevene, noon or fewe men ben siche ; and asaye hem bi
hem silf, for þei schulden have noon [1] evidence to seie þat
10 God haþ told hem þis. Þe first bileve þat we schulden
have is, þat Crist is God and man ; and how He haþ Him
bi his Goddhede, and how He lyvede here by his manhede.
And þus oure hope and bileve ben temperid in Cristen
men.

CAP. II

[CHRIST, NOT THE POPE, IS HEAD OF THE CHURCH]

15   But aftir þes two godliche virtues, we taken sumþing
as bileve, and sumþing bi comune croniclis ; and hopen
þat charité moveþ us here. After that Crist hadde dwelt
here long ynowȝ wiþ His apostlis, aboute þree and þritti
ȝeer, as Him likide, aftirward He was kild of þe Jewes,
20 and aftirward þe þridde day oure God aroos from deþ to
lyf. And aftir þe fourtiþe day fro þat He was schewid
to His disciplis, Jesus stiede in to Hevene, and rengnede
ever þere wiþ his Fadir. And so þe first part of þe
Chirche rengneþ þus in Hevene with Crist ; þe secounde
25 part slepiþ ȝit, as longe as Crist likiþ ; þe þridde part of
þe Chirche fiȝtiþ here aftir Crist, and takiþ ensaumple
and weie of Him to come to Hevene as He cam.

And ever more þe Hooli Goost governeþ wiþ hem al
Cristis Chirche ; for as þes þree persones of God ben o
30 God and not manye, so alle dedes and werkes of þe
Trinité mai not be departid from oþir. For as al þat þe
Fadir wole, þe Sone wole, and þis Goost wole,—so al þat
o persone doiþ, þes þree persones done. Aftir þat Crist
was stied in to Hevene, aboute ten daies, as He hadde

---

[1] omitted *CC*.

ordeynid, He sente doun þe Holi Goost, and movede
apostlis to do his dedes ; and þei wenten and prechiden
faste among Jewis and heþen men. But Jewis aȝen-
stonden hem faste, and heþene men token him wiþ wille,
and resceyveden þe Holy Goost, and bicamen Cristene 5
men. And þus apostlis of Crist filliden bi Goddis grace
þis world.

But longe aftir, as croniclis seien, þe fend hadde envie
herto ; and bi Silvestre preest of Rome he brouȝte in
a newe gile, and moved þe emperour of Rome to dowe 10
þis Chirche in þis preest. For, as the fend tauȝte þis
kyng, þis dede cam of greet almes ; for þei þouȝten not
how þe Chirche shulde sue Crist in his lawe. But trewe
men supposen here, þat boþe þis emperour and þis preest
weren moved of God bi tymes to trowe þat þei synneden 15
in þis dede. But bisie we us not where þei ben seintis,
and how þei were þus moved of God ; for al þis is byneþe
bileve, and men mai trowe it ȝif þei wolen.

Whan þis lif was þus changid, þe name of this preest
was changid ; he was not clepid Cristis apostle, ne hiȝ 20
disciple of Crist, but he was clepid the Pope, and heed
of al hooli Chirche ; and aftirward camen oþer names bi
feynyng of ypocritis ; as sum men seien, þat he is even
wiþ the manheed of Crist, and hierste viker of Crist to
do in erþe whatever him likiþ ; and summe florishen oþir 25
names, and seien þat he is moost blissed fadir. But
cause herof ben beneficis þat þis preest ȝyveþ to men ;
for Symon Magus travailide nevere more in symonie þan
þes preestis doon. And so God wolde suffre no lenger
þe fend to regne oonli in oo siche preest, but, for synne 30
þat þei hadden do, made devisioun amongis two, so þat
men myȝten liȝtlier in Cristis name overcome þes boþe.
For as o virtu is strengere if it be gedrid, þan if it be
scatrid, so o malis is strenger whanne it is gederid in
o persone, and it is of lesse strengþe whanne it is departid 35
in manye ; for þanne oon helpiþ aȝen anoþir to confounde
Anticrist.

And þis moveþ pore preestis to speke now herteli in
þis mater. For whanne þat God wole helpe his Chirche,

and men ben slowe and wole not worche, þis slouþe is to
be dampned for many causis in idil men.   And myche
more ben þei dampnable, þat letten Goddis lawe to shyne.
Þes men taken noo witnes of adversaries to þis Pope, as
5 ben Jewis and Sarasynes, Grekis and Yngdis, wiþ many
oþir; but þei taken þe lyf of Crist as bileve, and þeron
grounden hem; and þus þei seien, ȝif þis Pope contrarieþ
to Cristis lyf, he is þe moste fendis viker and Anticrist
þat is here; and sich Anticrist and noon oþir þenken
10 many þat Goddis lawe spekiþ of.

．　　．　　．　　．　　．　　．　　．　　．

And ȝif þou seie þat Cristis Chirche mut have an heed
here in erþe, soiþ it is, for Crist is Heed, þat muste be
here wiþ His Chirche unto þe day of dome, and everywhere bi His Godhede.   For siþ vertue of a kyng mut
15 be strecchid by al his rewme, myche more þe vertue of
Crist is comuned wiþ al His children.   And ȝif þou seie
þat Crist mut nedis have sich a viker here in erþe, denye
þou Cristis power, and make þis fend above Crist.   For
bileve techiþ us, þat noo man mai grounde þis viker
20 oonly on Cristis lawe, but on presumpcioun of man; and
sich hyenesse of emperours haþ destried her empire;
and, ȝif þat God wole, þes Popes shal destrie hemsilf, ȝhe,
here,—for no drede þei ben distried in helle bi jugement
of Crist.   And so whatever resoun men maken of Crist,
25 of Petir, or oþer good ground, it goiþ opinli aȝen sich
a pope for þe grete diversité; and so whanne þes men
failen resoun, þei tristen to mannis helpe, and feynen bi
ipocrisie how myche good þei don aȝen.   But God cursiþ
by Jeremye hem that affien þus in man.

CAP. III

[THE POPE IS NOT INFALLIBLE OR ELECTED TO BLISS]

30   Here men taken sumwhat soiþ, and doon dremyng to
þis treuþe.   Þei seien soþli, þat Cristis Chirche is His
hous to kepe His meyné;—and summe in þis hous ben
sones, þat shulen ever dwelle in Hevene and take her
fadris heritage, ȝhe, ȝif þei trespassen for a tyme,—and

summe ben servauntis in þis hous, al ȝif þei shulen aftir
be dampned. And so it is greet diversité to be in þis
Chirche; and of þis Chirche þes wordis ben soþli seid,
and notabli to mannis kynde. But whanne dremes come
aftir, þei maken a fals feyned tale. Þei seien,—whanne 5
Crist wente to Hevene, His manhed wente in pilgrymage,
and made Petir, wiþ al þes popis, His stewardis to reule
His hous, and ȝaf hem ful power herto bifore alle oþir
preestis alyve. Here þis dreem takun amys turneþ upso-
doun þe Chirche. For Petir was a trewe help wiþ Poul 10
and Joon and oþir apostlis; but noon of þes servauntis
dremeden þat he was heed of hooli Chirche, or þat he
lovede Crist more þan ony of his breþren dide.

It is licli to many men þat Petir lovede Crist more in
a maner þan ony of þes oþir apostlis, but he was tauȝt to 15 ·
strive not herfore; for oþir apostlis in oþir maner loveden
more Crist þan dide Petir,—as Poul traveilide more in þe
Chirche,—and Joon lovede Crist more hevenliche. For
Joones love was in quiet and clene, as seintes loven in
Heven. Which of þes is more hiȝ now is but foli us to 20
dreme. Wel we witen þat Crist wole taken, of what state
þat Him likiþ, a man, aftir þat he is worþi, to more blis or
more joie; but aftir bileve of Hooli Writt, þat telliþ of
Petre and oþir apostlis þat þei ben now blessid in
Hevene,—for noon fel but Scarioth,—taken we biside 25
bileve of many oþir, þat þei ben seintis, as of Clement
and Laurence, and oþir þat þe Legende spekiþ of. And
of summe we han more evidence, and of sum lasse, bineþe
bileve.

And summe þenken a greet evidence, þat if þe Pope 30
canonise þis man, þanne he mut nedis be seint in Hevene.
But trowe þei þis men þat wolen. Wel Y woot þat þese
popis may erre and synne, as Petre dide, and ȝit Petre
dremede not þus, to shewe þat men ben seintis in Hevene.
But it mai falle þat manie men þat ben canonisid by þes 35
popis ben depe dampned in helle, for þei disseyven and
ben disseyved. Afferme we not as bileve, þat ȝif a man
be chosen Pope, þan he is chosen to blis, as he is here
clepid 'Blessederste Fadir'. And many trowen bi þer

werkes þat þes ben depperst dampned in helle. For þei
chargen hemsilf as ypocritis, boþe in office and in name;
and so þei sitten in þe firste place here, and at þe laste
day of dome þei schulen be in þe laste place, þat is, þe
5 depperste place of helle. Holde we us in bondis of
bileve, þat stondiþ in general wordis and in condicionel
wordis, and juge we not here folili. But we mai seie bi
supposal, þat we gesse þat it is so; and whoever haþ
more evidence, his part shulde sunner be supposid.
10 But here ben þree grete heresies þat disseyven many
men. First, men supposen þat ech pope is þe 'Moost
Blessid Fadir'; but þis speche lastiþ but a while, til þat
þe Pope mai avaunce men. But heere we seien soþly,
þat þes men þat clepen hem blessid, disseiven hem and
15 flateren hem, for þei hopen to have wynnyng of hem.
For wheþir is þis Pope moost blessid in þis liif or aftir þis
lyf? He is not blessid in þis lif, for blis falliþ to þe toþir
lyf, and þis lif is ful of sorowe and synne, þat suffriþ not
blis wiþ it. And ȝif men speken largeli, many men ben
20 here more blessid þan þe Pope; for hyenes of þis state
makiþ not bi himsilf man blessid, for ellis ech pope were
blissed, al ȝif he were falsly chosen of fendis; and Scarioth
shulde be blissed, for he was chosen of Crist Himself.
And it is no nede to argue here for to disprove þis foli,
25 for it is more fals in himsilf þan ouȝt þat men shulen
bringe herof.

þe toþir heresie, þat comeþ of þis, disceyveþ many
simple men; þat ȝif þe Pope determine ouȝt, þanne it is
soiþ and to bileve. But Lord! where ech pope be more
30 and beter wiþ God þan was Petre? But he erride ofte,
and synnede myche; ȝhe, aftir he hadde take þe Holi
Goost. Lord! wher Crist clepide hym Sathanas, and
bad him go aftir Him, and ȝit þer was no cause of his
errour, wherfore Crist clepide him þus? And so whanne
35 Petre denyede Crist, and swore fals for a wommans vois,
he erride in þis foul synne; and þerfore he wepte aftir.
Also, aftir takyng of þe Holi Goost, Petre erride, as Poul
seiþ, whanne he wolde not dele with Gentiles for tendir-
nesse of þe Jewis. Lord wher men of worse liif mai

sunner erre in þer jugement! And ever þe moo þat ben
of siche, ever þe sunner mai þei erre; for Scarioth made
oþir apostlis to erre in companye of Crist, and it werc to
fals a feynyng, to seie þat holi Chirche hangiþ on þes, for
þis feyner can not teche þat ony of þes is of þe Chirche. 5

And of þis comen many heresies, as of assoilingis and
indulgencis, and cursingis, wiþ feyned pardons, þat make
many men have conscience and trowe more to þe Pope in
sich a cause þan þei trowe to þe Gospel. And men moten
erre here in bileve, and take ofte fals as bileve. Þis heresie 10
schulden men flee, for fals mainteynyng makiþ heretikes,
and to assente wiþ suche falseheed bringiþ in ofte heresies;
and Crist wole not assente wiþ þes, for þei mai not be
soiþ.

CAP. IV

[Monks, canons, friars have become a burden to the 15
Church. They are ever absorbing more wealth and land.
In supporting them the Pope ' semeth wood and blyndid
by þe fend. . . . Þus mai men see þat þis steward doiþ
more þan he haþ leeve to do; and þes newe ordris,
groundid on hym, and not on grauntyng of Cristis lawe, 20
ben a flok of þe fendis children.']

CAP. V

[MISDEEDS OF FRIARS]

And here men noten many harmes þat freris don in þe
Chirche. Þei spuylen þe puple many weies by ipocrisie
and oþer leesingis, and bi þis spuylyng þei bilden Caymes
Castelis, to harme of cuntreis. Þei stelen pore mennis 25
children, þat is werse þan stele an oxe; and þei stelen
gladlich eires,—Y leeve to speke of stelyng of wymmen,—
and þus þei maken londis bareyne for wiþdrawyng of
werkmen, not al-oonli in defaute of cornes, but in beestis
and oþer good. For þei reversen Goddis ordenaunce in 30
þre partis of þe Chirche; þei maken men to trowe fals of
hem, and letten almes to be ȝovun bi Goddis lawe; and
þus þei letten bi gabbingis office and lif of trewe prestis,

for þei letten hem for to preche, and speciali Cristis
gospel. Þei moven londis to bateilis, and pesible persones
to plete ; þei maken many divorsis, and many matri-
monies, unleveful, boþe bi lesingis maad to parties, and
5 bi pryvelegies of þe court. Y leeve to speke of fiȝting þat
þei done in o lond and oþir, and of oþir bodili harmes þat
tungis suffisen not to telle. For as myche as þei dis-
penden, as myche and more þei harmen rewmes ;—as þei
han, in þis laste journé þat Englishemen maden into
10 Flandres, spuylid oure rewme of men and money more
þan þe freris han wiþ hem.

And no drede to Englishemen but ne þei han procurid
þis iourney, boþe in preching, and in gedering, and in
traveiling of þer owne persone.

.   .   .   .

15 Also þes sectis inpungnen þe Gospel, and also þe olde
lawe, for þei chargen more þer owne statute, alȝif it be
aȝens Goddis lawe, þan þei done þe lawe of þe Gospel;
and þus þei loven more þer ordre þan Crist. As, ȝif it were
nevere so myche nede to go out and preche Goddis lawe,
20 to defende our modir holi Chirche, ȝit þer ordre lettiþ þes,
but ȝif þei han þer priours leeve, alȝif God bidde to do þis.
And comunly þes pryvat prioures letten þer felowes here
to go out ; and so, be þei never so riche, þei shulen not
helpe her fleishli eldris ; for alle þer goodis ben þe housis,
25 siþ þei han nouȝt propre but synne. And þis errour re-
proveþ Crist in Phariseis, þat siȝen þe gnat, and swolowen
þe camele, for þei chargen lesse more harm.

Also þes Phariseis chargen moche þer fastingis and
oþir þingis þat þei han founden, but keping of Goddis
30 mandementis þei charge not half so myche. As, he
shulde be holde apostata þat lefte his abite for a day, but
for leevyng of dedis of charité shulde he noþing be
blamed. And þus þei blasfemen in God, and seien, whoso
dieþ in þer abite shal nevere go to helle, for holynes þat
35 is þerinne ; and so, aȝens Cristis sentence, þei sewen an
old cloute in newe cloiþ.

.   .   .   .

CAP. VI

[THE CHURCH SHOULD BE PURGED OF FRIARS]

Lord! where þe Pope þinke good to conferme siche
newe ordris! Certis synne of siche children turneþ into
heed of þer fadir, as Helias sones maden þer fadir to be
punishid sharply of God. And generalli, whoso synneþ
for avantage of himsilf, his synne makiþ disavauntage of 5
þat þat he weneþ turne to good. As, þes two Popis han
now no more enemyes, ne more hid, þan ben þes freris;
for summe holden wiþ þe o Pope and many and grete wiþ
þe toþir; and þei enformen þer countreis to holde stifli
wiþ þer Pope. And no drede, ȝif cuntreis turne fro þe oo 10
Pope to þe toþir, þe freris wolden turne also, for þei
obeishen to þe puple. And þus love ungroundid in God,
but oonli in temporal goodis, mut nedis faile and do harm,
for al siche love is sinful.

Siþ þes sectis ben so harmful to oure modir hooli 15
Chirche, and, as bileve techiþ us, þe Chirche may be
purgid of þis, it were sumwhat for to speke of þis purging
of þe Chirche. For alȝif it shal not fulli be turned in þis
lyf, but first in Hevene,[1] ȝit it may be purgid in part, and
in þis purginge stondiþ mennis mede. And no man is 20
excusid here of consenting to þis synne, but ȝif he helpe
on sum maner; for ech man mai helpe sumwhat. Sum
men shulden helpe bi resoun þat is taken of Goddis lawe,
and summe bi worldli power, as erþely lordis þat God
haþ ordeyned, and alle men bi good liif and good preieris 25
to God, for in Him liggiþ þe helpe here aȝens þe cautelis
of þe fend.

[THE FRIARS ARE HERETICS]

Men han hem suspect of heresie for many causis.
First, for þei varien þus in bileve of þe sacrid oost. And
þus þei schulden telle at þe bigynnyngė what þing þei 30

---

[1] and *omitted*.

trowun þat it is,—wheþir it be Goddis bodi or not. And
here þei mai not be excusid; for mynystrel or joȝelour,
tumbler and harlot, wole not take of þe puple bifore þat
þei han shewid þer craft; and siþ freris craft stondiþ in
5 þis, to teche þe puple þer bileve, and þe puple trowiþ
comunli þat þis oost is Goddis bodi, here freris shulden
bigynne, and tellen men wher þis be soiþ. And ȝif þei
seien þat þis oost in no maner is Goddis bodi, flee þes
freris as heretikes, for Crist and his Chirche seien þe
10 contrarie.

Ȝif þei seien þat it is Goddis bodi, and manye freres
seien þe contrarie, þis word techiþ not þat þei gabben in
comune bileve of þe Chirche. And þerfore men shulden
abide witnes of þer comune seel, and bifore dele not wiþ
15 hem, but have hem suspect of heresie.

Ȝif þei seien þat þis oost is an accident wiþouten suget,
as colour and figure, and þus it is not Goddis bodi, wel
we witen þat olde bileve, groundid in þe wordis of Crist,
seiþ þat it is Goddis bodi, as þe Pope sumtyme seide.
20 And it is not ynowȝ þat freris erren in colour and figure
of þer abitis to prove þat þis sacrid oost is colour and
figure of breed. And þis defamynge shulde þe Pope
seke out wiþ greet traveile; for þes sectis han sclaundrid
him, as he and hise hadden errid in bileve.

. . . .

25 Aftir þis myȝte a man axe, siþ God tolde of newe
sectis þat shulen come into þe Chirche, to charge and
harm of þe Chirche, how groundiþ þis frere his ordre, and
in what tyme it bigan. And siþ o frere contrarieþ anoþer
in þis mater, and nouȝt is proved, men shulden avoide þis
30 frere til he hadde here tauȝt þe treuþe. Þis strif is mater
of gabbing and of synnyng among manie; and þus for
profit of þe Chirche shulden freris worche to quenche þis
strif. Carmes seien þat þei weren bifore þe tyme þat
Crist was born. Austyns seien þat þei weren many
35 hundrid wynters bifore oþer freris. Prechouris and
Menours seyn þe reverse. But noon groundiþ here his
word, as noon of þes newe ordris groundiþ þat he cam in
bi Crist; and but þis grounding be in dede, dremes and

confermyngis ben nou3t. On þis maner shulden trewe
men seke wisely þe soþe, and purge oure modir of apostemes þat ben harmful in þe Chirche. To þis shulde þe
Pope helpe, for to þis dette weren apostlis bounden, and
not to lordschippes of moneie, but in as myche as it 5
helpide herto. And siþ it lettiþ comunli, popis shulden
flee þis, as dide apostlis ; for ellis þei seiden wiþ oþer
foolis, þat helpe were harm, and good were yvel.

CAP. VII

[THE POPE HAS NO SPECIAL POWER TO BIND AND
    LOOSE]

Aftir þis shulden men wite of þe Popis power in assoilinge, in graunting of indulgencis and oþer privylegies, wiþ 10
cursing. For ri3t as þe Popis clerkis feynen þat þei done
miraclis whanne evere þei syngen, moo and more woundirful þan ever dide Crist or his apostlis, so in asoiling and
cursing þei feynen hem unknowun power ; and in fablis
of þis power þei blasfemen and harme þe Chirche. And 15
þus comeþ in errour into þe Chirche, as it doiþ of þe
sacrid oost ; for noon mai comprehende þis power, siþ it
is wiþouten noumbre, siþ Crist 3af þis to Petre, and oþir
popis þat camen aftir.

Here Cristene men bileven þat Petre and Poul and 20
oþir apostlis token power of Crist, but not but for to
edifie þe Chirche. And þus alle prestis þat ben Cristis
kny3tis han power of him to þis eende. Which of hem
haþ moost power, is ful veyne for us to trete ; but we
supposen of preestis dedis, þat he þat profitiþ more to þe 25
Chirche haþ more power of Crist, and ellis þei ben ydil
wiþ þer power. And þus bi power þat Crist 3af Petre
mai no man prove þat þis preest, þe which is Bishop of
Rome, haþ more power þan oþer preestis. For siþ oure
bileve seiþ, þat þer is noo power but of God, chesinge of 30
þes cardinalis 3yveþ not sich power to þe Pope. And it
sueþ not þat God mut 3yve, whan þes cardinalis han þus
chosen, but apostlis dedis þat popis doone shulden bere

witnes of þer power ; siþ fleyinge to Hevene of assoilid
spiritis, and comyng aȝen, bereþ no witnesse.

And wordis þat Crist seiþ in þe Gospel ben to liȝtli
undirstonden.   Crist seiþ to his apostlis ; Y am wiþ ȝou
5 alle daies unto þe ende of þe world. But what maken þes
wordis for þis Pope ? Þes wordis techen generali, þat
Crist shal be wiþ his lymes þat he haþ ordeyned to blis
riȝt to þe dai of dome ; but how shulden men wite þat þis
Pope is ony of hem þat Crist spekiþ to ? Certis þis Pope
10 woot not himsilf, and haþ litil mater to hope it ; for in
goode werkis and suynge of Crist shulde þis Pope grounde
his hope.

But ȝit in anoþir word þat Crist seide unto Petir,
groundiþ þis Pope his power, þat it is so myche over oþir ;
15 Crist bihiȝte to Petre, þat whatever he bindiþ in erþe it
shal be bounden in Hevene, and so of þis assoiling. But
þis resoun is ful of folie for many causis, whoso takiþ
hede. Soþly Crist seide þus to Petre, and so he seide to
oþer apostlis ; whi shulde Petre have power bi þis more
20 þan oþir apostlis of Crist ? Also men shulden wite here,
þat þes wordis þat Crist seide to Petir ben noþing for þis
Pope but ȝif he sue Crist and Petir in lyf. And suppose
þat al þis be soiþ ; ȝit eche preest of ony apostle shulde
have power to do good to þe Chirche, but not so myche
25 as here is dremed. For ellis Petre synnede many weies ;
for Petre uside not þis power ; who shulde excuse hem
of þis synne ?

Also men shulden undirstonde what it is to bynde man
above erþe. And men moten nedis seie here, þat þanne
30 a preest bindiþ man above erþe, whanne he bindiþ man·
after God, and not for fleish ne coveitise. And so þis
Pope shulde teche men þat he bindiþ þus above erþe, and
neiþer in þe erþe, ne undir þe erþe, but evene after þe
keies above ; but þis wole he nevere teche bifore þat
35 Gabriel blowe his horn.

.   .   .   .

Lord ! siþ Crist assoilide not þus, ne Petre, ne ony
oþer apostle, and þis Pope seeþ not in God þat He wole
þat it be so, what spirit shulde move þis Pope to feyne

sich assoilinge boþe fro peyne and fro synne, and aftir
chaffare þus þerwiþ? . . . For he mai not asoile here of
a litel bodili peyne, as myȝten Petir and oþer seintis;
how shulde he assoile soulis of þe peyne of purgatorie?

Cap. VIII

[Popes wrongfully claim divine sanction for their choice 5
of incumbents to benefices. Simony is rife in the settling
of these appointments.

Enforced private confession is contrary to the practice
of Christ and his disciples.]

Cap. IX

[CHURCH ENDOWMENTS SHOULD CEASE. POPE AND CLERGY SHOULD PRACTISE THE POVERTY OF CHRIST.]

It myȝte seme to many men þat myche of þis is hid 10
speche, and men shulden speke opinli to þe world, as
Crist dide, for to telle more clereli what is oure last
entent. For ȝif it were a trewe sentence, God myȝte
move men hereafter, boþe lordis and clerkis, to drawe to
þis sentence. And herfore we wolen seie opinli þe 15
sentence þat we conseyven: and ȝif God wole vouchesaaf, it mai aftir be declarid more. Oure ground is
comune bileve, þat Crist is boþe God and man, and so
He is þe beste man, þe wyserst man, and moost vertuous,
þat ever was or ever shal be. And He is heed of þe 20
Chirche; and He ordeynede a lawe to men, and confermede it wiþ his lyf, for to reule holi Chirche, and
teche how þat men shulde lyve; and al þis mut passe al
oþir, siþ þe auctor is þe beste.

And grutche we not þat many men þenken ful hevy 25
wiþ þis sentence, for so þei diden in Cristis tyme, boþe
wiþ His lyf and wiþ His lawe. Of þis ground we gessen
ferþere, how us þinkiþ þat men shulden do. But we
graunten at þe firste, þat if ony man wole shewe us þat
we speken aȝens Goddis lawe, or aȝen good resoun, we 30
wolen mekeli leeve of, and holde Goddis part bi oure
myȝte. For we ben wiþholden wiþ treuþe, and wiþ

Goddis grace shulen ever last þerinne. Us þinkiþ þat þe
Chirche shulde here holde þe ordenaunce of Crist ; and
ever þe streiter þat it helde þat, evere þe betir it were
to it. And þus bastard braunchis shulde be kutt fro þis
5 tree ; and þus þe Pope, wiþ his cardinalis, and alle preestis
þat been dowid, shulden leeve þis dowing and worldli
glorie þat þei han, and neiþer lyve ne do ouȝt, but ȝif it
were groundid in Cristis lawe ; for þat lawe is charité,
and groundiþ al þing þat is medeful. Ȝif þat God wolde
10 vouche-safe to ȝyve þes preestis of his grace, þat þei
wolden mekeli leeve þis, and lyve in Cristis poverté, þe
miracle were þe more, and more wolde profite to þe
Chirche.

Aftirward men þenken þat al þes newe sectis or ordris,
15 boþe possessioneres and beggeris, shulden ceese bi Cristis
lawe. And ȝif þei wolden leeve þes for charité, and lyve
purely aftir Crist, þer merit were þe more, and þei myȝten
encreese þe Chirche ; and ȝif þei wolden not do þus, þei
shulden be honestli constreyned. Both worldli goodis
20 and comunyng shulde be wiseli drawun fro hem, and
knyȝtis, wiþ lordis of þe world, shulden be confortid bi
Cristis lawe to stonde and defende þis sentence, as þei
diden aftir Cristis deþ; and trewe prestis shulden telle
þe comunes how þei shulde kepe charité, and obeishe
25 upon resoun, as Poul techiþ hem to do. And God myȝte
move summe of þes ordres to leeve þer ritis, and take
Cristes lawe, for þei hiden now ypocrisie, and ben ydil fro
many goode dedes. Lord ! what stiward were he þat
wolde ordeyne newe rehetors to ete mennes mete and do
30 hem harm, aȝens Cristis ordenaunce ?

Þe þridde point, of curatis, us þinkiþ shulde stonde þus.
Þei shulden lyve on þe puple in good measure as Poul
biddiþ ; but þe puple shulde not be artid to ȝyve hem
dymes ne oþer almes ; but þer goode wishes shulden
35 move to ȝyve hem freeli þat were nede, for þus lyvede
Crist with his apostlis. What preest shulde not be paied
herof ? And þus shulde þe Chirche drawe to acord bi
Crist, þat lediþ þe daunce of love. Ȝif oþir men wolden
be preestis, lyve þei þerafter, and shewe þei bi dede þat

Crist haþ made hem preestis, for þis passiþ lettris of
bishopis. And þus þe puple myȝte wiþdrawe þer almes
fro wickide preestis, and þe pride of preestis shulde be
stoppid, bi which þei envenymyn þe puple. Ȝif þis be
not doone anoon, ȝit it myȝte drawe to þe good; for 5
Cristis lyf was þe beste, þat shulde ensaumple alle oþir.

Here men arguen many weies aȝens þis sentence þat
here is seid, and speciali for þe Pope, þat þanne were
holi Chirche fordone, siþ Petre was Pope and many oþer
seintis, and who shulde contrarie þis? But here han men 10
seid ofte, þat it were good to obeishe to Petre, and þat
sich a captein were in þe Chirche; but name of þe Pope
hidiþ venym. Men seien þat it cam first yn bi folie of þe
emperour, þat reiside him an enemy boþe to God and to
þe world.   15

And ȝif þou aleggist seintis lyves, noon of hem is to
preise but in as myche as it acordiþ to Cristis lyf and
his lawe; and siþ Cristis lawe is more opyn, slepe þe
fablis, and rengne his lawe. It is no nede here to dreme,
how holi eende þes men maden, for men mai trowe it 20
whoso wole, and many ben seintis wiþouten þis trouþe.

Al oþer office of þe Pope myȝte be done mekely, as
myche as it wolde turne to worshipe of Crist and profite
of þe Chirche, by a trewe preest, as was bi apostlis, alȝif
þes bullis of leed slepten. It is licly þat Petre suede 25
more Crist in brennyng love þan diden oþer apostlis þat
weren wiþ Crist in Petris tyme, and so Petre was more
servisable, more meke, and more pore; for fervour of love
of Petre made him in þis more love Christ. But aftir þat
þe Chirche was dowid, no man hatiþ þis more þan þe 30
Pope; and þus he is not Cristis viker but raþir Anticrist
himsilf. Ȝif he wolde be meke and pore and servisable,
as Petre was, and take no more werk upon him þan þat
he myȝte wel do in dede, þanne he myȝte be Petris vicker,
bi grace of Crist heed of Petre.   35

As anentis þes newe ordris, þei semen alle Anticristis
proctours, to putte awey Cristis ordenaunce, and magnefie
þer newe sectis; and þus hem nediþ to have an heed oþir
þan Crist to susteyne hem. For Crist tolde not bi siche

habitis, ne siche ritis of Phariseis, but bi werkes of charité,
bi preching among þe puple.

CAP. X

[PAPAL CENSURE MAY BE DISREGARDED.]

Now were it for to speke last of censures, þat þe fend
blowiþ, as ben suspendingis, enterditingis, cursingis, and
5 reisingis of croiserie. But first Cristene men shulde
byleve, þat alle suche feyned censures don noon harm
a Cristene man, but ȝif he do harm first to himsilf. Bi hem
may his bodi be sleyn, and he be pursued many weies;
but Crist seiþ, þat mai not lie,—Blessid be ȝe whanne men
10 cursen ȝou, and whanne men pursuen ȝou, and seien al
maner of yvel aȝens ȝou, for me and my lawe. As Cristis
apostlis weren confortid, holde þou þe in Cristis lawe, and
sue þou him in maner of lyf, and drede þou not alle þe
censures þat Anticrist can blowe aȝens þee; but as he
15 meneþ to harm þee, he doiþ þee good maugree his. And
as þe assoiling serveþ of nouȝt, but as it accordiþ wiþ
Cristis keies, so þe cursyng noieþ not, but as Crist above
cursiþ. And herfore Crist tolde but litil bi cursingis of
þe hie bishopis, but confortide his disciplis of þes cursingis
20 and þes pursuyngis. For þei puttiden men out of
chirche, and pursueden hem in Cristis tyme, but apostlis
wolden not leeve to preche for al þis pursuynge.

And o confort is here; þat a man mai serve God in
clene wille þat he haþ, as longe as he haþ lyf, and ȝif his
25 wille lastiþ, aftir, whanne Anticrist haþ slayn his bodi, in
more blisse þan bifore, as oure bileve techiþ us. And þus
drede we hem not for censures þat þei feynen, but drede
we ever oure God, lest we synnen aȝens him. And so
double drede falliþ in sich cursingis of Anticrist. Oon,
30 lest we ben not worþi to have grace to cleve to God and
stonde stif in his mandementis,—and þanne God cursiþ
us; and þus cursing is to drede, for cursing of God for
oure synnes. Also men shulden be in charité, and loven
þes men þat cursen þus; and so men shulden drede þer
35 curs, lest it harme hemsilf and þe puple. For ȝif þei

cursen undiscretly, as þei don ever whanne þei cursen not
for love of þe Chirche, or for love of oþer men to whom
þei leien þis medecine, þanne þei cursen hemsilf first, al
ȝif þei knowun not þis foly. And bi sich blyndenesse in
cursing many curseris emblemyshen hemsilf, and þerwiþ 5
þe comune peple. Such cursing is to drede ; such drede
passiþ mannis lawe, and comeþ to lawe of charité, and
axiþ not curseris assoilinge, but Goddis purging, ȝif it
wole be.

As anentis suspendinge and enterdityng þat ben feyned, 10
we trowen þat þei doon myche good, and noon harm but
to foolis. For ȝif þei wolden suspende hemsilf fro alle
þingis but Goddis lawe, it were a graciouse suspendinge,
for hem and for oþer men ; for þanne Goddis lawe myȝte
freeli renne bi þe lymytis þat Crist haþ ordeyned. And 15
he is a cursid man þat leeveþ to do þat God biddiþ, and
for sich feynynge of censuris,—ȝhe, ȝif deþ sue aftir.

As anentis croiserie, summe of Cristis Chirche ben
enformed how þei shulden not trowe to þe Pope for ony
bullis þat he sendiþ, but ȝif þei ben groundid in Goddis 20
lawe. And þis grounding shulden men take wiþ reverence, and leeve þis leed. For men shulde take as bileve
þat þei shulden neiþer trowe to Crist ne Petre, but in as
myche as þei grounden bi Goddis lawe þat men shulden
trowe þus. For Crist telliþ [1] fulli in His lawe, how men 25
shulden trowe to Him and Hise ; and þus no þing untouchid in þis lawe shulde be dun or axid to do. But
who shulde axe more þan Crist, or more obeishe to þe
Pope þan to Crist ? And we ben certein þat Crist may
not axe oþir obedience ; whi shulde þe Pope ? Men 30
shulden bi hooli lif of Crist trowe þat His lawe is com-
pleet, and axe noon oþir ground of þis lawe, for Crist is
þe firste and þe laste. And so, ȝif þe Pope assoile men
a pena or *a culpa*, or whatever pardone he grauntiþ for
þing þat is not charité, forsake it as þe fendis bidding, þat 35
is contrarie to love of Crist. Wel I woot þe fend mai
feyne more pardone þan God wole graunte to ech man

---

[1] *So in CC*; *Arnold prints* lettiþ.

þat wole slee his broþir ; but God forbode þat we trowun
þis, as þe Pope may graunte to day, and to morowe per-
seyve his folye, and revoke þe formere errour. But who
shulde bileve siche bullis ? for wel we witen bi Goddis
5 lawe, þat God ȝyveþ þe Pope no power, but for to edifie
his Chirche, bi charité þat God haþ toold.

Crist was þe beste herd, and so He puttide his lyf for
His sheep ; and þe Pope mai not opinlier telle þat he is
Anticrist or a fend, þan for to putte many mennis lyves
10 for þis office þat he presumeþ. For Cristis lyf was myche
betere þan al þis office or þes popis. How shulde men
fiȝte for a persone, þat þei witen not where he be a fend,
or tauȝt of God to do þus ? Siþ þei ben certein of medeful dedis, certis þat man were a fool þat wolde take þis
15 uncerteine weie, and leeve þe certeyn witt and feyþ for
wordis ungroundid in Goddis lawe. And many þenken
þat þes prelatis þat ben upon Cristis side shulden have
joie of þis sentence ; for it is for alle good men. And if
ony can disprove it, men wolen revoke it, and treuþe
20 shal shyne, and it shal have moo witnessis. And þis is
more to Goddis worship.

But here men dreden blasphemye, and oþir cautelis of
þe fend ; þat men gon not bi resoun ne bi Goddis lawe
in þis mater, but putte þe Pope here heierste juge, as ȝif
25 he were God in erþe. And he, wiþ his part þat loveþ þe
world, quenche men þat speken þis, and axen noon oþer
proof þerof. And siþ þe fend haþ þe strenger part here
þan þe part of treuþe þat is wiþ Crist, Crist wole suffre,
for formere synne, þe fendis side have maistrie ȝit. But
30 in o bileve men resten, þat day shal come of þe laste
jugement, whanne þe fendis side shal lurke, and treuþe
shal shyne wiþouten lettyng ; and þat day abiden men,
bi reule of lawe þat Crist haþ ȝovun.

[CHRIST'S ' LAW ' ALONE IS TO BE FOLLOWED]

Þus bringinge in of sectis and of lawes þat Crist made
35 not, quenchiþ þe love of Crist and of His religioun here.
And þus men shulden stonde in þe mesure þat Crist haþ

ȝovun of þes two, boþe of sectis and of lawis ; for bringinge in of þes doiþ harm. And so marke þis as greet
synne, when men passen in oþer of þes, alȝif þe fende
coloure it, and medle good wiþ þe yvel ; for þus dide
Machamete in his lawe ; and þe fend doiþ þus comunly. ... 5
And þus, siþ men shulden love more Cristis ordenaunce
and his boundis þan ony þat comen after, and Crist haþ
ordeyned at þe fulle, men shulden leeve þes novelries as
contrarie to Cristis ordenaunce, and love þe mesure þat
Crist haþ ȝovun. For so diden Cristis apostlis.   10

Also whi shulden not love of Crist move men to holde
His boundis ? . . . we shulen drede Poulis sentence þat
who þat loveþ not Jesus Crist, he is cursid of God ; and
þis cursing is moost to drede. And generaly, worst þing
is more costly and more hevy ; and þus it lettiþ feble 15
weie-goeres to be taried wiþ such þing. And errour in
weiyng of þis love makiþ many fals weddingis ; as men
ben weddid wiþ þer habitis, and þer custumes and þer
singular maners, as ȝif þei weren Cristis comaundementis ;
and ȝit þei ben ful feble in kynde.   20

And men blasfemen in þis point, for þei putten a reule
of love to ordeyne an yvel þing to be more loved, aȝen
þe ordenaunce of God. And þis is opin blasfemy, siþ
God appropriþ unto Him to weie þingis, how þei shulden
be loved, and to make hem oþere betere or worse. And 25
þus auctours of accidentis hyen hem above Crist as ȝif
þei wolden maken a newe world, and change goodnesse
of þingis.

But þes goddis varien ; as oon loveþ o maner, and
anoþir loveþ anoþir, and hatiþ þe maner of his broþir. 30
And þis techiþ wel ynowȝ þat alle þes ben false goddis.

[CONCLUSION. THE CRAFT OF THE LOVE OF ' THINGS ']

And þus þe crafte of love of þingis is moost nedeful to
al oþer ; for no man mai come to blis but bi vertue of þis
crafte ; and no man mai synne but for errour in þis crafte,
as blessid men doone Goddis ordenaunce, and dampned 35

men loven þe contrarie. And alle þes newe ordris ben dividid in þer love, as oon loveþ oon and anoþer anoþer, and so hatiþ his contrarie. But Crist, whanne He lovede hoolliche His Chirche, wolde not make it faire wiþ þese
5 ordris. And eche man is holden to love liche after þat Crist loveþ, and to hate þat He hatiþ, and þanne is his hierste vertue stablid.

APPENDIX A

WYCLIF'S ENGLISH

THE description of Wyclif's English which follows has been based on the language of the writings in *MS. Bodl. 788*, *MS. Ashburnham XXVII*, and also *MS. Corpus Christi College 296*. The first of these MSS. contains the whole of the *Sermons* and *Þe Chirche and hir Membris*. On it Arnold based his text for these writings. The MS. probably belongs to the last decade of the fourteenth century. *MS. Ashburnham XXVII* contains the important tracts *de Papa* and *de Officio Pastorali*. Matthew states that this particular MS. is written ' in a charter hand of the fourteenth century'. The *Corpus Christi MS. 296* contains, among other writings, *Of Weddid Men and Wifis, Of Feigned Contemplative Life*, and *Of Servauntis and Lordis*, and belongs to the last quarter of the fourteenth century.

One cannot but be struck by the similarity of the language employed in these different MSS. There are, of course, discrepancies in orthographical and phonological details, but the broad linguistic features are identical. When we remember, further, that two of the MSS. were written down either in Wyclif's lifetime or shortly after his death, we are tempted to believe that they represent fairly closely the word-forms which Wyclif himself employed.

According to the evidence of these MSS. Wyclif employed a S. Midland Dialect closely akin to the SE. Midland of Chaucer. There are, however, some important differences. Wyclif's vocabulary contains fewer French words than that of Chaucer. This was to be expected from the different subject-matter of the two writers. Wyclif's language further manifests a strong preference for the unaccented vowel *i* in the plural of nouns, the 3rd sing. pres. indic. of verbs, and the ending *id* of the p.p. of weak verbs. There is also one West feature in Wyclif, i. e. the *u* in the ending of the p.p. of the strong verb—*fallun, takun,* &c.; cf. also *aȝenus* and the gen. plur. of *man, mennus.*

Wyclif seems to have lost all trace of the northern speech which he must have used as a boy. This is probably to be attributed to his long residence in the University of Oxford, and to his holding of parishes situated in districts employing Midland modes of speech. Lutterworth, it is to be noted, lies not very far from Oxford.

NOUNS. (i) The plural most often ends in *is* though *es* and *s* are also found: *discipis, pingis, cautelis; signes, Grekes; Latyns, confortours.*

(ii) Mutation plurals: *men, wymmen.*

(iii) Weak nouns: *iȝen.*

(iv) Double plurals: *lambren, breperen, children* (also *childre*).

(v) The gen. sing. usually ends in *is*: *popis bullis, goddis cause, soulis leche, fendis blast.* In *his modir sistir, per modir tunge* the OE. uninflected genitive has been preserved.

ADJECTIVES. (i) Strong: sing. *greet defaute*; plur. *grete heresies*; Weak: sing. *pe laste day*; plur. *pes olde ordris.* The usual rule is observed, namely, that the weak form is employed after a demonstrative or in the vocative; but the distinction was dying by the end of the fourteenth century. We get, for example, *sich fals freris, pis foul synne, both greet and stronge.*

(ii) Comparison. The comparative is formed by the addition of *r, er, ere,* to the positive: *liȝter, lyȝttere, sykerere.* The superlative is formed by adding *est, erst* or *erste: porest, depperst, blesserderste.* (Shortening of long root-syllables is seen in *sunner, depperste.*) The adverbs *more* and *moost* are also used in comparison: *more bisie, moost blessid.*

(iii) The definite article is the uninflected *pe*: *pe Pope, pe fendis lymes.* Note, however, that *pe* is not much employed in the plural. It is usually replaced by *pes.*

ADVERBS end in either *e, li,* or *ly: fastè, neverè; passingli, goostli; liȝtly, comounly.* The comparative is formed either with *more* or by the endings *re, er, ere: betre, hiȝer, sunner, bisiliere.* The superlative ends in *erst: depperst dampned.*

VERBS. (i) The usual endings of the indic. pres. are *e, ist* or *est, ip* or *ep; en: telle, tellest* or *tellist, tellip; tellen.*

(ii) The preterite of weak verbs ends in *ede* or *ide, edest* or *edist, ede* or *ide; eden* or *iden: lovede, lovedest, lovede; loveden: passide, entredist, clepide; killiden.* Note the addition of a weak ending to the preterite of a strong verb in *he felde* (= he fell), *pei felden.*

(iii) The infinitive ends in *e* or *en*; *e* is sometimes dropped:

the infinitives *heer, heere, heeren* all occur in one sermon. *Starin* (OE. *starian*) preserves the *i* of the suffix of OE. verbs in *-ian*.

(iv) The pres. participle ends in *yng(e)* or *ing(e)*: *brennyng, gretynge, preching, assoilinge.*

(v) The strong past participle ends in *en, un, yn*: *ȝyven, ȝovun, holpyn.*

The weak form ends in *ed, id*: *dividid, closid, blamed.*

(vi) The gerund: *Curiousté of science . . . is to dampne. It is to drede.*

(vii) The imperative: the distinction between sing. and plur. is lost: *loke þou* or *ȝe.*

STRONG VERBS

	Infin.	*3rd Sing. Pres. Indic.*	*3rd Sing. Preterite.*	*3rd Plur. Preterite.*	*Past Partic.*
Class I	holde(n) falle(n)	holdiþ falliþ	held fel(l), fyl[1]	holden fallen	holde(n) fallun
Class II	take(n)	takiþ	toke	token	takun
Class III	binde(n) fynde(n)	bindiþ	bond fond, foond	bounden	bounden founden
Class IV	bere(n)	bereþ, beriþ	bar	beren	boren, borun
Class V	ȝyve(n)	ȝyveþ	ȝaf	ȝavun	ȝovun (en)
Class VI	write(n) wryte rise	writiþ riseþ	wroot roos	writen risen	writun rysen
Class VII	chese	chesiþ	chees	chosen	chosen

PRONOUNS (i) PERSONAL.

Sing.	Nom.	y	þou	he, she, it.
	Obj.	me	þe	him, hir, it.
	Poss.	my	þi	his(e), her, his.
Plur.	Nom.	we	ȝe	þei.
	Obj.	us	ȝou	hem.
	Poss.	oure	ȝoure	þer, her.

[1] Cf. *felde* in (ii) above.

Note : (1) the dative occurs in *me þinkiþ* (= it seems to me) ; *Crist axide hem . . . what hem þou3t of þe kynd of Crist* ; (2) *bi himsilf* occasionally = by itself ; (3) *maugree his* = in spite of himself.

(ii) RELATIVE. *þat* for all cases and genders, e.g. *men þat here lyven.* Note *þe which* : *þe Confortour, þe which is þe Holy Goost . . . Who* is still mainly an interrogative or indefinite pronoun ; it is sometimes used compounded with *þat* : *who þat loveþ not Jesus Crist, he is cursid.*

(iii) REFLEXIVE. E. g. *þey shulden holden hem paied of sich form of sending. Crist, beerynge to him a cros, wente . . .*

(iv) DEMONSTRATIVE. Sing. *þis, þat* ; plur. *þes.*

APPENDIX B

I. WEST-MIDLAND PIECES

Lincolniensis, On the Seven Deadly Sins, Wyclif's Confessio, and the *Letter to Pope Urban,* which all occur in MS. Bodl. 647, are written in a marked W.Midland dialect. As the language of all these tracts is practically identical, only that of *Lincolniensis* has been analysed. In addition a few re-remarkable forms, occurring in the other pieces, have been noted.

LINCOLNIENSIS.

Inflexions :

VERB : 2 sing. *þou semes.*

3 sing. *seis, slepes, consentis.*

1st plur. *telle.*

3rd plur. *pursuen, schewen, contrarien.*

p.p. *cropun, knowen, punyschid, cleped, sought.*

imperative 2 sing. *seme* ; plur. *trowe.*

NOUNS : plur. *freris, munkes, prests.*

gen. sing. *Gods body, soule heele.*

DEF. ARTICLE : *þo.*

PRONOUNS : nom. plur. *þei* ; obj. *hom* ; gen. *hor.*

VOWELS : *o* and *u* occur frequently for E.Midland *a, e, au,* e. g. *bot, oght, connot, hor.*

SPELLING : *gh* written commonly instead of *3,* e. g. *noght, oght, sought, nyght.*

Note *c* in *horce.*

LETTER TO POPE URBAN. This possesses a single example of a nom. plural in '3', *meyne3*. Note the northern form *lastandly*.

WYCLIF'S CONFESSIO. 3rd sing. *hafs* = has. Nom. sing. *kirke*. Note the northern participles in *þo erþe trembled, faylande monnis voice*; *answerande for God*.

II. AVE MARIA [LAY FOLKS CATECHISM]

Dialect. S.Midland with westerly features.
Spelling. The most noteworthy feature is the use of *y* for E.Midland unstressed *e*. N.B. *chaumbyr, watyr.*
Inflexions. VERB : pres. indic. 3 sing. *savys, ys, contenys.*
pres. indic. plur. 1st pers. *suppose, take, trow.*
pres. indic. plur. 3rd pers. *gretyþ.*
pres. p. *livynge, dampnynge.*
strong p.p. *holpyn, knowyn.*
weak p.p. *divydyd.*
NOUNS : com. plur. *Seyntys, wordys*; also *maneris.*
gen. sing. *Elisabethis, Goddys.*
PRONOUNS : 3rd pers. sing. fem. *sche.*

Notice the W.Midland *u* in *furst, buth.*

APPENDIX C

NICHOLAS HEREFORD

HEREFORD possibly belonged to the Herefords of Sufton. 'By 1360 or thereabouts Nicholas was a widower and had gone up to Oxford.'[1] His career there is uncertain in its chronology, but in September 1374 he became bursar at Queen's and as such let certain rooms to Wyclif. Shortly afterwards he obtained from Gregory XI ·'the usual reward of a master's degree, "a dignity with prebend in Hereford"'.[2]

In the spring of 1380 Hereford probably began, at Wyclif's instigation, the translation of the Bible; in 1381 he obtained

---

[1] H. B. W. ii. 132.   [2] Ibid.

his doctorate, and in 1382 shared with Wyclif the condemnation of the Blackfriars Synod. He gave vent to his resentment
in *Lincolniensis* and *Vita Sacerdotum.* He also appealed from
the Synod to Urban VI and actually journeyed to Rome,[1]
where he was flung for his pains into St. Angelo's prison. In
1385 he was released by the Roman mob in an insurrection;
he subsequently returned to England, wrote various Lollard
tracts, and took part in Lollard missionary activity. He was
apprehended at Nottingham in 1386, but managed to escape
in 1387 and took part in a preaching campaign in the West of
England. 'Between the 30th March 1388 and the 16th
December 1389 Hereford is included in the many proclama-
tions and commissions issued by Richard for the destruction
of Lollard writings. He was then imprisoned by Courtenay,
probably along with Purvey, at Saltwood in Kent. There he
was "grievously tormented", so that he too in the end re-
lapsed, recanted at St. Paul's Cross, and became "a cursed
enemy of the truth".'[2] In other words, he obtained high
ecclesiastical office and persecuted his former associates.

Purvey was charged with being 'neither hot nor cold';
Hereford was always 'hot'—first in his advocacy of Lollardy,
afterwards in his zeal to suppress it.

WRITINGS BY HEREFORD

1. Bible Passages,[3] pp. 14, 16, 17.
2. *Lincolniensis*, pp. 38–40.
3. *On the Seven Deadly Sins*, p. 108.

The writer of *Lincolniensis* and *On the Seven Deadly Sins*
was a man of quick and warm feelings—as we know Hereford
to have been—who employed picturesque and outspoken
language: 'þo fend haves cast a boon and made þese houndes
to feght; and by a bal of talow lettis hom to berke'; he was
fond of alliteration: 'dryven wiþ þo devel for to drecche
men.' The tracts occur in MS. Bodl. 647, and are both
written in W.Midland—Hereford's native speech. The
vocabulary resembles that of the Old Testament in 'Hereford's' version, e. g. in the use of 'quyter' for 'filth'. We may

---

[1] This caused him to break off *the First Version* at *Baruch* iii. 20; see
p. 8, l. 4.

[2] H. B. W. ii. 136.   [3] See p. 7.

therefore assign these writings with a certain degree of confidence to Hereford.

Lincolniensis was probably written soon after the Blackfriars Synod of 1382. The second paragraph (see p. 38) seems an obvious reference to the persecution of Poor Priests set on foot by Courtenay late in 1382.[1]

On the Seven Deadly Sins is a tract on a familiar medieval topic which is made to serve as a basis for the expression of Lollard ideas. Workman ascribes the tract to the year of Hereford's return from Rome (1385). 'There is ', he says, ' a distinct allusion to the later fortunes of Urban VI in his identification of the Pope with Antichrist closed in a castle ; a wolf of ravin who "puts" many thousand lives for his own wretched life.'[2]

JOHN PURVEY

' Purvey was a native probably of Lathbury, a village near Newport Pagnell. The details of his career at Oxford are unknown, but Netter[3] acknowledges that he was " a noted doctor". From the date of his ordination—the spring of 1377—it may be inferred that he was born about 1354 and was at Oxford as a student when Wyclif's influence was at its highest. " As an invincible disciple", he " drunk deep " of " Wyclif's most secret teaching ", and became his " inseparable companion ",[4] living with him at Lutterworth as his secretary, and proving " the stout executor in all things of the doctrine of his master ".'[5]

Purvey probably took a hand in the completion of the First Version of the Bible after the flight of Hereford to Rome, and he seems to have commenced a revision of this version very shortly after its publication. He was still engaged on this when he joined Hereford and Aston in an unsuccessful preaching tour in the West of England in 1387. ' Between 1382 and 1395 he wrote a series of twelve tracts in English defending English Bibles. Of these the tenth was afterwards incorporated by him in his *General Prologue* as the epilogue to his gloss on *St. Matthew*.'[6]

---

[1] See note to p. 18, l. 17. [2] H. B. W. ii. 135.
[3] *Doctrinale*, i. 619. Netter also calls him ' pessimus glossator ', ibid. iii. 110; ' glossator Wicliffi ', iii. 127; and 'librarius lollardorum ', iii. 73 2.
[4] Knyghton, ii. 179. [5] H. B. W. ii. 137.
[6] Ibid. ii. 164.

In January 1395 Purvey assisted the Lollard knights in Parliament by supplying them with an appeal which they might lay before that assembly or bring to the notice of the citizens of London. He also wrote many tracts about this time, in one of which he set forth a scheme 'for utilizing the confiscated wealth of the Church for the establishing of fifteen new universities, a hundred alms-houses and the like, as well as 15,000 knights'.[1] As a result of this pamphleteering activity Purvey was arrested in 1400 and imprisoned in Archbishop Arundel's 'foul, unhonest prison' at Saltwood. He was brought before Convocation in the chapter-house of St. Paul's (28 Feb. 1401) and charged with promulgating heretical doctrines, and on 5 Mar. 1401 recanted. The next day he read a recantation at St. Paul's Cross and was rewarded in the following August by being presented to the living of West Hythe in Kent. He resigned this living 8 Oct. 1403, and after this his movements are uncertain.

'Shortly before 1405 a debate was held at Oxford on the lawfulness of vernacular Bibles, between the Dominican, Thomas Palmer, and a regent master, probably the noted Peter Payne. Purvey composed Latin and English records of the arguments advanced. The English version entitled *Against them that say that holy writ should not or may not be drawn into English* still exists.[2] . . . What afterwards became of Purvey we know not. That he was again thrown into gaol, possibly by Chichele . . . appears certain, for Netter tells us : "I have in my hands now a book taken from John Purvey in prison." In the third chapter of this work Purvey had claimed that women should be allowed to preach—a position which would justify the late date usually assigned to this imprisonment. It is possible that he was still living in 1427 when Netter wrote his *Doctrinale*, but this is uncertain. The chief evidence in favour is a doubtful monogram written in a small but clear hand, " J. Perney ", and also a Latin distich :

> "Christus homo factus
> J. P. prosperet actus"

both in a Lollard manuscript of 1427.

Thus Purvey passed away, either in some bishop's gaol or in hiding, with none to tell of his fate. From the way in which Netter speaks of him, as " one of great authority " among the Lollards, it is evident that his memory was reverenced and his

[1] See *Fasc. Ziz.*, p. 393.
[2] It has been called in this book Purvey's *Determination* : see pp. 21-3.

writings treasured. To-day, after long obscurity, he holds an established niche in the temple of fame as the translator of the first readable English Bible.'[1]

WRITINGS BY PURVEY

1. The *General Prologue* to the Second Version of the Bible, pp. 23–9.

2. Bible Passages, pp. 15–17.

3. Purvey's *Determination*, pp. 21–3

4. *Þe Grete Sentence of Curs Expouned* (?), pp. 34, 35, 77–9, 104, 105, 109, 110.

Purvey's *General Prologue* and *Revision of Hereford's Bible* are noticed in some detail on pp. 8, 9. His authorship of the *General Prologue* cannot be doubted.

'The *General Prologue* was written by a scholar of undoubted eminence; by a Lollard: and by a persecuted Lollard: and it was finished in 1395. Sufficient is known of all the Lollards to say with certainty that there was no other Lollard doctor or scholar holding out in 1395 except Purvey himself: they had all recanted earlier, and the date of their recantation is known.'[2]

Purvey's authorship of the able and interesting *Grete Sentence of Curs* is highly probable. From internal evidence[3] it seems to have been written in 1383. It manifests a close familiarity with Wyclif's ideas, and yet Wyclif's own authorship is precluded (1) by the manner of writing, which is less reasoned, more picturesque in phrase, and more profuse in proverbial sayings than an authentic work like *Þe Chirche and hir Membris*, written a few months later; (2) by the uncontroversial treatment of the Eucharist which appears in Cap. VII. On the other hand, Purvey was at this time Wyclif's secretary, drinking in 'his most secret teaching'. He would therefore be able to maintain that consonance with his master's ideas which is displayed in this fairly lengthy tract.

---

[1] H. B. W. ii. 169–70.

[2] Deanesly, p. 266. For a detailed examination of the *Prologue* see Deanesly, chap. x.

[3] There is a reference to the council of 'Þe erþe schakyng' (Blackfriars Synod, 1382), and Spenser's Crusade is indicated as being still in progress. See Cap. XXVI. S. E. W. iii. 329.

APPENDIX D

CHRONOLOGICAL TABLE

	1084 St. Bruno founds Grande Chartreuse.
	1098 Foundation of Cîteaux.
	1155 Arnold of Brescia burnt.
	1170 Murder of St. Thomas of Canterbury.
	1184 Waldensians condemned.
	1208 Crusade against Albigensians.
	1213 John surrenders to Papal legate.
	1221 The first Dominicans in England.
	1224 The first Franciscans in England.
	1274 Death of St. Thomas Aquinas.
	1305 Beginning of 'Babylonish Captivity' at Avignon.
	1307 First Statute of Provisors.
	1311 Council of Vienne.
	1316 John XXII Pope.
	1324 Marsiglio's *Defensor Pacis*.
	1327 Accession of Edward III.
	Simon Meopham Archbishop of Canterbury.
1328 c. Wyclif born at Wiclif-on-Tees.	
	1333 English tribute to Rome suspended.
	1340 John of Gaunt born.
	Chaucer born (?).
	Rolle's Psalter (?).
	1343 Parliament petitions King against papal provisions.
1345 (?) Wyclif goes to Oxford.	
	1346 Crecy.
	1349 Black Death.
	Thomas Bradwardine Archbishop of Canterbury.
	Simon Islip Archbishop of Canterbury.
	1350 Fitzralph's *de Pauperie Salvatoris*.
	1351 Second Statute of Provisors.
1353 c. Death of Wyclif's father. Wyclif becomes lord of manor.	1353 Statute of Praemunire.

1356 Poitiers.
1357 Edward refuses tribute to Pope.
Death of Ockham.

1358 (?) Wyclif Master of Balliol.

1360 Treaty of Bretegny.

1361 As Master of Balliol Wyclif appropriates living of Abbotsley.
Takes M.A.
Instituted Rector of Fillingham.
Leaves Balliol.

1361 John of Gaunt becomes Duke of Lancaster.
Great outbreak of pestilence in Oxford.

1362 Wyclif obtains prebend of Aust.

1362 Urban V Pope.

1363 Granted leave of absence to study at Oxford for degree in Theology.

1365 Appointed by Islip Warden of Canterbury Hall.

1365 Urban V demands John—tribute.
1366 Parliament refuses tribute to Pope.
Simon Langham Archbishop of Canterbury.

1367 Deposed by Langham.

1367 Wykeham Chancellor of England.

1368 Rector of Ludgershall.

1368 Wm. Wittlesey Archbishop of Canterbury.

1369 Takes B.D.
1370 Doubts on Eucharist begin.

1370 Sack of Limoges.
Gregory XI Pope.

1372 Takes D.D.
Enters service of Crown.

1374 Rector of Lutterworth.
Appointed to Bruges commission.

1374 Gregory XI demands tribute.

1375–6 *de Dominio Divino,
de Civili Dominio.*

1375 Simon of Sudbury Archbishop of Canterbury.
Courtenay Bishop of London.
1376 The Good Parliament.

1377 Trial in St. Paul's.
Gregory XI issues bulls against Wyclif and cites him to Rome.
Beginning of Poor Priests ?

1377 Richard II King.

1378 Tried at Lambeth.
de Veritate Sacrae Scripturae.
Appears before Gloucester Parliament.

1378 Urban VI Pope.
Haulay-Shakyl breach of sanctuary.
Great Schism.
Parliament meets at Gloucester.

1379	Beginning of Eucharistic controversy.		
1380 (?)	'Hereford' Bible begun. Wyclif condemned at Oxford.	1380	Poll-tax.
1381	Defends peasants in *Servantis and Lordis*.	1381	Peasants' Revolt. Wm. Courtenay Archbishop of Canterbury.
1382	Appeals to Parliament. Condemned by Blackfriars Synod. 'Hereford' Version finished? Suffers first stroke.	1382	Richard marries Anne of Bohemia, Letters patent against Lollard preachers.
1383	Attacks Spenser's Crusade.	1383	Spenser's Crusade. (May–Sept.)
1383-4	Many English and Latin works written.		
1384	Suffers second stroke (28 Dec.). Death (31 Dec.).		
		1388	Great Lollard activity.
		1393	Second Statute of Praemunire.
		1395	Lollard Activity in Parliament. Purvey's Revision completed.
		1399	John of Gaunt dies. Accession of Henry IV.
		1401	*de Haeretico Comburendo*.
		1407	Constitutions of Oxford.
1410	Wyclif's Works burnt at Carfax, Oxford.		
		1411	Convocation condemns 267 heresies of Wyclif.
1413	*Dialogus* and *Trialogus* burned at Rome.	1413	Death of Henry VI. Cobham condemned.
		1414	100 alien priories dissolved in England.
		1415	Council of Constance orders Wyclif's bones to be dug up. Hus burned.
		1417	Cobham burned.
1428	Wyclif's bones dug up by Fleming and burned.		

NOTES

I (PAGE 1)

PAGE **1**, line 12. *beestis skynnes* : i.e. the parchment on which papal bulls were written.

PAGE **2**, l. 10. *Crist spekiþ* : the doctrine of Necessitarianism.

l. 12. *Crist preieþ not* : a corollary of the doctrine of Predestination. If men are predestined by God for Hell, Christ's prayers cannot apply to them since His prayers must be granted.

l. 18. *þat bi þat hydeþ* : 'that conceals a spiritual meaning'.

l. 22. *Ever wite we* : see Introd., p. 68.

PAGE **3**, l. 9. *Go we nere* : a fundamental doctrine of Wyclif.

l. 16. *Lord, where þis Pope* : 'Lord, did this Pope Urban have', &c.

ll. 20–1. *a flye foot* : note the genitive *flye* ; see Appendix A.

l. 23. *þes newe ordris* : the four orders of friars, Carmelites, Augustinians, Dominicans (Jacobins), Franciscans (Minorites), were founded respectively in 1160, 1150, 1215, 1208. *Newe* means ' not mentioned in the New Testament ', and therefore unauthorized. The ordinances of the Pope are similarly condemned by Wyclif as *novelries* because they are not in the Bible.

l. 24. *þe Lawe* : i.e. the Bible.

PAGE **4**, l. 2. *Essees* : 'Essenes'; the form is possibly due to analogy with ' Phariseis and Saduceis '. ' Of the Essenes, whose centre was on the shores of the Dead Sea, the foundation principle was the old Gnostic or Persian idea of the malignity of matter. As part of their struggle to avoid pollution they rejected animal food, avoided wine and warm baths, and wore linen rather than wool because of its higher ceremonial purity.' Workman, *Evolution of the Monastic Ideal*, p. 91.

l. 3. *chanouns* : ' canons ', i. e. clerics attached to an abbey, collegiate church, or priory in receipt of church funds or *prebendae*. Wyclif was, for many years, a secular canon of the collegiate church of Westbury-on-Trim.

l. 9. *for to drynke* : ' to drink '.

l. 11. *3if man* : see Introd., p. 60.

l. 16. *Whoevere failliþ* : this idea, like the preceding one, is connected with Wyclif's theory of ' Dominion ' and doctrine of Predestination. Only those ' elected to bliss ' are in a ' state of grace ' ; and only they have a just title to their worldly goods.

PAGE **5**, l. 5. *O leprous man* : it should be remembered that leprosy was a very real thing in the England of Wyclif's day.

ll. 11–12. *to more werre* : ' to the end of further warfare '.

l. 14. *Þis Baptist*: Wyclif was called by his contemporaries *Doctor Evangelicus* because he stressed the authority of Scripture. To him earthly learning sank into insignificance compared with the inspired teaching of the Bible, and one of his chief Latin works, *de Veritate Sacrae Scripturae*, is a defence of Holy Scripture. But it should not be supposed that Wyclif seriously questioned the authority of Aristotle or of Plato, any more than other thinkers of his time. Plato, he considers, is to be preferred to Aristotle 'because he proceeds from the immutable to the fluctuating, while Aristotle reverses the process'.

l. 17. *is to dampne*: 'is to be condemned'.

l. 18. *han anoþer knowing*: 'have a different kind of know-ledge'.

II (PAGE 6)

PAGE 11, l. 28. *after his owne virtue*: A.V. 'according to his several ability'. Vulg. *secundum propriam virtutem*.

l. 31. *wrouȝte in hem*: Vulg. *operatus est in eis*.

PAGE 12, l. 6. *Wel be þe*: Vulg. *euge*. A.V. 'well done'.

l. 23. *bishopis*: Vulg. *pontifices*. A.V. 'chief priests'.

l. 24. *Picche Him*: Vulg. *Cruci-fige*.

PAGE 13, l. 2. *to leeve þee*: Vulg. *dimittere*. A.V. 'release'.

l. 8. *aȝenseiþ*: Vulg. *contradicit*.

ll. 9–10. *for domesman*: Vulg. *pro tribunali*. A.V. 'on the judgement-seat'.

l. 10. *Licostratos*: Vulg. *Lithostrotus*. A.V. 'The Pavement'.

l. 11. *Friday of Pask*: Wyclif reckoned according to ecclesias-tical time; therefore Friday would commence at sunset on Thurs-day.

l. 34. *above altogidere*: Vulg. *desuper contexta per totum*. A.V. 'from the top throughout'.

PAGE 14, l. 7. *into his modir*. A mistranslation. Vulg. *accepit eam discipulus in sua*.

l. 9. *were endid*: 'might be fulfilled'.

l. 11. *putting it aboute wiþ isope*: Vulg. *hysopo circumponentes*.

l. 24. *folk shulen wandre*: A.V. 'the nations (Gentiles) shall come'.

PAGE 15, ll. 9–10. *Þe flowinge of camels*: A.V. 'the multitude of camels'. Vulg. *Inundacio camelorum operiet te*.

PAGE 17, l. 6. The defects of Hereford's slavish following of the Vulgate are most apparent in this passage. 'Adversaries', for instance, might be either the subject or the object of the sentence, while the retention of the Latin participles renders the style thoroughly un-English.

ll. 9–10. *slayn the dwellers of it*: an absolute construction, with which Purvey's much neater method of rendering by a 'when' clause should be compared; see his advice on translation, *infra*, pp. 26-9.

ll. 19-20. *he baar hevye, or unworthili*: Vulg. *indigne tulit.*

PAGE 18. Sect. C. 'At one time there were not many parts of England in which lollard gentry could not be found. In the west, when Hereford, Aston, and Purvey preached in the churchyards, the knight of the manor often stood by armed for greater security. . . . Other lollard gentry " who will help poor priests in right of God's law " were also to be found, in spite of the law which put their lands under edict.' H. W. B. ii. 380.

l. 8. *for Anticrist*: 'because of Antichrist'.

l. 17. *oo greet Bishop*: probably William Courtenay, Archbishop of Canterbury, 1381-96; he induced Richard II to commence a systematic persecution of the Lollards in 1382.

l. 23. *wiþouten fablis.* See Introd., p. 41.

ll. 28-9. *þis lordship shal be taken*: see Introd., p. 60.

l. 32. *fals lawe þat þei han made*: i. e. Canon Law, which is not to be found in ' Goddis lawe ' and is therefore false or a ' novelrie '.

l. 33. *Emperours bishopis*: bishops appointed by the Emperor for secular services which they continued to perform. They were often more expert in civil law than in canon law or theology.

l. 34. *Pharisees*: cf. *Sermons*, S. E. W. i. 7 : ' And þes religiouse [monks] ben Pharisees, for þei ben divydid fro þe comoun maner of lyvynge bi her rotun rytys as Pharisees weren.'

possessioners: Wyclif's term for clerics holding property of any kind.

beggeris: ' friars ' (mendicants).

PAGE 19. l. 7. *nygromansye*: Wyclif apparently uses this word merely as a term of condemnation, not literally. Matthew (*English Works of Wyclif*) cites his tract ' De Contrarietate duorum Dominorum : *potest quelibet ars falsa vel non fundata in lege Domini ars nigromantica benedici*'.

l. 14. *Wit Sunday*: a philological guess ; ' Whit Sunday' actually means ' White Sunday '.

l. 24. *þe newe law*: the New Testament.

l. 31. *þe Bible in Freynsch*: for French verse translations in the Middle Ages see J. Bonnard, *Les Traductions de la Bible en Vers Français au Moyen Âge* (Paris, 1884) ; for prose renderings S. Berger, *La Bible Française au Moyen Âge* (Paris, 1884).

PAGE 20, l. 2. *þe pley of ȝork*: The York Play of the Paternoster unfortunately has not survived, but we know that it was regularly performed by the ' Guild of the Lord's Prayer '.

PAGE 21, l. 1. *Worschipful Bede*: Bæda (*c.* 673-735), historian and scholar, was for practically the whole of his life an inmate of Wearmouth and Jarrow monasteries. He wrote, besides his *Historia Ecclesiastica*, about forty other works, chiefly bible commentaries. He is the only authority for the life of St. Aidan, all later accounts being only amplifications of his. *Worschipful* is a rendering of

Venerabile, the epithet commonly applied to Bede since about a century after his death.

l. 2. *Seint Oswold*: Oswald (*c.* 605–42), King of Northumbria, had been converted to Christianity in Iona, whither he had fled on his father's death. After his return to Northumbria in 634, he sent to Iona for missionaries to convert his people, but the first of these were unsuccessful. Then in 635, *Aidan* was sent, and he became first bishop of Lindisfarne, and founder of the Northumbrian church. He was a close friend of King Oswald, who, as Wyclif relates, acted as his interpreter when he began to teach in Northumbria.

l. 10. *James Merland*: Jakob van Maerlant, a Dutch poet, who had made, in 1271, a verse translation of Peter Comestor's *Historia Scholastica*, a work containing much of the Bible. This he called *Rijmbibel.* (Deanesly, pp. 71–5.)

l. 17. *Sistrence* (i. e. *Cestrensis* ' of Chester '). Ranulph Higden, a monk of St. Werburgh's, Chester, who wrote the *Polychronicon*, translated into English by John of Trevisa. The passage referred to reads, in this translation (Rolls' Series, v. 224) :
' *For sevene wekes contynualliche his stomak hadd indignacioun of mete and drynke, so þat unnepe he myȝte eny mete holde and was streiȝt and schort breþed. But for al þat he sparede not þe travayle of lettrure and of bookes, bote everiche day, among þe detty* [debitum] *travaylle of service and of psalmes, he tauȝte his disciples in lessouns and in questiouns, and he tornede Seynt Iohn his gospel into Englisshe, and seide, " Lerneþ, my smale children, while I am wiþ ȝou, I wot nouȝt how longe I schal wiþ ȝow abyde".*'

l. 24. *A man of Loundoun . . . hadde a Bible* : H. B. W. ii. 189 suggests that this bible was an Anglo-Saxon version ; it is unlikely that any complete Middle English translation preceded that of Wyclif.

l. 29. *opone scolis* : public or common schools.

l. 30. *turnede the best lawes* : at the beginning of his laws Alfred placed the Mosaic Civil Code, Exodus xx–xxiii.

l. 33. *Richerde Ermyte*: Richard Rolle of Hampole, near Doncaster ; a hermit and mystic, who died in 1349. He wrote a prose version of the Psalms with a lengthy commentary. Deanesly, p. 442, suggests that *lessouns of Dirige* are Rolle's Latin *Novem lectiones mortuorum*. *Dirige* is the first word in the antiphon of the Matins of the Dead : *Dirige, Domine, Deus meus, in conspectu tuo vitam meam.*

PAGE **22,** l. 1. *sire Wiliam Thorisby* : see note on *Lay Folks' Catechism*, p. 165.

l. 12. *Ne auferas* : Ps. 119. 43.

ll. 18–19. *into a Parliment*, &c. : this Parliament met 27 Jan. 1395 ; to it the Lollards presented the famous *XII Conclusions*.

l. 23. *Duke of Lancastre* : John of Gaunt, Wyclif's patron during his political career.

l. 31. *Thomas Arrundel*: Arundel, Archbishop of Canterbury, 1396–1414; the determined foe of Lollards, stamped out Lollardy at Oxford by his Constitutions of 1407. H. B. W. ii. 340–59.

l. 33. *the biriyng of Quene Anne*: i. e. Anne of Bohemia, the young wife of Richard II. She died in 1394.

PAGE 23, l. 10. *Austyn*: St. Augustine of Hippo (A. D. 354–430), author of the *Confessions* and *de Civitate Dei*, was the greatest single influence on the medieval church. For the sermon see Migne, *Opera August.* vi. 310.

l. 14. *as Petir seide*: John vi. 68.

PAGE 24, l. 12. *leet hange him*: 'caused him to be hanged'.

l. 36. *to us Latyns*: 'to us who use the Vulgate'.

PAGE 25, l. 1. *Ebreu*: Purvey may have got his knowledge of the difference between the Vulgate and the Hebrew either from De Lyra (see note to p. 26, l. 28) or from the Oxford scholar, Adam Easton.

ll. 4-5. *convicte Jewis therbi*: because it 'comprehendith al the Elde and Newe Testament and techith pleynly the mysteries of the Trinité', &c.

ll. 20-1. *as fro uniust possessouris*: the medieval schoolmen were much concerned to reconcile the teaching of Plato and Aristotle with that of the Bible, and while they recognized the value of the ethical teaching of the great Greeks, were somewhat disturbed in their minds because this teaching preceded that of Christ.

ll. 25-6. *treuthis the filosueris founden not*: i. e. the philosophers did not fashion these ethical truths for themselves: God had laid them ready to be found.

l. 28. *Cipr.an*: Bishop of Carthage, †14 Sept. 258.

l. 29. *Lactancius*: a Christian apologist of the beginning of the fourth century.

Victorinus: bishop and martyr; mentioned by Jerome as having written commentaries on Genesis, Exodus, &c.

Illarie: probably St. Hilary, the celebrated bishop and theologian, †368. He wrote, among other works, *Commentarii in Psalmos*.

PAGE 26, ll. 6-7. *doon his fourme in art*: see Introd., p. xiv. The normal course in arts took seven years, after which a successful scholar became a Regent Master, and was allowed to enter on a seven years' course in Theology.

l. 23. *this symple creature*: i. e. Purvey himself. Elsewhere he refers to himself as 'a sinful caitiff', 'this scribler', 'poor caitiff', 'a simple creature of God'. Deanesly, pp. 276, 277.

l. 25. *comune glosis*: commentaries. 'The standard commentary ...known as the Gloss, was compiled by Walafrid Strabo, abbot of Reichenau, in the ninth century.' *Legacy of the Middle Ages*, 42.

l. 28. *Lire*: Nicholas de Lyra, a Norman Franciscan (†1340), wrote famous glosses on the Bible which Purvey made considerable use of. Lyra was a good Hebraist and demonstrated the necessity for the study of Hebrew. Like Wyclif he favoured the literal interpretation of Scripture.

l. 30. *elde dyvynis*: Wyclif was no doubt one. Purvey nowhere mentions the name of Wyclif.

PAGE **27**, l. 3. *not oneli aftir the wordis*: as in 'Hereford's' version.

l. 9. *resolucions*: the word is used in the literal Latin sense of 'loosening'; i.e. the compressed structure of the ablative absolute is 'loosened' into a subordinate clause.

PAGE **28**, l. 3. *the English Bible late translatid*: a reference to 'Hereford's' version.

l. 4. *Jerom*: author of the Vulgate, prefaced by the *Prologus Galeatus*, which Purvey's *General Prologue* is written in imitation of.

l. 18. *King Alured that foundide Oxenford*: cf. p. 21.

l. 21. *Frenshemen, Beemers and Britons*: Frenchmen, Bohemians (Czechs), and Welshmen. For the French Bible see note to p. 19, l. 31; for the Bohemian see Count Lutzow, *Life of John Hus*, p. 297; parts of the Bible had been translated into Bohemian by various writers by the first half of the fourteenth century. Nothing is known of a Welsh version; possibly this is a mistake due to some Latin reference to a 'Gallicum Biblum', with 'Gallicum' mistranslated as 'Gaelic'.

l. 30. *Cristene Teching*: *de Doctrina Christiana*, Lib. ii, Cap. 12; Migne, Tom. 3.

ll. 32–3. *that place of the Salme*: really Prov. i. 16 or Isaiah lix. 7 and 8.

l. 34. *the Greek word*: ὀξύς.

III (PAGE 30)

PAGE **31**, l. 19. *so many, as men seien*: 'This very precise calculation appears to be taken from the *de Civitate Dei* of St. Augustine, who (Lib. xvi, Cap. 3–9), reckoning the posterity of Shem at 27, that of Ham at 31, and that of Japhet at 15 (Gen. x), considers that the human race after the flood, was divided into 73, or rather, as he undertakes to prove by a particular argument, into 72 nations. Till the building of the tower of Babel, these nations had one common language; but after the dispersion which followed as a penal infliction upon that event, there came to be as many languages as there were nations' [Arnold's Note. S. E. W. i. 175.]

PAGE **32**, l. 3. *whanne þei ben preestis*: i.e. when they belong to the elect.

l. 32. *Ripe corn is moche*: Luke x. 2.

PAGE **33**, ll. 35–6. *oþer to turne to oþer peple*: 'either by turning (going) to other people or by working as Paul did'.

PAGE **34**, l. 11. *Ne take þei not of Cristis lyf*: 'let them not take the example of Christ's life to avoid work'.

Notes 159

l. 16. *how Petir lyvede* : ' He is lodged in the house of one Simon, a tanner, by the sea side.' Acts x. 32. 'Of a truth I perceive that God is no respecter of persons : but in every nation he that feareth him, and worketh righteousness, is acceptable to him.' Acts x. 34.

PAGE 35, ll. 1–2. *as Peter witnessep* : Acts iii. 6.

l. 7. *And Seynt Bernard writip* : in the powerful treatise *de Consideratione* (Lib. iv, Cap. iii), written to Pope Eugenius III.

PAGE 36, ll. 11–12. *kild as worse pan peves* : see p. 45.

l. 19. *Phariseis* : see note to p. 18, l. 34.

l. 22. *pe Sixte, wip Clementyns* : ' The compilation of the *Sixth Book of the Decretals* was made by order of Boniface VIII, and promulgated by him in 1297. . . .The *Clementines* were first published by Clement V at the Council of Vienne in 1312 ; they were afterwards given out in a fully digested form by John XXII in 1316. They treat of various points of canon law and church discipline and are supplementary to the *Sextus'* [Arnold. S. E. W. i. 205 note].

l. 28. *falsehede is more suspect* : ' the adducing of such laws causes those who use them to be all the more suspected of falseness '.

l. 30. *our modyr* : the true Church, *mater ecclesia*.

PAGE 38, l. 1. *Lincolniensis generaliter* : 'Grosseteste thus describes the friar and the monk who has left his cloister. Such a one, he says, is like a corpse come out of its tomb, wrapped in grave-clothes and driven forth among men by the devil '. Grosseteste was Bishop of Lincoln 1235–53, and first Chancellor of Oxford. His ' sharpe pistle' to ' Master Innocent' (the Pope's representative in England) was one of the most-quoted medieval documents, especially by Wyclif and Hus.

PAGE 39, ll. 4–5. *pei grucched*: a sudden transition to the members of the Blackfriars Synod of 1382, at which Wyclif's views on the Eucharist were condemned. See note to p. 88, ll. 2–3.

ll. 13–14. *nerepoles knyghtes schulde more scharply stonde* : this appeal is typical of the attitude of the early Lollards ; cf. II C. *Oo Confort is of Kny3ttis*.

ll. 17–18. *by Seynt Jon Baptist* : Luke iii. 14. The Vulgate has *milites* which often means *knights*.

l. 19. *Mauris* : probably St. Maurus, founder and abbot of the Benedictine monastery of St. Maur-sur-Loire, †584. The Benedictine ' rule' was notable for its severity. Cf. Chaucer, *Prologue*, 173 f :

> *The reule of seint Maure or of seint Beneit,*
> *Bycause that it was old and somdel streit,*
> *This ilke monk leet olde thinges pace,*
> *And held after the newe world the space.*

l. 31. *visitynge of prisouns* : St. Matt. xxv. 43 f.

PAGE 40, ll. 4–5. *prestes are dampnable* : ' priests are worthy of condemnation, if, when God shows them perils by which He means to punish the people, they keep them hidden'. *þo prophete* is apparently Jonah, whose story exemplifies the maxim.

IV (PAGE 41)

PAGE **43,** ll. 21-2. *here may Grekes be moved*: the question of the 'double procession' (i. e. of a procession from the Father through the Son, or a procession from Father and Son equally) had been a matter of keen debate between the Eastern (Greek) Church and the Western (Latin) Church ever since the Second General Council of 381. *Life of St. Anselm*, p. 180.

ll. 23-4. *þe toon seiþ Crist*: Christ says the one thing, i. e. that the Comforter comes from the Father; *and leveþ þe toþer*, and leaves the question as to whether it comes from Himself also.

PAGE **44,** ll. 25-6. *viker of Thomas in Inde*: the Christians found in Malabar by St. Francis Xavier called themselves 'Christians of St. Thomas', but the missionary work in Malabar was probably performed not by St. Thomas but by a Nestorian monk.

l. 26. *viker of Poul in Grees*: Head of the Greek Church. Wyclif seems to regard Paul as head of the Greek Church just as Peter was head of the Latin (Roman) Church.

ll. 26-7. *Soudan of Babilon*: the head of Mohammedanism.

l. 27. *þe rote*, &c.: this is one of the many references in Wyclif's works to the acceptance by Pope Sylvester of the Donation of Constantine.

PAGE **45,** l. 10. *þat 3e be not sclaundrid*: John xvi. 1. The word 'slander' is here used in the meaning 'to be a stumbling-block to, cause to stumble'.

ll. 26-7. *Sum men be sumnyd to Rome*: this refers very probably to Nicholas Hereford. See Appendix C.

l. 29. *freris killen þer owen breþeren*: see Introd., p. xxxiii.

l. 32. *þei defenden*: 'they maintain that it is lawful and praiseworthy for priests to fight in a cause which they pretend is God's'.

l. 37. *as unable*: 'as being incompetent'.

PAGE **46,** l. 17. *I ese gospellis ben passid*: the previous eleven sermons had dealt with *Feestis of Many Martiris*.

ll. 26-7. *as creaturis tellen a man his God*: 'as created beings reveal God to man, so natural phenomena [i.e. sleep, &c.] show men how they should serve God'.

PAGE **47,** l. 10. *ouþer worching or suffring*: 'either actively or passively'.

l. 12. *out-wittis*: the five senses. The 'outer wits' were so called to distinguish them from the five 'inner wits'; these, according to Wyclif, were 'Wyl, Resoun, Mynd, Ymaginacioun, and Thogth'.

PAGE **50,** l. 10. *deeþ is þe þridde þing*, &c.: cf. 'And so men seien þat þree þingis wole God have hid to men. God wole þat tyme of deþ be comunli unknowun to men, and whanne þe dai of dome shal be ... þe þridde þing ... is privyté of his ordenaynce, wheþer God have ordeyned to save þes men or ellis to dampne hem for her synne.' S. E. W. i. 236.

PAGE 51, l. 21. *telde hem unablité of her kyn* : 'showed to them the inability of their kin [to receive the Gospel]'.

PAGE 53, ll. 1–2. *popis wolen have þe firste fruytis* : 'against first-fruits Wyclif, with a personal interest in the matter, protested as " an unheard of thing, a damnable custom newly introduced ", as he rightly affirmed, by John XXII.' H. B. W. ii. 86.

ll. 2–3. *bishopis an hundrid shillingis* : some amounts recorded as having been paid are, for dedicating a church, 5 marks, an altar 40*s*., a churchyard £5. See *Registrum Sede Vacante* (Worc. Hist. Soc.) and Grandisson's *Register*, ed. Hingeston-Randolph, 1897.

PAGE 54, l. 6. *false ȝyvynge to alyens* : see Introd., p. xvi.

l. 10. *þes chirches þat ben aproprid* : i. e. parishes whose tithes were 'impropriated' to monastic communities who replaced the rector by a vicar.

l. 38. *and go to scole* : Wyclif himself, while an incumbent of Lutterworth and Ludgershall, studied at Oxford for his doctorate.

PAGE 55, ll. 16–17. *Bi my double kynde* : i. e. as God and man.

PAGE 56, l. 27. *þat þing þat holdiþ alle* : i. e. the Holy Spirit.

haþ science of vois : 'hath skill to produce a voice'.

PAGE 58, l. 8. *Him likeþ* : *Him* is dative case.

l. 12. *As Moyses heied* : Numbers xxi. 6–9.

V (PAGE 60)

PAGE 62, l. 17. *bi skile* : ' when put to the test of reason '.

l. 25. *þis lord suffriþ hee noȝt* : note the repetition of the grammatical subject.

PAGE 63, ll. 8–9. *þat makiþ a man servaunt to nouȝt* : 'good ' to Wyclif is 'esse '; 'sin ' is 'deesse ' or 'deficere in moribus ', cf. *de Dominio Divino*, Cap. 14.

l. 17. *þis grete chartre* : i.e. ' Goddis lawe ', the Bible.

PAGE 64, l. 5. *in þe Parlement* : which assembled 7 May 1382 ; see Introd., p.   .

ll. 10–11. *of what kynne privat sectis* : i. e. of whichever of the various orders of friars and monks.

PAGE 65, l. 3. *whoos contrarie freres han determined opinly* : ' the contrary of which friars have publicly asserted '. To ' determine', in scholastic language, meant to maintain a thesis in the teeth of argument.

l. 5. *Coventré* : Coventry at this time (1382) was a noted centre of Lollardy and disaffection. Swynderby in the autumn of 1382 went there from Leicester and stayed a year, busying himself in preaching Lollard doctrines. Coventry was also the place where John Ball was apprehended in July 1381.

ll. 7–8. *seculer lordis ... temporal goodis* : this is the 17th of the 24 *Conclusions* condemned by the Council of London. *Fasc. Ziz.*, p. 280.

ll. 8–9. *But siþ oure kyng haþ don so* : see *de Ecclesia* 332. Wyclif there gives instances of the recent confiscation of the temporalities of Bishops Bateman, Grandisson, and Lyle, and Richard's confiscation of alien priories. H. B. W. i. 264.

l. 26. *at his owne wille to ȝeve* : on the death of a bishop his temporalities passed for the time being into the hands of the king.

PAGE **66**, l. 4. *Crist biddiþ þe Iewis* : John vii. 24.

VI (PAGE 67)

PAGE **69**, l. 17. *God seiþ bi Ieremye* : Jer. xxv. 4.

l. 20. *God seiþ by Salomon* : Prov. i. 20–8.

PAGE **70**, l. 2. *taken over* : ' believe also '.

l. 29. *dyvysioun of þes Popis* : the Great Schism of 1378. Urban VI (1378–89) had only been elected Pope (8 April) a few months when the cardinals, who were mostly French and desirous of returning to Avignon, elected an Antipope Clement VII (30 Sept. 1378). See Introd., p. xxvi.

l. 30. *bi Poul* : Rom. viii. 28.

l. 33. *Y shal putte enemyté* : Gen. iii. 15.

PAGE **71**, l. 7. *Crist was most pore man*, &c. : the contrast between Christ and the Pope which now follows closely resembles that contained in ' Exposicio Textus Matthei xxiv, Cap. iii ' (*Op. Min.* 361).

PAGE **72**, l. 27. *nou he is neþer Pope ne prelat* : ' He ' is here used in the sense ' a man ', ' one '.

l. 33. *shewide it out* : ' proclaimed it '.

PAGE **73**, l. 3. *bitokeniþ wundirful* : Matthew suggests that Wyclif connected *Papa* with the Greek interjection of surprise' παπαί.

l. 19. *Seynt Petre dwelte* : Acts x. 6.

PAGE **74**, l. 24. *anentis assoyling* : cf. *Þe Chirche and hir Membris*, p. 130.

PAGE **75**, l. 14. *and þus he shal not dwelle* : i.e. he shall escape Purgatory by virtue of the Pope's indulgence.

l. 31. *be þis hert :* ' et in hoc legem evangelii omnes partes scripture alias excedentem '.

PAGE **76**, ll. 4–5. *for þus techis . . . sentence of Crist* : not in the Latin.

ll. 7–8. *boþe in spirit and in havyng :* ' omnem dominacionem mundanum abiciens '.

ll. 8–15. *for Crist seis . . . worldly hynesse* : the Latin has merely a reference to Matt. viii. 20 and 2 Cor. viii. 9.

ll. 19–22. *And Petir and Poule . . . fro Jesus Crist* : not in the Latin.

ll. 25–9. *til þo fende . . . ben partyneris* : not in the Latin.

l. 31. *if hit be skilful* : ' si oporteat '.

PAGE 77, l. 2. *he is an open Anticrist*: this is the last sentence of the Latin.

ll. 3–4. *And merciful entent . . . Sathanas*: not in the Latin.

ll. 5–7. *bot if he aske . . . Anticrist*: not in the Latin.

l. 11. *his olde holy entent*: 'sicut inceperat'.

ll. 12–14. *And Crist . . . fendis*: not in the Latin.

PAGE 78, ll. 4–5. *Simon Magus*: Acts viii. 18. See p. 122, l. 28.

l. 10. *collacion . . . institucion . . . induction*: 'institution', in canon law, is the final act by which a person, elected by a chapter, is appointed to a benefice; 'collation' differs from 'institution' in that it proceeds of the bishop's own motion; 'induction' is the formal ceremony by which a clerk already 'instituted' is installed in possession of a benefice.

PAGE 79, l. 5. *dede lede*: the leaden seal on a papal order.

ll. 26–7. *in Silvestris tyme*: Silvester, Bishop of Rome 314–35; supposed to have cured the Emperor Constantine of leprosy and to have been granted in return the temporal dominion over Rome and a great part of Italy.

PAGE 80, l. 6. *bi dyvysiouns and opere iapis*: 'by formal arrangement of the subject-matter and other foolish devices'. Wyclif desired that the preacher's discourse should follow the gospel of the day, verse by verse, a method known as 'postillization'.

PAGE 81, l. 5. *þey ben pure almes*: 'Omnes curati secundum legem domini debent pure vivere de corporali elemosina subditorum . . . patet, quod Christus eam cepit a devotis viris et feminis.' *de Off. Past.*

ll. 16–17. *Luk in his gospel*: Luke ix.

PAGE 82, l. 2. *but þey weren holdun*: 'but they were supposed in return to slay beasts and do hard service'.

PAGE 83, l. 18. *to his castel*: 'Antichrist has adopted a bold manner of providing for his castle'.

PAGE 84, l. 9. *Cayms castels*: 'caym' = 'Cain'; it is found by the initial letters of the four proper names Carmelites, Augustinians, Jacobins, Minorites. See note to p. 3, l. 23.

Cf. the 'Song against the Friars', Wright, *Political Poems and Songs*, Rolls' Series, vol. i. 266:

> *Nou se the sothe whedre it be swa,*
> *That frer Carmes come of a k.,*
> *The frer Augstynes come of a.,*
> *Frer Jacobynes of i.,*
> *Of m. comen the frer Menours ;*
> *Thus grounded Caym thes four ordours.*

l. 10. *Salomons temple*: cf. *de Ecclesia* 97 In cantu ecclesie die Dedicacionis sic canitur:

> *Rex Salomon fecit templum*
> *Cuius instar et exemplum*
> *Christus et ecclesia.*

l. 20. *collegies of studies* : it is interesting to note that Wyclif had himself, as Master of Balliol, impropriated the living of Abbotsley 7 April 1361. ' The document is still extant in which Wyclif reports on the 9th April 1361 that he has taken possession of the church and received oblations and " young pigeons " from the parishioners . . . . [The Vicar] was to retain sixty acres of glebe land, an annual pension from Balliol of " sixty pence sterling ", the usual fees and lesser tithes, together with " a suitable dwelling to be kept furnished containing a reception room, a sleeping chamber, a kitchen, a stable, and a granary ".' H. W. B. i. 79.

PAGE **85,** l. 11. *Non tamen,* &c. : ' I will not dare to assert that the body of Christ is that bread in essence or substance, corporally or identically. . . . For we believe that the body of Christ is present in the consecrated Host in three ways, that is, virtually, spiritually, and sacramentally.'

l. 17. *Here after þis witt* : Wyclif begins his sermon by relating the story of the visit of the two Marys to the sepulchre (Matt. xxviii). Then he says, ' Ech word of þis gospel bereþ grete mysterie' and proceeds to expound. In the same way men may ' large þis gospel ', i. e. go on expounding.

l. 30. *as Poul seiþ* : the reference is probably to 1 Cor. xi. 26 ff.

l. 31. *seiþ Austyn* : Serm. 272, vol. v, p. 1104, Benedictine edition : *Ista, fratres, ideo dicuntur sacramenta, quia in eis aliud videtur, aliud intelligitur. Quod videtur, speciem habet corporalem ; quod intelligitur, fructum habet spiritalem.* Quoted by Arnold.

PAGE **86,** l. 1. *bifore þe fend was losid* : see Rev. xx. 2, 3. It was a popular belief among various sects that the fiend had actually been released from his captivity in A. D. 1000.

l. 2. *accident wiþouten suget* : see Sectional Introd., p. 68.

l. 14. *herfore seiþ Poul* : 1 Cor. xi. 26 f.

l. 21. *as Austyn declariþ* : Serm. 229. The ' foure poyntes' are : ' threshing, which answers to conversion by preaching ; grinding, which represents the discipline of fasting and exorcism ; mixing with water, which is Baptism ; and baking, which corresponds to the flames kindled in souls by the Holy Ghost '. Arnold. S. E. W. i. 134.

PAGE **87,** ll. 15–16. *accydent wiþouten subgett* : see p. 68.

ll. 18–19. *by wittenesse of Jerome* : MS. H H. reads ' of Johan '. This seems the better reading, but note *Fasc. Ziz.*, p. 128, where Jerome is adduced as the *quintus testis*. ' Nos,' inquit, ' audiamus panem quem fregit Dominus . . . esse corpus Domini Salvatoris, ipso dicente . . . hoc est corpus meum.'

l. 20. *sithen þo fende was loused* : Rev. xx. 2 f.

PAGE **88,** ll. 2–3. *þis counseil . . . was wiþ erthe dyn* : the Council of Blackfriars which met 17 May 1382. ' As the proceedings were coming to an end, between two and three in the afternoon, a terrific earthquake was felt all over England but especially in

Kent. . . . Some of the bishops in their terror desired to adjourn the court. But Courtenay, " a valiant man and zealous for the Church of God reassured them. . . . The earthquake did indeed portend a purging of the realm from heresies." . . . Courtenay's happy inspiration saved the synod. Wyclif found it necessary to publish at once an interpretation in an opposite sense. The "earth-din", he maintained, was the outcry of the world against heretic prelates.' [H. B. W. ii. 267.] Wyclif ever afterwards dubbed the meeting the ' Earthquake Council ', ' concilium terraemotus ' [*Trialogus* 374]. In *Political Poems and Songs*, i. 250, occurs an interesting poem, ' On the Earthquake of 1382 ' ; one verse indicates the violence of the earthquake :

> *For sothe this was a Lord to drede*
> *So sodeynly mad mon agast ;*
> *Of gold and selver thei tok non hede,*
> *But out of ther houses ful sone thei past.*
> *Chaumbres, chymeneys, al to-barst,*
> *Churches, steples, to grounde hit cast ;*
> *And al was for warnyng to be ware.*

l. 5. *faylande monnis voice* : i. e. the earth spoke since man did not.

ll. 10–11. *aske . . . þis office* : ' ask clerics concerning this sacrament '.

PAGES **88–90**. *The Lay Folks Catechism* : Archbishop Thoresby of York, †1373, ' in order to improve the status of his parish priests and vicars ordered a catechism of the simplest character to be issued both in Latin and in English so as to be understood by all. . . . Thoresby's Instruction, or as it is more often called, *Lay Folks' Catechism* [E.E.T.S. 1901], was translated, or rather paraphrased, into rude verse by John de Gaytrik, a monk of St. Mary's Abbey. . . . Wyclif saw its value both for his own order of Poor Priests and for the instruction of the people. In consequence there was issued a version of Gaytrik's manual freely interpolated with Wyclif's views, sometimes with whole passages from his tracts.' [H. B. W. ii. 158.]

PAGE **88**, l. 29. *wordys of Gabriel* : Luke i. 26 f.

PAGE **89**, l. 2. *Elysabeth spake* : Luke i. 42 f.

l. 22. *Seynt Stevyn* : Acts vi. 8 f.

l. 24. *þe chaumbyr of his manhed* : Mary is thus described because in her womb Christ's fleshly body took shape.

PAGE **90**, l. 17. *as Ambrose* : ' in 386 St. Ambrose, besieged in the Portian Church at Milan by Arian sectaries, kept his followers occupied and in good heart by introducing the Eastern practice of singing hymns and antiphons. See St. Augustine's *Confessions*, Bk. ix, c. 7.' [K.S.]

l. 23. *placebo* : ' Vespers of the Dead, named from the first word of the antiphon, " Placebo Domino in regione vivorum " (Ps. cxiv. 9)'.

dirige : ' Matins of the Dead, named from the first word of the antiphon, " Dirige, Domine, Deus meus, in conspectu tuo viam meam (Psalm v. 9). Hence our word " dirge ".'

comendacion : ' an office in which the souls of the dead are commended to God '. [K. S.]

l. 24. *matynes of Oure Lady* : ' one of the services in honour of the Virgin introduced in the Middle Ages'.

The whole question of these accretions to the Church Services is dealt with by the late Mr. Edmund Bishop, in his essay introductory to the E.E.T.S.'s edition of the *Prymer*, since reprinted with additional notes in his *Liturgica Historica* (Oxford 1918), p. 211 f. [K. S.]

ll. 29–30. *deschaunt, countre note, and orgon, and smale brekynge* : ' The elaboration of the Church services in medieval times was accompanied by a corresponding enrichment of the music. To the plain chant additional parts were joined, sung in harmony either above or below the plain chant. " Descant " usually means the addition of a part above, " organ " and " countre-note " (= counterpoint) the addition of parts either above or below. All these could be composed note for note with the plain chant. But " smale brekyng " represents a further complication, whereby the single note in the plain chant was represented by two or more notes in the accompanying parts.' [K. S.]

PAGE **92**, l. 7. *Ordynalle of Salisbury*: ' An " ordinal " is a book showing the order of church services and ceremonies. In medieval times there was considerable divergence in the usage of different churches. But after the Conquest, and more especially in the thirteenth century, there was developed at Salisbury Cathedral an elaborate order and form of service which spread to most of the English churches of any pretensions. This was called " Sarum " or " Salisbury " use.' [K. S.]

l. 35. *þei demen it dedly synne a prest to fulfille*, &c. : ' For this construction, cp. Chaucer, *Prologue*, 502, ' No wonder is a lewed man to ruste "; Shakespeare, *Two Gentlemen of Verona*, V. iv. 108 f. "*It is the lesser blot . . . Women to change their shapes*, &c."' [K. S.]

PAGE **93**, ll. 11–14. ' They say that a priest may be excused from saying mass, to be the substance of which God gave Himself, provided that he hears one.' [K. S.]

ll. 19–20. *newe costy portos, antifeners, graielis, and alle opere bokis*: ' " Portos ", French " portehors " represents Lat. " portiforium ", a breviary convenient for " carrying out of doors ". The " antifener " contains the antiphons, responses, &c., necessary for the musical service of the canonical hours. The " graiel ", or " gradual ", was so called from the gradual responses, sung at the steps of the altar or while the deacon ascended the steps of the pulpit : but

the book actually contained all the choral service of the Mass.'
[K. S.]

l. 21. *makynge of biblis*: 'Wyclif in his *Office of Curates* (ed.
Matt., p. 145) complains of the scarcity of Bibles. *But fewe curatis
han þe Bible and exposiciouns of þe Gospelis, and litel studien on
hem, and lesse donne after hem. But wolde God þat every parische
chirche in þis lond hadde a good Bible!*' [K. S.]

PAGE **94**, l. 15. *Poule seiþ*: 1 Cor. viii. 1.

l. 24. *rownyngly*: 'in a whisper'; cf. 'Whenne Crist forȝave
Marie Magdeleyne hir synnes, he used not siche rownynge; and
whenne He forȝave Petir hise synnes . . . he usid not sich rownyng
in ere '. *Of Confession.*

l. 28. *Crist, alwitty*: cf. ' Et certum videtur quod Christus ecclesie sue foret negligens si hoc sacramentum foret sibi tam
necessarium et tamen non foret usque ad solucionem sathane
ecclesie declaratum '. *de Euch. et Poen.* Cap. 2.

PAGE **95**, l. 4. *þe keies*: St. Matt. xvi. 19.

þe Chairinge of Seint Petre: i. e. the feast of his first becoming
Bishop of Antioch; ascribed by Eusebius to the year 42. The
feast—*in cathedra Antiochena*— occurs on 22 February.

PAGE **96**, l. 3. *boles and my volatils*: Vulg. *tauri mei et altilia.*

l. 5. *toun*: Vulg. *villam.*

l. 9. *loste þes mansleeris*: Vulg. *perdidit homicidas illas.*

l. 28. *foure degrees ben in þis Chirche*: ' Frustra legeretur quod
Salomon haberet tot reginas, tot concubinas et tot adolescentulas,
nisi ut figurando Christum significet nobis suum coniugium '. *de
Ecclesia* 125.

ll. 36–7. *Goddis two lawes*: the Old and New Testaments.

PAGE **97**, l. 19. *as Josephus telliþ*: a reference to *The Wars of
the Jews*, Bk. vi. The destruction of Jerusalem took place in
August A. D. 70. Christ was probably crucified on 18 March A. D. 29.

l. 36. *þe chirche of þe fend*: ' The foreknown (*presciti*)—the
name he gives to the damned—form one body united with the devil
as head, just as the " predestined " are one body united with
Christ.' H. B. W. ii. 10.

PAGE **98**, l. 8. *but if þei lasten*: St. Matt. xxiv. 13.

VII (PAGE 99)

PAGE **100**, l. 32. *Seint Poul biddiþ*: 1 Cor. vii. 21.

PAGE **101**, ll. 6–7. *for þei ben breþeren in kynde*: i. e. all
descendants of Adam.

ll. 8–9. *Poul writiþ*: 1 Tim. vi. 1.

l. 28. *Seynt Petir techiþ þus*: 1 Pet. ii. 18.

PAGE **102**, l. 7. *bi Ieromye*: Jer. xxii. 3, 5.

l. 10. *by Ysaie*: Isa. i. 16.

ll. 16–17. *paien not þerfore but white stickis*: these were given
as tallies but very often not redeemed.

ll. 27-8. *sisouris of contré*: jurors of the country.

l. 33. *bi þe prophete Ysaie*: Isa. i. 15, 23.

PAGE **103**, l. 4. *And ʒit men of lawe*: cf. *Piers Plowman*, *Prologue*, 210-15:

> *ʒit houed þere an hondreth · in houues of selke,*
> *Seriauntz it semed · þat serueden atte barre,*
> *Plededen for penyes · and poundes þe lawe,*
> *And nouʒt for loue of owre Lord · unlese here lippes onis.*
> *Þow myʒtest better mete þe myste · on Maluerne Hulles*
> *Þan gete a momme of here mouthe · but money were shewed.*

ll. 14-15. *brynge hem in þraldom*: for Wyclif's views on serfdom see p. 99, l. 30 f.

l. 18. *lovedaies*: days for settling disputes by arbitration.

PAGE **104**, l. 5. *newe fraternytes or gildis*: see Introd., p. xxiv.

l. 6. *in þis curs*: i. e. the curse of the Church against 'conspirators'. The relevant passage in the document cited in the note to p. 109, ll. 6, 7, *infra*, runs : 'Alle false conspiratours ben cursed of God and man. Conspiratours ben þo þat by comyn assent don wrong or ony falsnesse to here neiʒeboris'.

l. 29. *leggyng on a wal*: 'placing [stones] on a wall'.

PAGE **105**, ll. 5-6. *sille betere chepe*: 'sell at a better bargain [for the buyer]'.

l. 6. *wel forþ it so*: 'easily do it'.

l. 19. *Raphael warned Tobie*: Tobit vi. 15-17.

PAGE **106**, ll. 5-6. *Seynt Petir biddiþ*: 1 Pet. iii. 1.

l. 19. *Alle þis seiþ Seynt Petir*: 1 Pet. iii. 1-7.

l. 20. *Seynt Poul spekiþ*: 1 Tim. ii. 8-15.

ll. 30-1. *in a pistel to Corynthis*: 1 Cor. xiv. 34, 35.

PAGE **107**, l. 1. *Poul biddiþ*: Eph. vi. 4.

l. 2. *God comaundiþ in þe olde lawe*: Ex. x. 2.

l. 6. *þe lond of biheste*: the Promised Land.

ll. 34-5. *so þat þei kepen*: 'provided that they keep'.

PAGE **108**, l. 15. *synne makes a mon noght*: see note to p. 63, ll. 9-10.

ll. 17-18. *suppose we to phisisians*: 'let us grant that physicians are right', i. e. presumably, when they say that a drinking-bout once a month is good.

ll. 18-19. *þat more gode comes*, &c. : the meaning becomes clear from Rom. vi. 1, 2, 'Shall we continue in sin, that grace may abound? God forbid. We who died to sin, how shall we any longer live therein?'

PAGE **109**. Sect. F. This passage is of great interest inasmuch as Wyclif played an important part in the famous case of breach of sanctuary at Westminster in 1378 when a knight, Haulay, was brutally murdered within the abbey, 'beside St. Edward's shrine', by the Keeper of the Tower, Alan Buxhill, at the head of forty soldiers. Haulay had captured in 1367, during one of the expeditions of the Black Prince into Spain, a Spanish grandee, the Count of Denia. The count was brought to England but returned to Spain shortly afterwards to raise his ransom, 60,000 florins (about £9,500). He left his son with Haulay as a hostage. Ten years passed, and just as there seemed some likelihood of this enormous ransom being paid, Parliament decided to exchange Denia's son for an English prisoner in Spain. On hearing of this decision of Parliament Haulay concealed his hostage and was therefore flung into the Tower. After nine months he escaped, and sought sanctuary in Westminster Abbey with the result described above.

The outrage was keenly resented by the Church and formed one of the main subjects of discussion at the Parliament of Gloucester (Oct. 1378), and Wyclif defended the Crown's action, arguing that 'neither God in his omnipotence nor the Pope in his sanctity could grant a local exemption from actions for debt'.

ll. 6–7. *Alle peves . . . ben cursed*: Maskell (*Monum. Ritual. Eccl. Angl.* ii. 286) prints, from an early printed copy of the *Sarum Manual* in the Bodleian Library, an incomplete version of the 'Grete Sentence of Curs' which is 'expounded' in this tract. This document is headed: 'Isti sunt generales articuli *maioris excommunicationis* in lingua materna, et dicantur hoc modo', and the clause here 'expounded' runs: 'Also we denounce acursed all open theves and robberes, and all that them receyve wytyngly, or gyve them help or counseil'.

l. 8. *foure tymes in þe ʒeer*: in the document referred to in the preceding note these are thus enumerated: 'that on is the fyrst Sonday of Advent, that other is the first Sonday of Lenten, and the nexte Sonday after Witsonday, and the first Sonday after the Assumpcyon of our Lady'.

l. 22. *Westmynstre, Beverlé*: Westminster Abbey and Beverley Minster both had special rights of sanctuary. Beverley possessed a famous stone chair or Frith [peace] Stool which, according to Leland, bore the following inscription: *Haec sedes lapidea Freedstoll dicitur, i. e. pacis cathedra, ad quam reus fugiendo perveniens omnimodam habet securitatem.*

PAGE 110, l. 13. *medefully*: the Latin version has *veraciter*.

ll. 17–21. *Alle þes questiouns . . . Goddis wille*: not in the Latin.

ll. 24–5. *love is in mannis herte*: the Latin evades the point: *Et sic, cum non queritur de loco amoris sed de subiecto eius, patet quod subiectatur in potencia volitiva et terminatur obiective in diligibili quod amatur.*

PAGE 111, l. 12. *clerkis, . . . munkis*, &c.: not specified in the Latin.

l. 28. *þes two versis*: Ps. cxvi. 16, 17.

VIII (PAGE 113)

PAGE 115, l. 2. *so many . . . weren langagis*: see note to p. 31, l. 19.

ll. 6-7. *Genasareþ . . . wounderful birþe*: Wyclif apparently connects ' Genasareþ ' with Gr. γεννάω = *to beget*.

l. 10. *Wit Sunday*: see note to p. 19, l. 14.

l. 15. *Aquyla*: Aquila, a native of Sinope, translated the O.T. into Greek at some time during the first half of the second century. He strove to find a Greek equivalent for every word and particle of the Hebrew text, and carefully endeavoured to reproduce Hebrew etymologies in Greek.

l. 16. *þis name [Pope]*: see note to p. 73, l. 3.

PAGE 116, l. 4. *Crist doubliþ þis word Martha*: this shows the meticulous way in which the words of Scripture were scanned. Cf. *Ave Maria*, p. 89, ll. 5-7, where a special interpretation is put on the fact that Gabriel omitted Mary's name in his greeting of her.

l. 21. *bi Matheu*: Matt. vi. 25.

ll. 25-6. *And þis is sumwhat here in erþe . . .*: ' This life may be lived to some extent here on earth, but in its perfection only in heaven '.

l. 37. *þis lif mote nedis laste*: *Civ. Dom.* 164 ' vita contemplativa propter sui perfeccionem . . . non excidit in via sed manet perfeccior in patria [Heaven]; vita autem activa propter sui imperfeccionem non intrat patriam '.

PAGE 117, l. 5. *þe laste word*: ' Mary hath chosen the good part which shall not be taken away from her '. Luke x. 42.

IX (PAGE 118)

PAGE 120, l. 1. *þat haþ þree partis*: Sancta ecclesia catholica . . . est tripartita ; una est triumphans, sicut Christus caput universalis ecclesie et beati alii, sive angeli sive homines iam defuncti. Secunda pars huius matris est militans ecclesia ut predestinati hic in corpore viantes. Et tercia pars ecclesie est predestinati mortui in purgatorio dormientes. *de Fide Catholica*, p. 99.

l. 22. *Belial*: 2 Cor. vi. 15.

l. 24. *ech membre of þe fend*: the *presciti*, i.e. foreknown by God as damned. The devil is their head as Christ is Head of the elect.

l. 27. *of þre þingis*: see note to p. 50, l. 10.

l. 29. *ech man shal hope*: ' debemus autem hoc *sperare* et credere cum formidine de gracie perseverancie '. *de Ecclesia* 25.

l. 33. *þis hope, bineþe bileve*: ' this hope, which does not amount to belief'.

PAGE 121, l. 19. *Him likide*: ' it pleased Him '.

PAGE 122, l. 9. *Silvestre preest of Rome*: see note to p. 79, ll. 26-7.

l. 15. *bi tymes*: ' after a time '.

l. 28. *Symon Magus*: cf. p. 78, ll. 4-5.

l. 31. *made devisioun*: the Great Schism ; see note to p. 70, l. 29.

PAGE 123, l. 5. *Yngdis*: Indians.

ll. 13–14. *and everywhere bi His Godhede*: i. e. God is omnipresent.

l. 26. *for þe grete diversité*: 'because it is so contrary [to the idea of such a Pope]'.

l. 29. *by Jeremye*: Jer. xvii. 5.

l. 30. *Here men taken*, &c.: 'men take something that is true, and add inventions to this truth'.

ll. 31–2. *Cristis Chirche is His hous*: cf. 'In hiis est domus Dei quos predestinavit'. *de Ecclesia* 6.

PAGE **124**, l. 1. *summe ben servauntis*: i. e. the well-intentioned *presciti* who though *in* the Church are not *of* it.

l. 26. *Clement*: Clemens Romanus, according to common tradition, one of the first bishops of Rome, if not the first, after the apostles, and certainly a leading member of that Church towards the end of the first century.

l. 27. *Laurence*: archdeacon of Rome and martyr under Valerian A. D. 258.

þe Legende: the *Legenda Aurea* of Jacobus de Voragine, Archbishop of Genoa in the thirteenth century.

PAGE **125**, ll. 37–8. *Petre erride, as Poul seiþ*: Gal. ii. 12 ff.

PAGE **126**, l. 8. *have conscience*: 'give reverence'.

l. 24–5. *Caymes Castelis*: see note to p. 84, l. 9.

ll. 25–6. *Þei stelen þore mennis children*: an Oxford University proclamation of 1358 contains the following charge against the friars : ' By apples and drink, as the people say, they draw boys to their religion '. Fitzralph [Brown, *Fasciculus*, ii. 473] tells us, ' An instance came to my knowledge this very day. As I came out of my inn [at Avignon] an honest man from England, who has come to this court to get a remedy, told me that immediately after last Easter the friars at Oxford abducted in this manner his son, who was not yet 13 years of age, and when he went there he could not speak with him except under the supervision of a friar '. [H. B. W. i. 93 and ii. 103.]

ll. 26–7. *þei stelen gladlich eires*: cf. *de Blasphemia* 212, where the friar is told that, according to Gal. iv. 2, the *heres* should be under the tutelage of the father: *non extraheret filium a parente fideli*.

l. 27. *stelyng of wymmen*: in *de Blasph.* 235 Wyclif applies to friars the verse from 2 Tim. iii. 6 *penetrant domos et captivas ducunt mulierculas*. Cf. Sermones iii. 219.

PAGE **127**, l. 2. *londis to Flateilis*: Hereford charged the friars with causing the Peasants' Revolt. *Fasc. Ziz.* pp. 292, 293 ; Wyclif charged them with recruiting for Spenser's Crusade. See note to ll. 9–10, and cf. Cap. 7 and 8 of *de Fide Catholica*.

l. 5. *pryvelegies of þe court*: the ecclesiastical courts, cf. Introd., p. xxvii.

ll. 9–10. *þat Englishemen maden into Flandres*: this refers to Spenser's Crusade into Flanders, prepared 1381–2, launched May

1383, and ignominiously abandoned Oct. 1383. It was led by Bishop Spenser of Norwich, *pugil ecclesiae,* who had distinguished himself previously by suppressing with a stern hand the revolutionary peasants of his diocese. The 'crusade' was an incident in the struggle of Pope and Antipope. Philip van Artevalde, the commercial friend of England, head of the republic of Ghent, acknowledged, like England, Urban VI. He had suffered a reverse at the hands of the Flemish subjects of the French king, who acknowledged Clement, and Spencer's Crusade, which was blessed by Urban, was designed to punish Flanders for this reverse.

PAGE **128**, l. 3. *Helias sones*: 1 Sam. ii. 12 f. and iv. 10–22.

l. 24. *as erþely lordis*: a reference to Wyclif's desire that king and nobles should reform the Church.

PAGE **129**, l. 16. *accident wiþouten suget*: see Introd., p. 68.

l. 33. *Carmes seien*: the Carmelites claimed to have been founded by the prophet Elijah when he retired to Mount Carmel, and the Augustinians looked upon St. Augustine [354–430], Bishop of Hippo, as their founder. *Prechouris* are 'Friars Preachers' or Dominicans, and *Menouris* 'Friars Minor' or Franciscans.

PAGE **130**, l. 12. *whanne evere þei syngen*: i.e. sing mass.

ll. 17–19. *noon mai comprehende . . . þat camen aftir*: 'none may "grasp" this power since it has no limits, for the whole string of Popes has [so they say] possessed it'.

ll. 21–2. *but not but for to edifie*: 'but only in order to build'.

PAGE **131**, l. 15. *Crist bihiȝte to Petre*: Matt. xvi. 19.

ll. 34–5. *bifore þat Gabriel blowe his horn*: i. e. on the Judgement Day. The expression seems to have been proverbial; cf. 'And I wote wel þat Gabriel schal blow his horne or þei han preuyd þe mynor'. [Proposition in a syllogism] *The Clergy may not hold Property* (Matt., p. 382).

PAGE **132**, l. 27. *of þis ground*, &c.: 'we will express a further opinion, based on this ground [the law of Christ], as to how it appears to us that men should act'.

PAGE **133**, l. 15. *possessioneres and beggeris*: 'monks and friars [mendicants]'.

ll. 22–3. *as þei diden aftir Cristis deþ*: a vague reference to the communism described in Acts ii. 44, 45; iv. 32 f.

l. 25. *as Poul techiþ*: Rom. xiv. 1–9.

l. 29. *rehetors*: this is a rare and obscure word. It occurs also S. E. W. ii. 229. The O.E.D. explains as 'a servant of some kind'.

PAGE **134**, ll. 13–14. *þe emperour*: Constantine; see note to p. 79, ll. 26–7.

PAGE **135**, ll. 3–4. *censures, þat þe fend blowiþ*: Wyclif had himself suffered from these, e. g. the Papal bulls of 1377. See p. 67, l. 29 f.

l. 5. *reisingis of croiserie*: e. g. Spenser's Crusade.

l. 15. *maugree his*: 'in spite of himself'.

ll 16-17. *but as it accordiþ wiþ Cristis keies*: i. e. Christ's powers of 'binding and loosing' as distinguished from Peter's, symbolized by the keys entrusted to him.

PAGE **136,** l. 6. *is to drede*: 'is to be dreaded'.

ll. 6-7. *such drede . . . comeþ to lawe of charité*: 'such fear makes one refrain from employing human laws and substitute the law of charity'.

l. 22. *þis leed*: the leaden seal of the bull.

l. 23. *þei shulden neiþer trowe to Crist ne Petre*: Arnold [S. E. W. iii. 362] remarks: 'There must surely be an error of the scribe here'. There is, however, no error. Wyclif has merely expressed, in a most striking way, his belief in the paramount authority of Scripture as 'Goddis lawe'. Men are not to follow even Christ except in so far as they do so on the authority of Scripture *(but in as myche as þei grounden bi Goddis lawe,* &c.). 'Goddis lawe' furnishes a complete rule of life.

l. 34. *a pena or a culpa*: 'from the punishment or from the sin.' This provided a topic for centuries of theological discussion, i. e. whether the Pope could absolve a man from the sin itself, or merely from the punishment or from neither.

PAGE **138,** l. 5. *Machamete in his lawe*: the Koran of Mahomet. Mahomet received his Christian teaching from the Nestorian monk, Sergius of Bussorah.

l. 16. *weie-goeres*: in his Latin works Wyclif shows a fondness for the term *viatores* as a synonym for *Christians*.

l. 18. *habitis*: the Carmelites wore a white garb over a dark brown tunic ; the Augustinians a black dress and a leathern girdle ; the Dominicans a black cloak and hood over a white woollen gown ; the Franciscans a grey habit with a hempen cord round the waist. Commenting on this variety of dress Wyclif says in *de Fundatione Sectorum*: 'Unde videtur sectis istis difficile fingere . . . quare in colore et figura taliter variatur. Deridenda quidem est ista ficticia quod nigredo dolorem de peccatis significet, albedo cordis mundiciam, et russetum laborem assiduum in ecclesia militante.'

l. 26. *auctours of accidentis*: i. e. the friars, who, by their belief in Transubstantiation, made a world of new 'accidents' or qualities.

l. 32. *þe crafte of love of þingis*: see p. 119, ll. 27-41.

GLOSSARY

abite, habit, dress.
acord, harmony, accord.
afflen, to trust.
after, according to.
alargid, extended.
algatis, alʒatis, in every way, wholly.
alienen, to dispose of.
Almaine, Germany.
al-oonli, only, solely.
alþof, although.
alwitty, omniscient.
alyens, aliens.
alʒif, even if.
amersy, to fine.
anentis, concerning.
apertli, openly.
apostata, apostate.
apostemes, imposthumes, abscesses.
artid, constrained.
asaye, to try.
aseeþ, satisfaction.
assoile, to absolve; to refute.
auctor, author.
austerneté, austerity.
auʒte, [he] possessed, owed.
averous, greedy, avaricious.
avoutrie, adultery.
aʒens, towards.
aʒenseiþ, gainsays, contradicts.
aʒenstonde, to withstand.
aʒenward, on the contrary.

baptym, baptism.
bedrede, bedridden.
besantis, bezants, talents.
besien, to busy.
bi, of, concerning.
biclippen, to embrace.
bie, to buy.
bigrucche, to begrudge.
biheste, promise.
biheten, to promise.
bikenes, ensigns, standards.

bileve, belief.
blaberen, blabre, to babble.
blasfemes, blasphemers.
bleckid, blackened, stained.
boles, bulls, oxen.
bolnen, to swell.
bonere, gentle, courteous.
bourdis, jests.
brenne, to burn.
brocage, brokerage, jobbery.
but-ʒif, unless.

calengen, chalengen, to accuse, charge, claim.
cɔn, [I] know, [he] knows.
canel, channel.
caryone, carrion, corpse.
cast, device.
cautel, craft, cunning, trick.
cavellacions, cavillings, quibbles.
chaffaren, to bargain.
chaffarynge, trading.
chaffere, wares, merchandise.
chargen, to put a load on, to care for, to charge.
chargeouse, charious, burdensome.
chepe, bargain.
chesoun, cause, reason.
clepid, called.
cloute, rag, clout.
cloutə, to join, patch.
clowtyd, patched, joined.
collacion, appointment to a benefice.
comunyng, sharing, participation.
conscience, consciousness, recognition, conscience.
contek, strife, debate.
contré, county, barony.
cope, canopy, vault.
coragious, courageous.
corier, currier.
covenable, fitting, suitable.
coveytise, covetousness, greed.

croiserie, crusade.
croniclis, chronicles.
cropun, crept.
cumpas, circle, circuit.
cunne : *see* kunne.
cure, cure (of souls).
curious, busy, dainty.
custome, public due.

dalf, [he] dug.
dampnable, worthy of condemnation.
dedeyn, indignation.
defaute, fault, error, want.
defenden, to forbid, defend.
deme, to judge.
depen, to baptize.
depraven, to depreciate, defame.
destried, destroyed.
deul, mourning.
discreet, judicious.
dispeiren, to despair.
dispendid, spent.
disseyved, deceived.
docken, to cut short.
dolle, dull.
dom, judgement, justice.
domesman, judge.
doon . . to, to add.
doren, [they] dare.
doump, dumb.
dowe, to endow.
dowynge, endowment.
drecche, to vex, torment.
dreden, to fear, dread.
dressen, to direct.
dronkelewe, given to drunkenness.
drowun, [they] drew.
dymes, tithes.

Ebreu, Hebrew.
edifien, to build.
eire, air.
eires, heirs.
eisil, vinegar.
either, or.
elde, old.
emblemishen, to blemish, defile.
empugnen, to fight against.
endid, fulfilled.
enke, ink.

enpeche, to prevent, hinder.
ensaumple, to be an example of, give an example to.
entent, meaning.
enterditingis, interdicts.

failen, to fall away, lack.
fallen, to happen, fall.
fast, closely.
fautour, supporter.
fel, dire, base, fierce.
fend, fiend.
fillen, fullen, to fulfil.
florishid, flowery, grandiloquent.
folili, foolishly.
fonnyd, infatuated.
fool, foolish, silly.
foorme, example, model.
forwhi, because.
forfendide, [he] forbade.
fraunchise, freedom.
freris, friars.
fyl, [he] fell.

gabbe, to lie.
gabbyng, prating.
gatis, ways.
gendrure, begetting.
gessen, to be of opinion.
geste, story.
glose, gloss.
gnastinge, gnashing.
good, property, possessions.
goost, spirit.
goostly, spiritually.
governaile, authority, management.
greesis, steps.
greggen, to aggravate.
Greu, Greek.
groping, touch.
grucchen, to grumble, murmur.
grucchynge, unwilling, reluctant.

halewynge, consecration.
half, side.
harlot, buffoon, rascal.
harlotrie, buffoonery, jesting, ribaldry.
heerde, shepherd.
heeryng, praise.
heierste, highest.

herre, hinge.
heryen, to praise.
hestis, commands.
hele, health.
hereris, hearers.
heyng, exaltation.
hevy, with displeasure, angrily.
heȝen, hye, to exalt.
hilen, to cover, conceal.
hilyng, clothing.
holden, to consider.
hooris, whores.
hopen, to expect.
hyenesse, pride, exaltation.
hynen, servants.

iaies, jays.
iapis, jokes, tricks.
iȝen, eyes.
impungnen, to impugn.
in cas, in fact.
intuycioun, intuition.

jeestis, stories.
joȝelour, jester, buffoon, juggler.

kerve, to cut.
knacke, to sing with trills and flourishes.
knackeris, trill-singers.
konynge, learned, versed, skilful.
kunne, to know, know how.
kunnyng, knowledge, skill.
kynde, nature, kind.
kynde, akin, acceptable.
kyndely, naturally, by nature.
kynne, kind, manner.

lastandly, constantly.
laste, to last, continue (last out), endure.
leche, doctor.
leese, to lose.
leeve, to let, permit.
leggyng, laying.
leggen, to allege, cite.
leien, to lay.
lerid, learned, lettered.
lemman, concubine.
lepre, leprosy.
lepre, leper.
lesinge, lie.

lesyng, losing, loss.
letten, to prevent.
lettingis, hindrances.
leven, to believe.
lewid, ignorant, unlettered.
leyȝe, to laugh.
liflode, livelihood.
liggen, to lie.
like (*with dat.*), to be pleasing to.
liȝe, to tell lies.
liȝtli, easily.
lorellis, good-for-nothings.
losengerie, flattery.
louse, to let loose.
louten, to bow.
lumpis, congeries, crowds.
lurke, to hide.
lymes, limbs.

Machamete, Mahomet.
manassen, to threaten.
mandement, command.
manhed, humanity, being human.
manquelleris, manslayers.
margery-stone, pearl.
mater, matter, cause.
maugree, in spite of.
mawmettis, idols.
mede, reward, desert.
medeful, deserving reward.
medle, to mix.
mene, mean, middle.
mercymentis, amercements.
mesure, measure, amount.
meve, to stir, urge, move.
meyné, retinue, household.
moeblis, goods, personal property.
more, moor.
more, greater.
moost, most, greatest.
muk, trash, dirt.
myche, great.
mynen, to undermine.
myȝte, power, might.

nameli, especially.
neiȝe, to draw near.
nemme, nempne, to name.
nere, nearer.
nereþoles, nevertheless.
next, nearest.
nobleie, nobility, noble rank.

nobut, except, unless.
no drede, certainly, doubtless.
noien, to harm, vex, harass.
nurshe, to nourish, rear.
nyle, will not.
nyse, foolish.

obeschen, to obey.
of, by, from.
onehead, unity.
oo, one.
oost, host.
open, clear, plain.
or, before.
ordeyne, to ordain, appoint.
ournynge, adorning.
ouȝte, [he] owed.
over, further, moreover, besides.
overcomynge, victorious, triumphant.

pagynes, pages.
paien, to satisfy, please.
panter, snare.
passen, to exceed, surpass.
passingli, exceedingly well.
paynim, pagan.
peiere, to make worse, impair.
pens, pence.
pese holes, pea-pods.
peyne, penalty.
picche, to put, place, transfix.
piling, pillaging, robbery.
ple(e, lawsuit.
plentevouse, plenteous.
plete, to go to law.
podel, puddle.
poot, pot.
pouste, power.
pows, pulse.
presumpcioun, presumption, usurpation.
privé, pryvé, secret.
priven, to deprive.
proces, narrative, exposition.
proctours, proctors.
profide, offered.
propre, own.
provendris, prebends.
pursue, to sue, make one's suit.
pursuing, prosecution.
purvyance, providing, providence.

queer, choir.
quenche, to destroy, oppress.
queyntely, cunningly.
quyc, alive, quick.
quyter, filth, pus.

raveyne, robbery.
rebelté, rebellion.
refute, refuge.
regalie, royal power, royalty.
rehetours, retainers, followers.
reisingis, raisings.
religiouse, those bound by a monastic vow.
rengne, to reign.
renne, to run.
rentes, revenues.
repreven, to reprove.
reseten, to harbour, receive.
resset, refuge, harbour.
reume, rewme, realm.
riȝtwisnesse, righteousness.
rownyngly, in a whisper.
rowte, to snore.
rugge, back.
ryken, to reckon.

sachil, wallet, satchel.
sadde, grave, sober, resolute.
saif, saved.
sample, example.
sauter, sawter, psalter.
savo(u)ren, to relish.
say, [he] saw.
Scarioth, Iscariot.
schapellis, chapels.
schent, reviled.
schrewe, to curse.
science, knowledge.
sclaundre, to be a stumbling-block to.
scole, company, band.
seel, seal.
seke, sick.
sensible, perceptible by the senses.
sensouris, censors.
sentence, meaning, sense.
shapen, to create, set about, fashion, form.
shope, [he] created.
sillide, [he] sold, gave.
singulerly, alone, only.

sisouris, jurors, assizors.
siþ, since, afterwards.
skile, reason, ground.
slee, to slay.
sleeris, slayers.
smyttid, infected.
sofymys, sophisms.
soget, suget, subject, substance.
soiþ, truth.
somewhat, something.
sotil, subtle.
soþely, truly.
sounen, to pertain to.
speckid, speckled.
sporis, spurs.
sprengen, to sprinkle.
spuylen, to despoil.
stablynge, establishing, strengthening.
starin, to stare.
steien, stye, to climb, ascend.
sterve, to die.
stirte, to start.
stoole, robe.
stressid, distrained.
stronde, stream, rivulet.
suen, to follow.
sum, one.
sumdel, somewhat.
suppose, to think, be of opinion.
syker, sure, secure.

taried, hindered.
taterynge, chatter, prating.
terminen, to determine.
tiffynge, adornment.
to, too.
tolde, [he] counted, reckoned.
toon, one.
tosquatte, to flatten, crush.
toþer, other.
traveilinge, labour.
travel, labour, travail.
traveler, labourer.
triste, trust.
tumbler, acrobat.

þankful, gratuitous.
þeefli, like a thief.
þerto, in addition.
þinkiþ, it seems
þrist, thirst.
þrof, throve.

unablité, incapacity, inability.
unfrədom, servitude.
unkynde, unnatural.
unmesurabli, immoderately.
unneþe, scarcely, hardly.
unpees, strife, war.
unriʒtwisnesse, unrighteousness.
unskilful, unreasonable.
unworchipe, to deprive of dignity.
up, upon.
upsedoun, upside down.
us, use.
utter, outer.

verrey, true.
viker, vicar.
vitilers, victuallers.
volatils, birds.

waki, to watch.
war, beware.
warien, to curse.
weiyng, weighing.
wende, to go, travel.
werre, war.
what, whatever.
wher´e, whether.
wil, wel, well.
wilfully, willingly.
wille, desire.
wite, to know.
witt, meaning, mind, understanding, knowledge.
wiþholde, to keep, preserve, maintain.
wiþoutenforþ, on the outside.
wlatien, to abominate.
woode, mad.
woodnesse, madness, violence.
woot, [he] knows.
worche, to work.
word, saying.
wos, whose.
wriþen, plaited.
wynnyng, profit.

ʒaf, [he] gave.
ʒede, [he] went.
ʒelde, to yield, give.
ʒemon, yeoman.
ʒhe, yea.
ʒok, yoke.
ʒovun, given.

yvel, ill, evilly, badly.

81
83
86
58